PAS

Church Point
Pittwater

THE HOUSE

THE HOUSE
at Salvation Creek

SUSAN DUNCAN

BANTAM
SYDNEY AUCKLAND TORONTO NEW YORK LONDON

Note: Some names in this book have been changed to protect the privacy of individuals.

A Bantam book
Published by Random House Australia Pty Ltd
Level 3, 100 Pacific Highway, North Sydney NSW 2060
www.randomhouse.com.au

First published by Bantam in 2008

Addresses for companies within the Random House Group can be found at www.randomhouse.com.au/offices

National Library of Australia
Cataloguing-in-Publication Entry

Duncan, Susan (Susan Elizabeth)
The house.

ISBN: 978 1 86325 648 3 (pbk.)

Duncan, Susan (Susan Elizabeth)
Women journalists – Australia – Biography.
Dwellings – New South Wales – Pittwater
Pittwater (N.S.W.)

920.72

Cover painting 'Tarrangaua' by John Lovett
Cover and text design by saso content and design pty ltd
Chapter openers feature a pencil study for a linocut 'View from kitchen window at Tarrangaua' by David Preston
Typeset by Midland Typesetters, Australia
Printed and bound by Griffin Press, South Australia

Excerpts from the diaries of Dorothea Mackellar, the two poems 'My Country' and 'Peaceful Voices' and Mackellar's recipe for Spiced Cottage Cheese Custard are reproduced by arrangement with the licensor, the Estate of Dorothea Mackellar, c/- Curtis Brown (Aust) Pty Ltd.

Random House Australia uses papers that are natural, renewable and recyclable products and made from wood grown in sustainable forests. The logging and manufacturing processes are expected to conform to the environmental regulations of the country of origin.

10 9 8

For my mother, Esther,
who has never lost her courage

AUTHOR'S NOTE

Unlike *Salvation Creek*, in *The House* I have made only a small attempt at trying to stick to an accurate chronology. Life on Pittwater slides along at an easy pace and we follow the call of every season – summer twilight races, autumn shoreside picnics, winter fires and spring cleaning. The years don't really matter much. More important by far, is that we are still around to experience them.

PROLOGUE

A LONG TIME AGO, but still barely more than ten years, I had another life. In the fast lane. But death changed all that. My brother, John, and my husband, Paul, slid slowly away within three days of each other and nothing was ever the same. Grief sent me mad for a while, although I only understand that now.

I blunted the razor edge of loss in the shadowy secrecy of an illicit affair and the bottom of a wine bottle – or two or three. Which is just about as ugly as it gets. Was that the goal, I sometimes wonder, when I look back? To wipe myself out, forever?

Then one day I sat across a desk from a doctor and heard the words we all dread. 'You have cancer,' he said. 'It's malignant.'

There it was. Wipe-out. And I finally understood I didn't really want the end at all. Such hideous irony, that I needed the threat of death to fall in love with life. Ironic, too, that cancer gave me a wisdom I doubt I would have learned otherwise. Life is precious. Catastrophes happen. Make every moment count.

In those first terrifying days after my diagnosis, I hesitantly stretched one foot forward. Gently tapped the earth with my toes. Like my mother does now she is old, making sure there are no bumps and she won't fall. And I began again. No falls for me, not this time.

By some strange, miraculous stroke of – what? Luck? Fate? Maybe both. It certainly had nothing to do with good planning – I bought a boxy, pale-green tin house on the edge of a secluded bay about forty-five minutes north of Sydney's CBD. Waterfront property usually costs the earth. Not this home, though, because most people want to drive into a garage at the end of the day, not jump into a small, unstable aluminium boat to navigate dark waters in the blue light of the moon. Friends told me I was mad. 'Too isolated,' they insisted. 'Who wants to go home by boat? Where will you find an early morning café latte? How can you manage without restaurants?' As if they were the fabric of life. I ignored their dire warnings. Risked everything. Because sometimes that's the only way to ever make a real commitment.

My tin shed hovered over the green waters of Lovett Bay, close to where a creek named Salvation tumbled in a delicate waterfall to the sandy tidal flats. It is one of five bays on the western foreshores of Pittwater that spread like fingers poised to grab Scotland Island, which rises like a mossy hill out of the waters beyond. It is an ancient landscape of ragged burnt-orange escarpments, soaring sea eagles, leaping fish and timber jetties.

To get here, we park our cars at Church Point then catch a ferry or clamber into a tippy boat for the final leg home. Called 'tinnies', they are mostly banged up aluminium tubs with outboard motors hanging off the back. Pull the engine cord, grab the throttle, rev to the max, then fly through the water like a winged chariot. Laughing. Even when there's a gale and the water's so rough every wave feels like a concrete hump hit at speed.

Mostly, our houses perch about forty-five feet beyond the high tide line, which is the legal building boundary. A few older homes, though, are built at the water's edge and have historic rights to be there.

The north side of Lovett Bay, where I live, backs on to the wild Ku-ring-gai Chase National Park. From a distance, it is as still as a painting. Up close, it teems with life. The bush never rests, not even at night when you hear the heavy drumbeat of wallabies on their age-old tracks, or the scream of a barking owl. And all around, always, there is the faint chorus of the water.

I moved into the tin shed only three weeks before being told I would lose a breast and all my hair. And perhaps my life. For a while, I thought I'd made a hideous mistake, that my friends had been wise after all. But slowly I learned a new set of values that had nothing to do with the fast lane, or proximity to café latte. I learned that if you are weak of body and spirit, you can still find strength by being useful in a community, a community that takes you out of your own messy despair, re-anchors you in normality and puts you in touch with optimism.

I learned that control is an illusion, that it is better to embrace change than to fight it. I learned to let go of wanting and, instead, focus on being. I learned that when you are forty years old, the best years are ahead, not behind, which is what we are so often told. I learned that when you are past fifty, adventure lurks in every moment if you look for it. I learned that it is cynicism that kills passion, not age. And after a lifetime of flitting, I learned where I belonged. And with whom. I learned all this in my simple tin shed where I sat on the deck on cold winter nights with a cup of tea and a blanket over my shoulders, breathing in the briny smell of oyster shells, wet sand, sea grass and mangroves. The fresh clean of high tide. Savouring the smallest details of a world I thought I might have to quit soon. But I am still here. So far so good.

In time, I began a friendship with Barbara, the woman with beautiful blue eyes who lived in a pale yellow house called *Tarrangaua*, on the high, rough hill at the mouth of the bay. And she passed on her love of the bush, her passion for all things Australian, as we drank tea together on her elegant columned verandah in the late afternoons. We talked about everything but death in those days, although it shrilled silently between us because she, too, had cancer. She died late on a hot autumn night, as gracefully as she had lived.

For a while, her husband Bob and I were friends, helping each other through his grief and my fear. Then, returning from a dinner party one starstruck night after a wild storm, he stopped the tinny near the crumbled shore of Woody Point and kissed me. We married on a brilliantly sunny June day in 2001, on a lovely old boat in the middle of Lovett Bay, surrounded by family . . . and, of course, dogs. It was a new beginning. A relationship that grew out of respect and friendship. The strongest of all foundations.

And this is what came after.

1

FOR NEARLY TWO YEARS after we marry, Bob's pale yellow house on the 'high rough hill', which is the Aboriginal meaning of *Tarrangaua*, stays empty. I know he prefers the grand isolation of his home high above the waters of Lovett Bay to my shacky shed hovering over the shoreline, and yet I cannot bring myself to give up my house, where the earth, sky and sea surge through walls of glass. Where the moon prances on the bedroom floor and the sun spears rainbows of light on the timber deck.

Tarrangaua, too, has its own particular beauty. It was built in 1925 for the rich and reclusive poet Dorothea Mackellar, and is a solid, quietly authoritative house – stately, even – made of bricks and terracotta tiles and surrounded on three sides by a gracious verandah. Through the day, light and shadow play on textured walls. It can look sombre, though, when the sun is masked by clouds and the spotted gums and ironbarks, rigid sentinels that enclose the building, turn black in the rain.

Mackellar, who built the house as a summer retreat, was born in 1885. As she grew older, she led a lonely life, thwarted by death and lost love – and, later, alcohol – but she had the courage, and the heart, to write a poem that evoked the raw passion of a young nation tired of being seen as Britain's grubby apron. In a single line, *I love a sunburnt country*, she embraced a land of *droughts and flooding rains* and made fools of an establishment that continued to yearn for *green and shaded lanes*. As though England's ordered gentility was the promised land and *home*, and Australia nothing but a far-flung, feral *colony*.

The poem, 'My Country', first published in 1908, made her famous and she was invited to recite it over and over throughout her life. It gave her a sense of achievement, a sense she would leave a worthwhile legacy.

My Country

The love of field and coppice,
Of green and shaded lanes.
Of ordered woods and gardens
Is running in your veins,
Strong love of grey-blue distance
Brown streams and soft dim skies
I know but cannot share it,
My love is otherwise.

I love a sunburnt country,
A land of sweeping plains,
Of ragged mountain ranges,
Of droughts and flooding rains.
I love her far horizons,
I love her jewel-sea,
Her beauty and her terror –
The wide brown land for me!

A stark white ring-barked forest
All tragic to the moon,

The sapphire-misted mountains,
The hot gold hush of noon.
Green tangle of the brushes,
Where lithe lianas coil,
And orchids deck the tree-tops
And ferns the warm dark soil.

Core of my heart, my country!
Her pitiless blue sky,
When sick at heart, around us,
We see the cattle die –
But then the grey clouds gather,
And we can bless again
The drumming of an army,
The steady, soaking rain.

Core of my heart, my country!
Land of the Rainbow Gold,
For flood and fire and famine,
She pays us back threefold –
Over the thirsty paddocks,
Watch, after many days,
The filmy veil of greenness
That thickens as we gaze.

An opal-hearted country,
A wilful, lavish land –
All you who have not loved her,
You will not understand –
Though earth holds many splendours,
Wherever I may die,
I know to what brown country
My homing thoughts will fly.

Mackellar built *Tarrangaua* when she was forty years old and employed a married couple, who lived in a cottage on the property, to care for it. Although we are told it became her favourite home, it remained empty for months at a time.

Houses, though, are oddly living things. When they are deserted, they begin to die. *Old* houses are especially vulnerable, like old people. Unless there is someone to notice a crack, a leak, mould clinging to long undusted furniture, a slow rot sets in. They get a smell, too, of neglect, like the dank smell that floats from the pages of a book left unopened for too many years. Bob and I are aware we cannot leave *Tarrangaua* echoing emptily forever, yet the idea of tenants is abhorrent. To sell it is unthinkable.

One day Fleury, a great friend and neighbour who has a travel business, asks if we'd ever think of opening *Tarrangaua* for tour groups.

'What kind of tours?'

'Small groups, mostly from the US. I take them to see the Aboriginal rock carvings on the Ku-ring-gai plateaus and give them a short Indigenous Australian history lesson. They get back on the bus to go somewhere to eat. Maybe you could provide lunch or morning tea? Sitting on the lawn at *Tarrangaua* would be quite special.'

'I'll talk to Bob about it,' I reply, my mind already spinning with possibilities.

It is more than a year since I sat in a crackling, slippery chair with a needle in my hand, being swamped, drop by agonising drop, with a poison that was supposed to save my life. My soul shifted during those grey days where we patients marked time with empty eyes, too frightened to look beyond the moment. I used to crane to see the sky through a window, always careful not to rip the needle from its slot. And later, when I stepped from the chemo ward outside into the physical world, everywhere I looked I saw the small miracles of daily life.

I doubt I will ever again have the kind of strength it takes to drive through peak hour traffic to a suffocating cubicle in a high-rise building to toil all day sealed off from birds, flowers, trees, the sea, sky, wind and earth. So Fleury's idea is appealing. It gives me the opportunity to work – a powerful ethic instilled from childhood – but on my own terms and in an environment that I believe sustains me.

Bob is hesitant and for a while I wonder if he is unwilling to tamper with what has inevitably become a shrine to another life.

'It is a way of breathing energy into the house. Without disturbing it,' I suggest.

He is still noncommittal. I mull for weeks, writing lists with plus and minus columns.

'Be a chance to do some cooking,' I say one day. 'Could be fun.'

'It's a lot of work. Do you know what you're doing?' Bob asks, sighing loudly.

'Haven't got a clue. It's a challenge, though, don't you think? And there's no real downside. If it doesn't work, we pull the plug.'

'A challenge? Yeah, well, challenges keep you young.'

'And they're harder to find as you get older.'

'You could go back to journalism?'

'No. Well, maybe an assignment here and there if it appeals. But that's all. I cannot bear the thought of working unsatisfyingly anymore. I sometimes look back and wonder what the old rat race was really all about.'

'You must have enjoyed it once. And it paid the bills.'

'Yeah, well, now I'd rather live more lightly with less.'

'It can be a mistake,' Bob adds seriously, 'to turn your hobby into a business. It can kill the passion.'

Instead of listening carefully, as I usually do, I plunge into a new career.

2

Much has changed since 1999, when I moved to this sleepy little enclave where there are only five houses.

My friend Veit, with the ceramic blue eyes and gentle humour who helped me through chemo, has quit his job at the boatshed next door, lured by fishing for lobster somewhere near New Guinea. He dreams of untold wealth, so the rumour goes. We don't know for sure. When boaties move on, they begin again without the past weighing them down, which is part of the seduction of the sea, I suspect. You can reinvent yourself in every port.

Jack and Brigitte, who live behind the *Tin Shed*, have a third son. He is tall and strong though barely two years old. Stef and Bella, who bought the house at the mouth of Salvation Creek, are no longer weekenders. The city, for them, has lost its gloss and they come home to the peace of Lovett Bay each night. Bella leaves us from time to time to work for the International Red Cross in Bosnia, Jerusalem, Timor, China. Lovett Bay, when she returns, brings her back to sanity.

Raoul and Larnce work at the boatshed now, so different from each other they could be from separate planets. Raoul is dark. Dark skin, dark hair – occasionally, dark mood. Larnce is golden: hair, skin, even his eyes, when they catch the yellow of the sun in the late afternoon. He threshes through the bays in a wild, mauve fibreglass boat he calls the *Ghost Who Whomps*. Nose pointing to the sky, his bony backside finely balanced on a sliver of the stern, engine roaring. Constantly on the edge of flipping, as though he is as immortal as the Phantom himself.

'You go too fast, Larnce, too fast,' we all tell him when we pass by.

He shrugs, a cigarette hanging from his fingers. He looks at the burning tip then back at us. 'Always something's gonna get you,' he says. But you can tell he thinks he's invincible.

At weekends, Raoul brings his little boy, still a toddler, to play in the bay. By early afternoon, you have to watch where you step. He falls asleep suddenly and haphazardly, on bare floors, dirt, grass, concrete steps. Even, once, on the roof of a boat cabin Raoul was painting, his scruffy blanket clutched tightly under his chin, his smooth face angelic.

The boatshed belongs to a new couple, Michael and Mary Beth. They have a young son and Michael has three grown sons and two daughters from a former marriage. Michael is whippet thin with a long face and flowing hair. He works like a demon, as though a moment of rest is a moment wasted. He comes from a family of ten children, two of them fostered. His father, he told us not long after he arrived, worked two jobs to provide for his brood – all day as an accountant, then as a cleaner in the hours before dawn.

Like his father, Michael also has two jobs. He spends mornings at the boatshed, where tired yachts and boats are scraped, painted and restored – even, in some cases, made glorious, like the wooden cruiser with rot so deep and sustained it seemed she would never float again. The boys worked every day, hard and fastidiously, repairing what they could and rebuilding what was beyond saving.

A year later, *Blaxland* slid into the water like a dowager queen, gleaming, her lines sharp and refined. Truly resurrected. In the afternoon, Michael jumps in his car and drives to Manly, where he works as a psychiatric nurse. Which is another form of restoration.

Mary Beth, who is also a mental health nurse, is from the US and has a Yankee accent thick as mud. She is good-hearted and tender. Blunt, too, if she thinks it is the only way you'll get the message. Then her blue eyes focus, her hips thrust forward, her arms fold across her chest like an iron gate. That's how she stood the day a local politician told her he was amazed at what he called the new civility of people who live offshore.

'You've got rid of all the ferals,' he told her, his tone ripe with approval.

'Oh, they're still here,' she replied, her blue eyes glacial. 'It's just that we take care of them.'

Bob and Michael are similar men. On hot summer evenings they stand, slightly slumped, on cool concrete, beer in hand, the setting sun framing them like electricity. They stare, not at each other, but at white-limbed mangroves dancing on the far shore, at an incoming tide filling the empty bowl of Salvation Creek. Proud, in a silent way, of their day's darg. Neither man ever gives in, only paddles harder. It is the bond between them, this quiet understanding of how to go about daily life in a way that is satisfying.

'In the States,' Mary Beth says, 'we'd call Bob a good neighbour.'

'Here, we call Michael a great bloke,' I reply.

Not long after they take over the boatshed Andrew, Michael's son from his first marriage, who is lean like his father and has the same hawkish face, brings home a pup from the dog shelter. Jessie, she is called. She is brindled with brown, grey, black and white. Long-snouted with light-tan eyes and fur soft as mink. At first she is shy and skittish, slow to trust. Perhaps because beginning life in a dog shelter is rarely a good start.

'Got some cattle dog in her,' we say. 'Bit of kelpie, maybe?'

Then we notice she moves with the silence and stealth of a dingo. She has the same aloofness as a wild dog, too. We didn't hear even a light thump the day we found her on the table on the verandah, licking the cream bowl as though she had every right. Soon, she rides the bow of Andrew's tinny with the grace of a dancer. Before long, she and our tarty little terrier, Chip Chop, get into trouble.

The complaints begin. Chip Chop is locked up, Jessie learns what a leash is. They still escape from time to time, but always by accident. When they do, Brigitte is immediately on the phone or banging at the back door. She's a furious guardian of our wildlife, although her passion faltered the day a brush turkey shat on her keyboard. A friend, dressed in a cloche hat and white overalls (for tick protection) and clutching a frail butterfly net, tried to help her catch the beady-eyed bird with its scrawny yellow neck and bulbous head. Chasing. Pouncing. Chasing. Pouncing. It escaped in a hysterical flap up to a power line, where it pitched backwards and forwards, clinging to the narrow wire like a red-faced drunken sailor, until she gave up and went home. The keyboard never recovered.

Mary Beth's father, old Bob, lives at home with his daughter and son-in-law but he is peripheral in our bay life, confined to bed, his heart worn thin by the years, his body reneging on even the most basic instructions. He is cared for by a string of family and hired help. We all know he is there, waiting for death, urging it to *come get me*! But death is taking its time.

'Wanted me to get his suit ready the other day,' Mary Beth says.

'What for?' she asked him.

'For the funeral!' old Bob shouted at her, as though she were an imbecile.

'Why would I burn a perfectly good suit?' Mary Beth shouted back. And together they laughed and laughed. Death, by then, was her father's friend.

He died one cold winter morning. Not in bed, as we all thought he would, but in the car after a visit to the doctor.

'I parked at Church Point,' Mary Beth told the story later. '"Come on, Dad, let's go," I said. But when I looked at him, his head was slumped, his face smooth as wax, like he was cold as the morning. I felt his pulse. Nothing. Put my hand under his nose. Not a breath. I'm a nurse, I know what death is. So I got out of the car and called the ambulance. "My dad," I said, "has just died in the car. Can you come?" Then I called Michael. Sobbing.'

Michael jumped in the boat he calls *Bethie*, after his wife, and flew across the water. At The Point, locals gathered around to comfort Mary Beth. She bought a coffee from the café in the General Store at Ferry Wharf, lit a cigarette as she waited for help, tears streaming down her face.

'Then I went back to the car, to sit with Dad.'

'Can I have a puff of that?' old Bob asked.

'Dad! You're supposed to be dead! The ambulance is coming because you're dead!'

'Dead or not, I'd still like a puff.'

His pacemaker, it turned out, had kicked in, saving his life. His time wasn't finally up until a year later. By then he was cursing the pacemaker from dawn to dusk.

There have been so many changes in so few years in this little cluster of houses in Lovett Bay, and yet I suspect that I have changed more than all else. I do not racket heavily like I did once, trashing through days and nights in a blur of booze and desire. I have a knowledge, now, that comes from an intimacy with death and grief and fear. Hard won but priceless. Live so there are no regrets.

Sometimes I pick up a book that turns out to be about searching for the key to happiness. Once I would have devoured it. Now I set it aside for a civilised thriller or to revisit a classic. For this short period of my life, I need no gurus. And I have learned that only I hold the key.

I am not smug, though, because I am aware the unexpected can drop like a hailstorm from the sky and steal joy in a flash. And if you are not careful, it might take years to rediscover it.

Fleury's first tour group is due in November, on Melbourne Cup Day. Lunch on the lawn for one hundred corporate wives on a junket with their husbands who have a golf day scheduled. Not quite the *small* group we anticipated.

'No problem,' I tell Fleury airily, wondering where I'm going to find one hundred plates, knives, forks and spoons.

'What about tables and chairs?' Bob asks.

'Chairs are easy. Saw some blue plastic ones on sale the other day. Tables are harder. Thought I'd round up all the tables in the bay.'

'I could use the timber from the old deck and build three trestles,' Bob offers. 'Make 'em big enough for ten people each.'

I am amazed, as always, at being married to a practical man. My father was so technically inept we wouldn't even let him turn the radio on. 'Thank you. That'll get us sorted completely.'

I come up with a ridiculous, overly complex menu from flicking through glossy food magazines. The recipes all seem to have at least fifteen ingredients, each one of them expensive. Naturally, I've never cooked any of the dishes before and it doesn't occur to me to do a practice run.

Lisa, from Elvina Bay, agrees to help on the day. She is bouncy and blonde and holds nothing in. Laughter, she always says, cures most ailments. She is a master cook, catering local weddings and parties, and she never shirks when there's a fundraiser, or the fire brigade is doing a back-burn before the heat of summer turns the bush tinder dry. She coddles the fireys, making them exotic sandwiches and homey cakes. It's food so luscious, there's never any trouble finding volunteers.

Marie, from Scotland Island, is quietly efficient. Not so much a cook as a subtle, dark-haired and aloof major-domo, she sees the details, aims for perfection, and is scrupulously careful to waste nothing. 'Scrape the pan,' she tells me as I rush around. 'The dog will eat it.'

And there's my friend and neighbour Caro, who studied to become a divorce lawyer and then turned her back on the petty squabbles of people who married before they grew up. She searched instead for finer pursuits, spurred on by the clear-sightedness of nearly anyone who has had cancer. She offers to lend a hand, as long as she doesn't have to stir anything. Which is weird because she's a great cook. Just doesn't have the confidence to do it as a job. *Neither do I!* But I bludgeon my fear. Confidence is everything, and planning and preparation – right?

Every night for a week before the big day I wake up in a cold panic. The nightmares are all the same. Not enough food. Prepare it for the wrong date. Can't find the plates. A couple of days before the guests are due, I dream about returning home from the supermarket to find crowds of people hanging around, bored, hungry and cranky. All I have is four small, raw chickens. I turn on the oven but it won't heat up. I'm screaming *no, no, no* when Bob wakes me. I'm wet with sweat. Breathless.

'This lunch isn't worrying you, is it?' he asks, frowning with concern.

'Nah! Hot flush, that's all.'

I buy more and more food. Bob shakes his head without saying a word. He offers to help but my mind swizzles in increasingly confused circles. I forget *why* I thought I needed so much parsley. And what's the chutney for again? The pantry is stacked with old jam jars full of it. Quadrupled the recipe.

The day before the lunch I halve fifty spatchcocks to marinate in lime zest, harissa, crushed garlic and salt flakes. It takes four hours to make one hundred fat veal meatballs stuffed with camembert, rolled in breadcrumbs and oven-roasted. Sprigs of fresh rosemary and crushed garlic are layered between delicate lamb cutlets to be barbecued on the day. I slow-roast beetroot and carrots in honey to serve cold. Spend the entire afternoon char-grilling vegetables on the barbecue – sweet potatoes, red capsicums, zucchini sprinkled with chopped garlic, mushrooms with a whiff of chili – until Lovett Bay smells like a restaurant and everyone wants to know what's going on.

'A party?' the boys in the boatshed ask hopefully.

'Nope. A lunch. A tour group. We're having it up the hill.'

Their faces sag with disappointment.

'There'll be leftovers,' I add, to cheer them up.

The fridge bursts with neatly packed and labelled containers, but the stainless steel bowls I bought hoping they would magically turn me into a professional chef are still stacked, unused, on the kitchen table. I can't decide if that is a good or bad sign.

Dessert will be easy, I tell myself before turning out the bedroom light. Lemon cakes, the kind you make in a food processor in a few minutes. They never fail. As I pull over the bedcovers, the smell of garlic and onions fills the air. From my hands. It takes about three days to scrub it away.

At four am before it's light, I creep out of bed. Count forty-five eggs, soften five and a half pounds of butter in the microwave and zest twenty lemons to make five cakes, doubling the quantities with each one. Twenty slices to every cake. It takes twice as much time as I allotted, time that pounces forward in half-hour increments instead of minutes. My stomach is roiling with anxiety.

By the time Lisa arrives with one hundred golden-crusted bite-size meat pies, the cakes are lined up. Only one has sunk a little alarmingly in the middle, pulled out of the oven before it was cooked. Impatience. A lifelong affliction, like plunging in without thinking about the details – or possible consequences.

'We can save that cake for last,' I tell Lisa when she looks at it uncertainly. 'Only use it if we have to.'

'Tell me again why you wanted the pies,' she asks, looking at the kitchen sink, which is head-high with dishes.

'Melbourne Cup Day tradition,' I explain. As I say it, I remember we always had chicken sandwiches on Cup Day. I've got it mixed up. Meat pies go with the football. Bugger. I break out in a wave of hot flushes, spin a few times.

'You alright? Think you might do well with a cuppa,' Lisa suggests, putting on the kettle.

'Feel a bit stressed,' I confess. 'Everything changes when people are paying for something. What if it all goes wrong?'

'Well, we fix it. I mean, what's the panic? Is anyone going to die?'

I hear my own words coming back at me: *If it's not life threatening, don't sweat it*. That's how I try to live. But I forget. 'No, of course not,' I smile.

Bob comes in for a cuppa. The knees of his faded jeans are caked with dirt. He's been kneeling somewhere, fixing something. He offers to chop the parsley lying in a deep green mound on the kitchen bench. I hand it to him with a grateful sigh. What's it for again? Then I remember he hasn't had breakfast. I'm about to ask him what he'd like, but he's already putting two slices of bread in the toaster.

At nine o'clock, Bob and Lisa carry the food containers past the boatshed to Bob's rusty old ute parked at the bottom of the hill. The boys put in their orders for leftovers: spatchcocks and lemon cake. There's no mention of vegetables.

At *Tarrangaua*, Caro, Fleury and Marie set the tables on the verandah, arrange flowers and fold crisp white napkins. We crank up the music. Tony Joe White belts out 'Polk Salad Annie', a song about a poor girl who lives on weeds from the riverbanks. I squirm. The largesse of lunch seems suddenly indecent.

A breeze floats along the verandah like a cool spirit. Splendid yachts, a derelict working boat with a sexy, svelte hull, motor cruisers, old ferries and boats wreathed in grunge and bird shit rock on green waters. The window of a homemade houseboat we call the *Fruit Box*, which never moves off its mooring, winks in the light. Tree tops foam like gold tipped waves. Who cares about the food? To be here is privilege enough.

Fleury organises water jugs, plates and servers, moves tables to strategic positions to serve food and drinks. Lisa sets up the kitchen like an army canteen while Marie and Caro polish cutlery borrowed from every nearby household, iron out creases in the tablecloths, sweep gum leaves that have flown in on the wind like butterflies.

Friends Geoff and Jacqui arrive with a basket of glorious roses from their mountain garden. Marie arranges them in vases on tables, cupboards, the old pianola, the mantelpiece. It feels like the house has woken from a long, deep sleep and has dressed for the occasion in its best party clothes.

'Ferry's coming,' shouts Lisa from the verandah.

'Here, Caro, you cook the asparagus. You do it better than anyone else.' I shove a large box at her. 'It's got me stumped. There's too much.'

Caro's brought her mother's old asparagus cooker, which is big enough for a couple of bunches. She laughs. 'This won't do it!' she says. 'What we need is a huge saucepan.'

She climbs a ladder and passes down a gigantic stockpot from the top shelf of the pantry. '*Almost* big enough,' she says. Then she lifts the box onto the bench and reaches in to begin snapping the ends off each spear. 'We'll tie them in lots of small bundles and stand them up,' she announces.

'Go, girl!'

Bob grabs the tongs and lays the naked little spatchcocks on the grill in orderly lines, tucking in their wings and legs tidily. Fleury's husband, Stewart, who's dropped by out of curiosity, gets ready to barbecue the lamb cutlets, so small and tender they're barely more than a bite each. Lisa arranges the dreaded meatballs on a large platter, cutting them in half.

'No-one's gonna eat a whole one, Susan,' she says. 'They're bigger than footballs!'

Marie and Lisa pour cool water, soft drinks or wine, as guests arrive, offer a bite-size pie. 'Melbourne Cup tradition,' Lisa explains, smiling. I decided not to confuse her with the truth.

Mid-afternoon, Fleury organises a sweep, which has the Americans, Brits, French, German and Italian dames flummoxed. They understand winning, though, and when the race begins, the budgie yabber of a boozy lunch hushes.

I stand back and raise a glass to my brother, a larrikin gambler who graced racetracks with Beau Brummel elegance, in a silent toast. As I will at this time every year. *Wish you were here. Wish we were dressed to the max to hit the Spring Racing Carnival, our race books marked up and every horse a lay-down misère winner.* Then I turn away from the television before the race ends. Too many tears. Too many memories. Better keep busy. Dirty plates are stacked from one end of the kitchen to the other. If my mother were around, she'd say *leave them!* I've always wondered how she thinks they'll get done. By magic? I turn on the tap and fill the sink. If my mother has a secret trick, I wish she'd pass it on.

An hour later, guests tackle the uneven sandstone pathway down to the ferry. Too late, I remember the wobbly stone on the bottom step at the fork. Meant to ask Bob to fix it.

'Lisa! Anyone really pissed?' I call out. She's clearing tables on the verandah.

'Just a couple,' she replies.

'Shit! We'd better help them on the steps.'

'Wouldn't worry,' she says. 'If they're pissed they won't hurt themselves. I'd be more concerned about the sober ones.'

And we laugh and laugh.

'Doesn't matter how many precautions you take,' Lisa adds, coming in with a tray load of coffee cups, 'if there's going to be a bolt out of the blue, nothing you can do will stop it.'

We line up on the verandah waving goodbye as the ferry slides past. Pittwater looks sublime. I feel possessive and protective.

'Well,' says Lisa, hands on her hips, her curly blonde hair looking only slightly frizzy, 'that wasn't too awful. But were you expecting a few more people?' She looks at the leftovers.

'Thought I'd make extra so everyone could take some home,' I lie. Bob's about to tell the truth but my black look stops him.

'So what was all the parsley for?' he asks.

'Decoration.' It's another lie. I remembered far too late that it was supposed to go in the meatballs.

When we've shared the leftovers amongst the helpers, the neighbours and the boys in the boatshed, finished the dishes, mopped the floors and re-settled the house into its customary solitary state, Bob and I wander home a little unsteadily along Lover's Lane to the *Tin Shed* by the light of a torch. An owl hoots, over and over. *Boo-boo. Boo-boo.* It's a lonely, mournful sound. Once it would have made me cry.

I tell Bob the truth about the parsley when we're in bed. Lying can get to be a habit – and there's no point. Trust is a very thin thread.

'House looked good, though, don't you think? Like she'd fluffed for the day?' I say in the darkness.

Bob grunts. Rolls over to wrap his arms around me. I squeeze tightly against him. Until a dreaded hot flush pounds in. He wipes the sweat from under my eyes with the ball of his thumb. Slides across the bed so I can throw off the blankets. Within a minute, his breathing falls into the steady rhythm of sleep. As I lie there reliving the day in my mind, I begin to think about the pale house on the *high rough hill* slightly differently.

It feels like only a minute or two has gone by between the Melbourne Cup lunch and Christmas Day. When I was a kid, a withered old bloke with missing teeth and a turtle head used to tell me, 'Time speeds up as you get older.' He ran the dusty corner store in the country town outside Melbourne where my parents owned a pub. Every visiting Sunday, when I was allowed out of boarding school – after church and back before dinner – I'd swing open the creaky door with its busted flywire and step into the gloom to buy two shillings worth of black cats.

He was a frugal old codger who'd survived the Depression and only turned on the electric lights after sunset.

'Youth is wasted on the young,' he'd despair, as he separated four black cats for each penny with knotted, arthritic fingers. He had jelly beans, jubes, freckles and mints in glass jars on the pitted counter. Black and white striped humbugs and red, green and gold traffic lights wrapped in clear paper. But the chewy black cats with a powerful taste of aniseed were my favourites.

I didn't believe him about speeding time. I was not even a teenager and the days seemed to drizzle between one school holiday and the next. Now I am in my fifties, I understand what he meant. About youth being wasted on the young, as well.

This first Christmas Day since Bob and I married, the weather is nervy. Winds swirl indecisively, cool from the south for a moment, then blasting hot from the west. Boats swivel on their moorings, confused. White caps foam and froth. We are edgy, too. It is the bushfire season and fires are wreaking havoc north and south of us, destroying homes, livestock, land and lives. It is calamitous. All night a westerly wind flicked ash and soot our way, fogging the sky, thickening the air. The smell of roasted eucalyptus seeped into our hair, our skin. Now it hangs off us like a spare set of clothing. Our little bay has escaped so far, but for how long?

We are planning to have lunch on the verandah at *Tarrangaua* instead of at home in the *Tin Shed*. A salute to the past. Another easing of feeling that I have somehow stolen another woman's life and I have no right to be standing in her kitchen. The *usual suspects*, as my mother always refers to them, are coming for roast turkey and pudding. Bomber and Bea, tanned almost black from slogging around the waterways on their boot-shaped emerald green barge, *The Trump*, fixing moorings. Marty, my brother-in-law from my first marriage, and his beautiful partner, Witch. The blind Buddhist nun, Adrienne Howley, whom we all met when she kindly visited *Tarrangaua* to talk to Barbara who hadn't much longer to live. Barbara had wanted to know more about the poet. The nun had nursed Mackellar for nearly eleven years and could answer most of her questions.

And, of course, my mother, Esther, is with us, as she is every year. Already Bob and I know she is not keen on the nun – feels her turf is threatened and she might have to battle for the single-minded attention she is used to. Adrienne, also in her eighties, is wise enough to stay out of her way, which isn't hard because we have given her a room at *Tarrangaua*. She sits, each morning, as still as a statue in a cane chair on the verandah, her hands folded in her lap. Wearing the deep maroon robes of a Tibetan nun. At peace.

In the *Tin Shed*, down the hill, my mother rises, as she's done for as long as I can remember, before dawn. I hear her footsteps going to and from the bathroom. The loo flushing. The kettle boiling. The smell of toast cooking and the acrid scent of instant coffee.

'I don't disturb you, do I?' she asks.

'No, not at all,' I fib every time. Because I know it is impossible for her to change her habits.

20

It is a small group gathering for Christmas lunch this year. Suzi and Lulu, the daughters of my first husband, Paul, are celebrating with their father's side of the family. Bob's son, Scott, can't get time off from his job in Pittsburgh, in the US, where he's a chemical engineer. Bob's three daughters, Kelly, Meg and Nicole, are based in Victoria. Kelly, a nurse, is on duty over Christmas and New Year. Meg, an engineer like her father, plans to drive from Melbourne on Boxing Day. Nicole, with two young children, finds it less stressful to spend Christmas at home.

Pia, a great friend and long-time Christmas stalwart, refused to budge from her new northern New South Wales paradise and who could blame her? 'I'm having a sandwich on the beach with anyone who wants to join me,' she explained.

Stewart and Fleury and their two daughters will come for pudding, bringing their guests – a tradition since I moved to Pittwater. And any neighbour who feels like floating in for a drink, or just to escape their own mayhem, is welcome.

Five minutes after we all sit at the table to begin lunch a hot gust explodes down Salvation Creek, blasting the nun's fresh prawns down the length of the verandah. We watch, open-mouthed. The prawns look alive, like a dream sequence in a B-grade movie. Then the phone rings. Somehow we know it isn't going to be a distant friend calling to exchange greetings.

'Akuna Bay is on fire,' says a neighbour. 'You'd better prepare.'

Akuna Bay, on Coal and Candle Creek, is in the heart of the Ku-ring-gai Chase National Park. When the wind blows from the west Lovett Bay always takes a direct hit. That's the course it blew in 1994, when all the houses in our little enclave burned to the ground. Except *Tarrangaua*.

'It is a strange house, that one,' an old-time resident told me a while after I moved here. 'It's only ever caught fire once. In the 1960s, in a small section of the north east corner, and it was easily put out with barely any damage done. No other bush fire has come near it. And there have been plenty! Seems to have a spirit protecting it. Or something.' I think of his words as smoke hazes the sky behind the hills and escarpments, hoping they will be true again.

'Better get the pumps ready,' Bob says, pushing back his chair.

'Better get the leaves off your roof,' Bomber replies, standing up.

'Better rake the lawn and sweep the leaf litter away from around the house,' Bea adds, smoothing her dress over a stomach iron hard with muscle.

'What can I do?' asks the nun.

'Better say a prayer,' I suggest.

'What about me?' Marty asks.

'You'd better direct operations, Marty. Save those tired old knees of yours in case we have to make a dash for it.' I look at Witch, dark-eyed, tanned and dressed in pure white linen. Her soft, city hands wave in query.

'Better start making sandwiches, Witch. Think the grand repast has turned into a picnic. Oh, and make a few – if the fire gets here, we'll have hungry fireys everywhere.'

My mother looks up from her plate. Sighs. The oysters will have to wait. 'I'd better have a whisky,' she says, to veil the inadequacy of old age.

Bomber changes into a pair of Bob's paint-stained shorts and a tatty shirt, jams his feet into a too-small pair of battered Dunlop tennis shoes. He grabs a ladder and broom and climbs to the roof, sweeping from a 30-degree angle, treading carefully and trying not to crack the terracotta tiles. Leaves drop from gutters and valleys in the roof line, falling in avalanches that lie three inches deep. Bea and I fill large plastic garbage bags with leaf litter. The wind rockets. Trees bend. Our throats grow hoarse with smoke.

Bob unrolls hundreds of metres of hose from house to shore. It lies on the track like a fat blue snake with a glittering nozzle head. He sets up a pump on the pontoon to pull water from the bay. The pump is so powerful it would empty the rainwater tanks in minutes.

22

Witch makes strong, earthy-smelling pots of tea, over and over. Offers glasses of iced water. The sandwiches, thick with ham and turkey, are wrapped and waiting.

When Bomber comes down from the roof, the two men test the pump. Bob starts the engine while Bomber holds the hose. We watch it swell until it suddenly kicks in his hands. Water sprays the bush for a hundred feet, drenching it. We are ready. And we wait.

Late in the afternoon, the nun's prayers are heard and a sea breeze kicks in. Our good fortune, someone else's tragedy. Like my Uncle Frank always says: 'If you're doing it good, someone else is doing it bad. If you're doing it bad, someone else is doing it good. Life's a cycle.'

'Worst Christmas ever,' Bea said after they sold *The Trump* and retired to twenty-five acres on the Central Coast a few years later. 'But really, really good, too.' And we laughed. As you do when you come close to disaster and somehow escape.

By February, the nation is still reeling from the worst bushfire season in history. The dry weather we thought would soon move on has become a permanent resident. It is officially a drought.

Already, the towering spotted gum in the normally damp gully in the elbow of the back track where a fungi forest once reigned weeps a resinous brown fluid. The eucalyptus trees that tower above the house are parched and haggard, as though engulfed by a terrible sadness. It's been more than two years since the waterfall in the south west corner of Lovett Bay flooded in foaming white torrents. Soon, we hope, the drought will break. It always does.

Since I retired from full-time work, my mother calls me nearly every morning. She doesn't often have anything new to say, but the connection, I think, makes her feel secure. Reminds her she is not alone.

'I don't want you to worry,' she begins one late summer day.

'Ok. I won't,' I reply calmly, squishing down anger at being manipulated. Because it is an old game – of course she wants me to worry.

'I've had another fall. Broken the other wrist. But I'm alright. Nothing to worry about. Just wanted to tell you.'

My irritation, so quick to flare with my mother for no reason I will ever really understand, subsides in a wave of shame. 'Do you want to come and stay for a while?'

'No. No. I'm managing beautifully.'

'Might be time you moved out of that house.'

'You're not putting me in some home somewhere,' she shoots back. 'I may be old but I'm still capable.'

So I do not ask how she will manage alone in a large house with steps, a house that is two hours away at the foot of the Blue Mountains. I do not offer to stay with her for a while. I do nothing except call her for a few days to make sure she is coping. I am not, I am aware, an ideal daughter, the kind she dreamed would nurse her through her old age. She may have hammered in her idea of family – 'It is the one place where no matter what you've done, no matter how long you've been away, it must always open its door to you' – but in the selfish way of children, I took that to mean *I* could always come home. Not that, one day, it might be the other way around.

'Could find her a place around here,' Bob says, after I indulge in another bout of guilt and still do nothing about it.

'You don't think that might be a bit close?'

'Nah. There's a moat.' He looks up. 'Not an Olympic swimmer or anything, is she?' he adds.

'Got a nice style in the water. Think the distance might be a handicap though.'

'That's alright then.'

I begin quietly looking around for a place in a retirement home for her. But I say nothing. With my mother, timing is of the utmost importance.

A year after we begin our tourist lunches at *Tarrangaua*, they are beginning to lose their novelty. I have learned there is a deep chasm between trained chefs and amateur cooks like myself. Budgets and too many clients wanting too much for too little are wearing out my enthusiasm. I am not helped, either, by my idiotic compulsion to over-cater.

One day, when the wind is blowing cold and hard from the south and hitting the verandah full on, we set up the tables inside. Half an hour before the guests are due, Fleury calls to say the leader of the group insists they all dine outside. She is from Belgium, apparently, where she eats inside all the time.

'There's a gale!' I tell Fleury.

'I know, but she doesn't care.'

I put the phone down. We have moved sofas, tables and chairs to accommodate extra tables. Now we're supposed to move them all again.

'No way,' I mutter darkly to Lisa, who sighs with relief. 'There's only one set of rules here and they're mine.'

Halfway up the steps with her group, Fleury phones again, her voice shaking with anger.

'Now she wants to eat inside!'

'Don't worry. I didn't move any tables. It would have been madness.'

'Thank God,' Fleury sighs.

'What's this dame like?'

'A nightmare,' she whispers.

When the Belgian woman arrives, she rushes straight into the kitchen and tells us she wants lunch on the table in five minutes.

'Madame,' I say, barely able to remain polite, 'you are here because Fleury is a friend. This is not a regular business. Lunch will be ready when it is ready.'

She turns away from me and blasts off a fusilade of complaints in French to her friend.

'Je parle français, madame,' I say, although truthfully I've understood the gist of her conversation and not the specifics.

She spins towards me in horror then bolts out of the kitchen. Half an hour later she insists on leaving in a water taxi.

'Now I've got to find her a goddamn private car as well,' Fleury groans, reaching for her mobile phone. 'Jesus. I'd hate to be her husband.'

The moment the Belgian woman leaves the room, the atmosphere switches from quiet gloom to relaxed chat. Guests stick their heads inside the kitchen to apologise for their colleague's behaviour, to thank us for lunch. I smile, nod. But it is too late. I have reached the denouement.

Bob and I look at each other after the last tipsy guest has piled into a water taxi in ridiculously high heels, and although he says nothing, I know what he's thinking. *Why on earth am I doing this?* It's taken a week to clean and do the food preparation and it will take two days to swizzle both houses back to normal. Cooking is my passion, the lunches my whim, but Bob cannot see me work without offering to help.

'You were right, you know,' I tell him. 'The fun evaporates when you turn a hobby into a job. I don't want to be around people like that mad Belgian woman. They steal your energy and shatter your peace.'

He nods but stays silent.

'The house needs people, though,' I continue. 'It will die if it's left empty for years at a time.'

A month later, around the same time as my mother calls to say the plaster has been removed from her wrist and the doctor reckons she's healed as beautifully as a woman with young bones, Bob casually mentions finding tenants for *Tarrangaua* could be difficult.

'They need to be fit enough to cop the steps,' he says.

'Never know unless we have a go,' I reply.

We ask the local real estate agent to put the house on her books. 'It's a difficult property,' she tells us. 'There's a good market for low maintenance beach shacks. Houses like *Tarrangaua* . . . well . . . it might take a while for the right people to come along.'

'Been empty for a couple of years now. A few more months won't matter,' Bob says.

'By the way, I've looked at a couple of retirement villages that might be suitable for Esther,' I tell him.

'Have you told her anything about all this?'

'Nope. She has a morbid fear of what she calls "old people's homes". I think it's better if I talk to her face to face.'

Over the next few months, though, she sounds so well and happy on the phone, the idea of moving her to a place where she will manage more easily loses its urgency. Like my mother always says, 'if it ain't broke, don't fix it'.

Towards the end of winter, the real estate agent says she has found tenants for *Tarrangaua*. Bob and I temporarily move up the hill to prepare the house. Cleaning furniture, emptying cupboards, repairing fly-screens, touching up paintwork and writing a list of anything that might flummox the uninitiated in the vagaries of Pittwater living. Such as the wise use of tank water and caring for a septic system so it stays happily in balance and neither pongs nor overflows.

We camp like holiday-makers, turning out the lights and sitting on the floor with firelight dancing on the walls, playing music until late. I am not entirely at ease, but nor do I feel like a trespasser.

Chip Chop, my trollopy little Jack Russell, is already familiar with the house. When I travelled, as I still do occasionally, on assignments for *The Australian Women's Weekly*, Bob and Barbara took care of her, making sure she didn't rampage through the bush as though it was her own private game park. On our first night up the hill, she leaps straight onto the sofa and falls asleep in a cushioned corner with a loud, ecstatic sigh.

A few weeks after the new tenants, John and Therese, lug the last of their clothes and all of their computer equipment up the steps, they call to ask if we would like to join them for dinner. We have seen them on the water in their tinny, but aside from a quick nod or a wave at a smiley bald-headed bloke and a skinny little woman with laughing blue eyes, there's been little contact.

On the night we get together, John barbecues a whole duck to serve with pieces of lime and chili. When he unwraps it from the foil at the table, none of us says a word. It is cinder black, and shrivelled to the size of a large potato.

'Wonderful,' we all trill after a minute or two, trying to find small bits that are still edible. Because we do not know each other well enough yet to understand if the truth might offend or hurt.

'Hottest blooming barbecue I've ever known,' John says eventually.

'What did you expect? Bob's a combustion engineer!' I explain.

'Ah!'

John is a shiny-headed . . . what? Renaissance man best describes him. Lawyer, writer, businessman, sailor and who knows what else? He came to Pittwater on holidays as a child and never forgot it. One day, he is not sure why, he decided he would like to return.

Therese is deeply Irish even though she's lived in Australia for more than thirty years. She is a social worker, unafraid of the seamier moments in people's lives. Once, she brought down the wrath of her board of directors when she let a homeless man sleep on a bench in the garden of the community centre where she was boss. 'It's bridge day,' they screamed at her, implying that the sight of a shambling alcoholic in need of a bath and clean trousers would be too confronting for the well-dressed women who played cards there every Wednesday.

'This is a *community* centre,' she replied, unmoved. She fetched him fresh clothes, made fifty phone calls until she found a place for him to sleep, then cleaned up the mess he had left behind. Her compassion should have shamed her colleagues, but all they felt was sullied.

'Pound for weight, she's stronger than any woman I've ever seen,' says Bob with approval. He has watched her carry a case of wine up the hill, slim as a teenager, barely more than five feet tall. His tone is rich with respect.

I am at ease that first time we return to *Tarrangaua* on the occasion that becomes known as 'the night of the black duck'. I am a guest, which I am familiar with. But Bob feels strangely disoriented. 'I keep wanting to check the oven and fill the wine glasses,' he whispers. 'And John's sitting where I always sit!'

And it is the moment I finally understand that the *Tin Shed* will never be home to him.

A year later, Bob makes one of his endless trips along Lover's Lane to get a tool from his shed at *Tarrangaua* and something inside me gives way.

'Should we give your house a go for a while?' I ask him. The rental lease is due to expire. We expect John and Therese to move on. Even though he has the chance to leap in with a loud *yes,* he holds back.

'It wouldn't bother you?'

'No. Not anymore.' And I hope it is true.

We tell John and Therese our plans over a dinner of slow-roasted pork with crackling rubbed with preserved lemon, fennel seeds, garlic and sea salt.

'Don't worry,' they say gaily, when we apologise if it's going to cause any inconvenience. 'We'll just move into the *Tin Shed*.' And we swap houses. It's as easy as that.

A week before moving day, I pile cookware, crockery, cutlery, serving dishes, glassware and bowls into the wheelbarrow and push each load along the rough bush path we call Lover's Lane. It runs behind the *Tin Shed* to *Tarrangaua*. According to local legend a doctor who ran a home for mentally disabled men fell in love with Dorothea Mackellar and cut the path from his house to hers. It was an unrequited love, from all accounts. Only a single, isolated sandstone chimney remains of his dwelling, and the tangled residue of a once ordered cottage garden: wisteria, two magnolias, hydrangeas. Plants that survived the firestorm of 1994. Tougher, in the end, than the house.

Bob cleared the pathway in the days not long after Barbara died and I began cooking for the two of us. Most evenings, he walked slowly along the track, bottle of wine in hand, shoulders hunched, his weathered face creased more deeply, it seemed to me, than just a year earlier.

At first, our dinners were awkward. We were wary. Not of each other, but of saying something thoughtless. It took the passing of time to dull the raw edges and, oddly, the familiarity of routine – oddly because I used to loathe predictability and lived for excitement. I am old enough now, though, to look back regretfully at so much effort wasted on worthless pursuits. I cannot help wishing I'd directed my energy more profoundly and less recklessly when I had it in abundance.

The wheelbarrow hits a gnarled and hard root of a spotted gum. I take a deep breath. Grunt. And bounce over it. Every day, stronger and stronger. Chemo is more like a bad dream from another lifetime.

Bob's shed is dusty, thick with spider webs and tools flung on benches. Bare floorboards, some of them sinking. Grimy windows and gaps between the timber. It is chaos.

'Where's all this stuff going to fit?' he moans as I unload another wheelbarrow load of kitchen equipment.

'What about the cupboards in the hallway? They're huge.'

'That's where I keep my old business files.'

'Oh.'

It makes me suddenly unsure, forces me to question whether what we are doing will be for the best. We are not *beginning* in a new house, we are picking up the past. In a different way, of course, but it's unshakable. There is the indelible print of another woman's life and it will always be there.

Barbara and Bob had the bed made for them in Australian cedar. They found the bedside tables on a jaunt through country Victoria. Bob and his son carried up the huge cedar chest of drawers from the boat on a stinking summer day. Eighty-eight steps. Will Bob drift back in time when he pulls a pair of socks from the drawers, when he lays a book down on the bedside table before turning out the light? Will I feel I have moved in with a ghost?

My head spins. I have made so many moves in too few years. The *Tin Shed* is perfect. Why change the order of things? Because Bob needs his shed, I reply to myself silently. Because going up and down the hill five times a day will get more and more exhausting. Because home is where Bob is and the rest is just building material. Because to resent Bob's past is childish and irrational. We all have pasts. My own is not particularly noble. And Barbara was a friend. To be reminded of her is a good thing. She was a fine woman with impeccable instincts. And because *Tarrangaua* is old and, like old people, it needs tenderness to keep sparkling.

'I'll only take *half* the hallway cupboards, then,' I tell Bob firmly.

Bob nods. A good relationship, he tells me from time to time, is built on many things. Trust is the baseline, with the ability to compromise not far behind. To win every round in a relationship can sometimes mean losing the marriage.

We swap houses on a fine day in late spring 2003 with the help of Bob's mates, six sunny-faced blokes from an engineering factory in Mona Vale.

'Not the kind of move you need a barge for,' Bob explains. 'Next door, really.'

Next door and up a mountain, I think to myself. But I say nothing. And there's Bob's old white ute, freckled with rust. No matter how heavy the load, it just gets gruntier. The blokes still have to carry sofas, beds, sideboards, tables and chairs down the steps from the *Tin Shed*, across the rutted slipway of the Lovett Bay boatshed and along a dirt waterside pathway to the bottom of the sandstone track. Nothing is light. My father always told me to buy stuff to *last*. 'You buy it once,' he advised, 'and you have it forever.'

But I was young then, and the idea of keeping something forever was unthinkable. What did *forever* mean, anyway? So I bought my share of new and trendy. Through the years, I've kept the timeless pieces and flicked the fashion fads. Should've listened to him when I had the chance. Although he was a realist about the usefulness of parental wisdom: 'You've got to make your own mistakes. Only way anyone ever learns.' His face, as he said it, was always full of sad resignation, as though he'd made a million of his own mistakes and wished he could save me from the ones he understood were ahead, but knew he couldn't.

At the waterfront, the blokes tightly strap the first load into the back of the ute. It's a 35-degree incline and the track is rough as hell.

'Would've been a cinch if we'd left all the furniture where it was,' Bob says.

'Yeah, but it's your house. If I don't have my own stuff around me, I will feel like a guest.'

'Fair enough.'

The ute goes uphill frontways over red kangaroo grass that grows down the middle of the track like a mohawk haircut. There's no turning circle at the house and Bob treasures his lawn, so he reverses down. It's like driving backwards into the stratosphere. All you can see in the rear-vision mirror is an empty lapis lazuli sky. Bob stares into the side mirrors to get his bearings but it's still tricky. Too far to the left and he plunges into a deep drainage channel. Too far to the right and he careens into knotty bush. Lose concentration and he'll end up in the bay.

By late afternoon, Bob looks haggard. He's done about thirty trips. There's an ominous thunk under the bonnet of the old ute, but it never falters. Nor does Bob. He's going home and he's happy.

'Those blokes are buggered,' I tell Bob when it is all, finally, done. The smiles are gone. The boys sit, shoulders hunched forward, arms wrapped around bony knees, heads hanging in exhaustion. Except for one. The fitness fanatic.

'Going for a run,' he says. 'To have a look around the bush.'

We groan, tell him to settle. He ignores us and takes off, tall, skinny and indefatigable.

'Bloody glad you didn't want the pianola moved,' says Troy, trying to grin but too tired to pull it off.

'I'll get tea and cake on the go.'

'A beer might go down a bit better,' he replies, forlornly.

On our first evening at *Tarrangaua*, we sit on the verandah as the sky segues from blue to pearly pink. There's a bottle of champagne on the table but it stays unopened. Five scruffy kookaburras line up on the rails, looking for dinner. They fly away in disgust when we ignore them. Two king parrots, a male and female, land in an explosion of red and green, like performers in a medieval play. The white cockatoos, louder than banshees, salt the bush on the other side of Lovett Bay. At dusk, two brown wallabies with rusty chests edge their way cautiously onto the lawn, wide-eyed and beguiling.

'Not bad for openers,' I say to Bob, reaching for his hand.

'It only gets better,' he replies with a smile.

Then we head down the hill to Stef and Bella's for dinner. 'Too hard to cook after a move,' Bella had insisted. 'I'll take care of food for all of you.'

John and Therese are already there. Their bed is made, they tell us, and they are looking forward to another chapter in Pittwater living. 'Not as far to come to dinner now,' John says to Bella. 'Easier to get home, too.'

'I love Pittwater,' I mutter later, when we're stumbling up the hill, exhausted and slightly pizzled. 'It's family without the baggage, and they're always there.'

'Yeah. They're great neighbours, great friends. But nothing beats family.'

Early the next morning, not long after the kookaburras and cockatoos shatter the dawn quiet, I walk down the hallway past a photograph of Bob and Barbara where their heads are touching and Bob's dark eyes are almost closed. Her blue eyes are filled with laughter.

'Well, he's back,' I tell the photograph. 'And I'm here too. Hope that's ok.'

I am full of bravado but despite Bob's careful courtesies, sleeping, dressing, reading and resting feel like trespassing in another person's inner sanctum. Vaguely voyeuristic. For a long

while, I hesitate to open bedside drawers even though I know –
because I have cleaned them – that they are empty of the remnants
of another life. Only indifferent flotsam remains – cedar balls to
ward off moths and silverfish, fragrant paper lining cupboards. But
it is impossible, now and then, to hold back the guilt of still living
when Barbara does not.

In the kitchen, I fill the kettle. Through the window, Lovett Bay
ripples with light. Same tawny bay. Same orange escarpment. Same
empty sky. Yet utterly different. Up here on this *high, rough hill*
where there are no houses close by, the physical world embraces
tightly. No wonder Mackellar made *Tarrangaua* her refuge and
retreat.

3

I EXPECT, OVER TIME, to find a way to live comfortably with Barbara's ghost in *Tarrangaua*. But I do not expect to move in with two lingering spirits, if that doesn't sound too theatrical – certainly that is how it feels. I don't mean to suggest that each night the hall-ways are full of ghostly traffic. Although Barbara, pragmatic, analytical, unemotional even, was convinced she once saw the ghost of Mackellar on the hillside, clothed in russet brown, her face hidden under the brim of a wide straw hat. And sad, so sad. It is simply the pervasive sense of the past.

Not long after I put away my pots and pans and books, I find myself intrigued, as Barbara was, by Mackellar and her life, far beyond reading a poem or two. As I grow older, I have begun to wonder if it is our neglect of the past that sometimes invites calamity. When I sit at the table near the kitchen door with tea and cake, I wonder if Mackellar followed similar rituals. I am curious about a few old brick footings in the bush. What were they part of? How did the concrete garden seat, with 1938 stamped on it, come to be here? Did Mackellar bring it? Old houses awaken curiosity, and this one is so rich with history. What was life like when Mackellar lived here? How would Pittwater have looked before electric lights, speedboats and garbage barge collection days? Who lived around here when she did? How did she spend her time?

Barbara's imprint, too, is all around. She collected Australian pottery from the twenties, thirties and forties – Remued, Campbell, Bendigo, Diana, McHugh – in blues, browns and greens. A frog, too, fat and emerald. He is quite rare, I am told, because he was manufactured to be used as a doorstop and most of them, naturally, shattered.

At first the vases look dark and ugly and I leave them on shelves only because they are part of Barbara's life. Gradually, though, I begin looking beyond the murky browns and muddied greens, to the subtle celebration of the Australian landscape. Vases decorated with slim gum leaves. Bowls with possums and koalas, gumnuts and kangaroos, most of them clumsily worked and some so badly fired they leak when you fill them with water for flowers. But they represent the beginning of a shift from a nation that admired Royal Doulton and Wedgwood, which is probably what appealed most to Barbara. She was deeply passionate about all things Australian and after a while, to my eye, the clumsiness transforms into a pleasing naivety.

One particular type of plate, known as 'Give Us Our Daily Bread', eluded her. It is oval-shaped with a slightly raised lip to prevent the bread from slipping off. It was primarily made by two companies, Bendigo and Lithgow Pottery. The most prized, though, is from Lithgow Pottery because this business, which began in 1880 as an adjunct to the Lithgow Valley Colliery Co, operated for just seventeen years. Anything intact is rare and sought-after, but especially the 'Daily Bread' plate.

'If we can find a plate at the right price, it will close the circle,' Bob says, knowing, even as he says it, that it will make no tangible difference, but nevertheless mean a lot. It becomes a routine for us to wander through antique shops when we drive through small country towns. *Looking for Barbara's plate.*

One day we are filling in time at Nundle, an old goldmining town south east of Tamworth in New South Wales, wandering through a hodge-podge of used and new in a wonderfully eclectic shop. 'Look, threepences and sixpences,' I say, pointing to a cabinet full of them. 'Need a few more for the Christmas puddings. Think they must get swallowed. Or something.' As we go to the counter to pay for them, Bob asks, more out of habit than hope, if there is a Lithgow 'Daily Bread' plate anywhere.

'Yes. Just one,' says the owner. He walks to a tall cabinet, pulls a chair to stand on, reaches for a dusty plate on top.

'Can't be a real one,' Bob whispers. 'It's got to be a mistake.'

But the plate is genuine. It is marked Lithgow, with a simple drawing of a kangaroo. And the price is fair.

'Where did you get it?' Bob asks.

'From my mother. She was a dealer, but she could never bear to sell anything, so she really didn't do too well. You're the first people who have ever walked in and asked for Lithgow pottery. It's been sitting there for years.'

When we're in the car, *Barbara's plate* cushioned in yards of bubble wrap, Bob shakes his head. 'You just never know, do you? You never have the slightest idea of what you might stumble across unless you ask the question.'

Whenever we return from even just a few days away, I am struck by the differences between living *up the hill* and *down the hill*. Before I lived in *Tarrangaua* – even before I knew Bob and Barbara – I would look up from the tinny as I passed on seagull grey days when rain fell in a mist so light it clung like sweat to your skin, and it looked almost ghostly, even a little forbidding, penned behind spotted gums with trunks as smooth as prison bars. *Tarrangaua* is such an aloof building, a house that sets the tone instead of embracing yours, as though it has a force or will of its own. Brogues feel more appropriate than thongs, tweeds preferable to sarongs. I fight hard in the first few months not to succumb to its subtle pressure to dress (and behave?) more decorously than in my usual jeans and scruffy T-shirts.

After a while, the deep verandah, which casts a veil-like shadow over windows and doors, becomes my favourite place. I am drawn to it even on cold days. It is wondrous to sit there, watching life. Birds, people, dogs, boats, bait fish in boiling pools, the quicksilver glitter of jumping fish. Clouds scudding, light changing. And the bay: flicked by the wind, mill pond smooth, frosted sometimes, or glassy in the thin evening light of late autumn. I have learned to read even the lightest winds by watching the water darken where air, no stronger than a breath, passes over it. Then, at sunset, golden slabs of light pour in and the veil is lifted.

The verandah, which can only be described as grand, becomes my buffer zone between the physical and material world. There are eight round, perfectly plain concrete columns that take two arms to embrace them. By some strange illusion, they look muscular but not clumsy and they frame the view as though it is a series of large paintings. I stay here for hours, as I once did with Barbara, sipping tea. Reading, or dreaming. Or simply giving thanks. Enfolded by the peace. Peace, the holy grail. Craved by all of us who have known *fraught*.

My father, I remember, would often look at my brother and me as we played loud games. 'What do I have to do around here to get some peace?' he'd shout, but never in anger. We understood instinctively that he loved our incessant chirruping. I don't think he ever really found peace himself, though. If he had, he wouldn't have needed to dive into the brandy some mornings and beer bottles each night until he could barely stagger to bed. He must have had demons, my father, somewhere in his head and heart. I once asked my mother if she had any idea what they might have been, and her face closed down. Snapped shut quicker than a finely sprung jewellery box. 'No,' she said. 'He just liked a drink, that's all. Life doesn't have to be complicated, you know.' But it almost always is.

Peaceful Voices

I fortunate, I know a refuge
When the strained spirit tires
Of town's metallic symphony
Of wheels and horns and wires:

Where through the golden empty stillness
Cool-flowing voices speak,
The alto of the waterfall,
The treble of the creek.

From far, beyond the headland's shoulder
Southeasters bring to me
Reminder of earth's wanderings,
The strong voice of the sea.

I happy, in a leafy fortress
Listen to hidden birds
And small waves of a making tide
Mingling their lovely words.

Dorothea Mackellar wrote this poem not long after she built *Tarrangaua*. It was published in a book, *Fancy Dress*, by Angus & Robertson in 1926. I am as sure as I can be that it refers to Lovett Bay. *Tarrangaua* was the first home Mackellar had that was truly her own. Until she built it, she'd always lived with her parents. She found the land, originally nine acres, commissioned Hardy Wilson, a leading – although controversial – architect, to design the house, and made it her summer retreat. I can't help wondering, sometimes, if she felt, like I do, a lightness of being when she stayed here.

I no longer sleep with fists and teeth clenched, like I once did. I do not wake with my heart pounding in fear that the sniggering little monkey in my head will return to point and sneer: *Look at the mess you've made! Of everything!* The grief that once flooded in on the scent of the same aftershave my brother used, or the sound of 'Danny Boy', my first husband's favourite lament, is gone now, packed tightly away so I am free to feel sadness but not succumb to it. Even the sadness, I sometimes think, is as much for a long-gone era as the pain of loss.

Here, too, I have learned to squish the little caterpillar of discontent that once wormed its way into so many moments, shouting *I want, I want, I want!* What is, after all, so desirable about the unattainable? Nothing. Unless you are looking for ways to punish yourself. Sometimes, though, I feel a stirring of restlessness, vague yearnings for I know not what. It would be a lie to pretend they don't exist, these sudden rushes of desire for something *else*. They fade as quickly as they flood in, and I forget them. Until the sun goes down in a spectacular blaze that reminds me of the bigger world, and the restlessness returns. Am I missing something integral by wallowing in so much contentment? Or perhaps, more accurately, am I inviting ill-fortune back into my life by living so joyfully? Who doesn't, here and there, fear attracting the wrath of the gods?

When friends visit *Tarrangaua*, most of them use the back door and walk into what was once the laundry. It's a kitchen annex now, with a second stove and a large sink where Bob washes his hands after working in his shed or the garden. Through a doorway, a short passage leads past a large pantry to the kitchen. The front, formal entrance is almost secretive. Two stairways are built into a solid sandstone wall wide enough to comfortably support large pots filled with hydrangeas or gardenias. When you climb the steps, either from the eastern or western ends of the house, the eye is drawn to whipped water and formidable escarpments, as though the building's designer would prefer you to admire the landscape instead of the house. A rare impulse for an architect, it seems to me.

There are three sets of double glass doors opening into the main living room, one around each corner of the verandah and one perfectly centred. Each of them has plain, round brass knobs that fit into the palm of your hand, although one is roughly dented as though it has been banged hard.

'Are there keys for all the doors?' I ask Bob one day when I'm cleaning one of the large keyholes where a mud wasp has made a nest. I poke out the dirt and it falls onto the floor, making an awful mess. The carapaces of spiders, food for the hatching wasps, scatter, blown by the breeze.

Bob takes my hand and leads me to a drawer in the kitchen where he pulls out a basket filled with odds and ends. Tweezers. A very small glass bottle with a white plastic screw-top filled with soil and labelled 'Simpson Desert Sand 1997'. Plastic discs to put under the legs of heavy furniture to stop them scratching the floor. And keys, mostly shiny and new.

'But this,' says Bob, picking out a long, thin key with an oval head like a cartoon character, 'is original.' He passes it to me while he searches for more. It has a brass tag, perfectly round, neatly engraved with 'FRONT DOOR'. 'Most of the keys have similar tags,' Bob says, 'although some are missing.'

'How carefully ordered this household must have been in Mackellar's day,' I add. 'What's the bottle of sand about?'

'Barbara and I went camping there. It was . . . one of the best times.'

Once, the grandson of Mackellar's caretaker came to visit when Bob and I were still living in the *Tin Shed*. I was only casually interested in his stories about the house at the time. I had no idea that one day I would think even the smallest details worth noting. He told us there used to be a sleep-out with blue-green shutters at the eastern end of the verandah. 'Miss Mackellar spent most of her time in that room,' he explained. 'Even when she wasn't around, I was never allowed to go in there.'

The shutters are gone, replaced, at some time, by glass. Light must have filtered through those shutters, though. Bright slashes on the floor, like rungs on a ladder. The sea breeze still drifts in lazily, making it a cool refuge in the heavy heat of a summer day. It is my study now and, to me, sacrosanct. No-one, not even Bob, is allowed to come in and fiddle around unless invited. I have no idea why I feel the need so firmly for my own space. That is just the way it is.

Bob has calculated that the house is built from sixty thousand bricks. An amazing statistic when you remember that every brick had to be shipped by barge and then carried up eighty-eight steps to the building site. After the 1994 fires, Barbara found a skeleton of a horse near the waterfront. Worn out, she thought, from hauling those sixty thousand bricks. But George Bennett, who came to live here with his parents in 1946, laughs when I ask him if it is true. 'That horse,' he says, slapping his thigh. 'Oh, that horse. Worse tempered horse I ever knew.'

George was just sixteen and working for Andy Anderson, who owned a quarry in Lovett Bay, when he first encountered the horse. Every day a cart would be loaded with stone and sometimes logs, and the horse brought over to be hooked up.

'It was a stubborn, cunning animal with a terrible habit of standing on your foot and shifting all its weight to one hoof so you couldn't get out from under it,' George says. But when he complained, Andy shrugged, as though it was the result of George's inexpert horsemanship.

'One day I was sick and Andy had to make a delivery. The horse pulled his usual stunt and flattened Andy's foot into the ground. Andy flew into a rage and shot it. Just like that. Then he tied its legs together and attached a bag of rocks to weigh it down and dragged the carcass to the bay. Only it didn't sink. It floated.'

George laughs. 'But that was just the beginning! Miss Mackellar decided to go for a swim and she banged smack into the carcass. She was outraged and swam ashore to threaten Andy with the RSPCA and all sorts of legal action. Andy decided to get rid of the evidence by blowing it up with a couple of sticks of gelignite. You've got to remember,' he says with a hint of nostalgia, 'times were very different then.'

The gelignite blew the horse to pieces. 'Dismembered bits floated to Scotland Island, into Elvina Bay, and as far as Towlers Bay, carried by the tides. A few bones got stuck on the shore at Lovett Bay and Andy gathered them up and threw them into the bush where they wouldn't be seen.'

Then he tells me that Dorothea Mackellar originally wanted to buy land at West Head. There had been much talk about developing an exclusive country club, casino, golf course and hotel there. Those plans were dropped in 1929 and the land eventually became part of the Ku-ring-gai Chase National Park in 1951.

'West Head was a remote and wild area in the twenties, not suitable for a single woman. Her father wouldn't let her go ahead with buying the land. That's where she really wanted to be, though. Not Lovett Bay,' George says.

George is seventy-six years old when we talk around the table in his Mona Vale home where he now lives with his wife, Thelma. His garage is filled with exquisite models of sailing ships and replicas of the boats he owned during his years in Lovett Bay, authentic in every detail down to the fabric in the sails. He may not be able to go to sea anymore, but he can still dream of the old days.

'That house you live in,' he says when I get up to leave, 'it is very strange, you know. Very strange. Not like any other house I've ever known. Can't explain why. It just is.'

'Did you know Dorothea Mackellar well?' I ask.

'No-one knew Miss Mackellar well around there. She kept to herself. She never swam across the bay naked, though, I'll tell you that, red bathing cap or no red bathing cap.'

He is referring to an old story about the poet stripping and swimming to the south side of the bay for Sunday morning gin and tonics with the actor Chips Rafferty and his wife, Quentin. Mackellar wore a red bathing cap so the ferry drivers would see her clearly.

But Mackellar was in her sixties when George first lived here, and the naked swimming story dates from the 1920s and thirties. So I say nothing. History is individual and often flaky. Anyway, it is such a feisty story I want it to be true. It hints at such passion and rebellion under the surface of the very correct *Miss Mackellar*.

'She often swam in the bay. That's certainly true,' George continues. 'Not to see Chips and his wife though. They didn't buy the house in Lovett Bay until the 1950s. No. She kept a very beautiful forty-foot timber launch on a mooring. I can't remember what it was called. Oh, it was a beautiful vessel. She always referred to it as her library because it was full of books. She'd swim to it day after day and climb aboard, staying until it was too dark to read. Then she'd swim back to shore. I tried to buy that boat after she died but I couldn't find where it had been taken to. Oh, it was a beauty.'

He looks up from his hands folded neatly on the table, pale and soft now that he is retired from outdoor manual work. 'She had to be rescued once. Miss Mackellar, I mean, not the boat. She swam so far into the bay she didn't have the strength to make it back to shore. One of the ferry drivers tried to rescue her. He was a terrible drinker, that bloke though, and he was too drunk to heave her on board. He'd pull her up, and drop her. Pull her up and drop her again. Eventually, he threw her a line and towed her to Church Point. She crawled to the shore, got into the ferry and he delivered her back to Lovett Bay. We laughed about that day for years.'

He pauses, his blue eyes staring out the window.

'But there was no red bathing cap. Not when Chips was around. That's for sure.'

Another winter creeps in seamlessly. Days are warm and sunny, bone dry. On Scotland Island, where residents can hook into mains water, the queue to fill tanks is growing longer. Only the nights are true to the season. The moment the sun sinks, air glides down from the escarpment, refrigerator cold.

I nestle more deeply into the bed. Bob's side is empty. He will be in the kitchen, reading yesterday's paper with a mug of tea and porridge with fruit and yoghurt. He'll bring me breakfast soon, as he does every morning.

'You don't have to do this,' I told him once.

And he grinned and shook his head. 'Don't you understand?' he said. 'It's my quiet time.'

Chip Chop's furry little barrel body lies in the crook of my legs. I once thought she might be cold but she creeps up from her bed even on the hottest nights. I rub her ear and she stretches, licking her lips with a loud, smacking sound.

One moody morning when the skies are bruised and the morning gloom is overwhelming, the bedroom feels oppressive, suffocated somehow.

'Should we get rid of the old water tank? It's all I see through the window,' I suggest, although it comes out more like a complaint.

'It's a big job,' Bob says.

'Yes, but the back of the house is a mess. Old guttering, tiles, plant pots – everything chucked under the tank stand. Spiders everywhere, dust and dirt.'

He is silent.

'It is ugly. It makes the room so dark,' I say finally. 'It's the first thing I see when I wake and it shuts out the physical world.'

I am homesick, I suddenly realise, for a flaming orange escarpment and an azure blue bay: my first sight when I opened my eyes each morning in the bedroom in the *Tin Shed*. The realisation makes me feel ungrateful, like a spoiled child. I regret my request instantly.

That night at dinner, Bob, who's rarely yearned for more than salt and pepper on his food, wonders if a herb garden might go well in place of the tank.

'Thank you,' I say. And he smiles.

It didn't rain that day, although we thought it would. Even the weather bureau predicted showers. Instead, the gloom drifted away and if any rain fell, it was out to sea where it didn't do us any good at all.

One day, cleaning out one of the high storage cupboards in Bob's office, I find a plastic bag – the flimsy, supermarket kind – filled with broken bits of china. They are mismatched and old. I cannot imagine why they have been saved.

'What are these?' I ask Bob when he comes in from his shed for lunch, sawdust hanging off his clothes. Flecks in his hair.

'Barbara found them. After the 1994 fire uncovered Mackellar's old rubbish dump. Thought they revealed a bit about the poet and her taste so she kept them.' He turns and points at a blue and white plate on the wall behind him. I've dusted it often, without any curiosity. 'Barbara searched for years to find that. It matches one of the broken bits. It's English. She would never tell me what she paid for it.'

I reach for the plate, turn it over. 'J. T. Close', it says on the back. 'W. Adams and Sons. Late M.' There's a floral stamp that looks like a coat of arms. 'Nett Border No.' is written in the space for a motto. A search on the internet reveals it is earthenware dated between 1855 and 1864.

'So we know what her dinner service looked like. I wonder what else she had in the house.'

'Check Barbara's files. She found an inventory. Tells you everything.'

Barbara's documents are stored in the high cupboards in Bob's office. He gets a ladder and passes down neatly labelled, cardboard legal file boxes. In my office, I begin flicking through the papers. Slowly at first because I cannot shake off a sense that I am prying. So much of the material is personal as well as historical. Some yellowed press clippings fall to the floor. Curious, I read odd little snippets on one of them. Sports results. A weather map. Shipping schedules. A crossword. What was so important that she tore it out and then filed it? I flip it over, and there it is. A story about Bob when he raced yachts off the bleak coast of Victoria.

'Come and have a look at this,' I call. He is in his office, next door, which is a maelstrom. Like his shed. Creative people, he insists, are never tidy. His paperwork is meticulous, though, his files religiously maintained. The mess is superficial.

'Didn't know she kept all that stuff,' he says. And he falls silent.

'I'll make a cup of tea,' I say, to give him time alone.

He nods, and doesn't move.

'Thought she didn't much approve of my sailing,' he says a few minutes later, pulling up a stool to the kitchen bench, wrapping his hands around his mug. 'Wonder why she kept the clippings?'

'Probably because she loved you and everything you did was important to her.'

'You can spend a lifetime with a person, think you know her all the way through. But you never do, do you?'

I return to Barbara's files a few weeks later. Her notes are carefully researched and indexed. Her goal, to leave a clear history of how *Tarrangaua* evolved, meant she sifted through the archives of the Mitchell Library piecing together a moment here, an event there. Like a puzzle. She had an eye for detail, an ability to organise. How does Bob cope with my excesses and chaos when he has been used to order and restraint? We are such different women.

I have always been bureaucratically inept although I coped, like most of us do. Until cancer and chemo. Some synapse burnt out then and now when I look at figures, they morph into hieroglyphics, no matter how hard I try. Or perhaps it's menopause. Whatever, it's fact. So when we married, I handed Bob the muddled details of my financial life with a loud sigh of relief. To be truthful, they were more chaotic than muddled. When you are told you have cancer, bank statements lose their power.

'Just one thing,' I said to him, handing over my ratty files.

He looked at me quizzically.

'My mother always told me a woman has to keep her financial independence. She meant a jam tin on the mantelpiece with enough money stashed inside for her to be able to stand up for herself if she ever had to. I feel the same way – but in current terms.'

Bob nodded. 'You forget, Susan, I have three daughters.' And I felt my face flush.

My father knew about my mother's private bank and occasionally, if he'd had a particularly bad run at the racetrack, he'd ask her for a loan to 'tide him over'. She always gave it to him.

It took Bob twelve months but now my records are meticulous.

Caro is shocked when I tell her on a morning dog walk that Bob handles our finances. 'You're a feminist,' she accuses.

'No. A realist. He's competent with figures and I am not. I write the letters.'

Barbara's research says that from the middle of the eighteenth century land in the Pittwater area was being divided into grants for settlers. One of them, Joseph Carrio, was granted a parcel of forty acres on the north side of Lovett Bay for the sum of forty pounds. It was rocky and steep with poor soil, but he owned a boat he called *Maid of Australia*, which he filled with timber to sell for firewood in Sydney. As well as tree ferns and staghorns. Then he'd return with supplies for 'settlers living on this side of the bay'.

When the land was stripped bare and no longer useful, he sold it to a woman called Eliza Bell. By the time Dorothea Mackellar bought two separate lots at Lovett Bay, they were owned by Henry Bartholomew Pickering and Fanny Elizabeth Pickering. The transfers took place on different days – 12 June (Henry) and 28 July (Fanny) – 1925. The transfers were precisely noted by the Registrar General in handwritten script, using pen and ink, on 16 June at 32 'mts pt' (minutes past) three o'clock in the afternoon and 6 August at 49 'mts pt' three o'clock in the afternoon. The titles were transferred to 'Isobel Dorothea Marion Mackellar of Sydney, Spinster'.

The word 'Spinster' makes me slightly nervous. When I was young and moody, my mother often warned that no-one would want me for a bride unless I improved my humour. I would end up a *Spinster!* she threatened, as though there could be no worse fate. 'I can always marry God,' I would retort, furious that it always seemed to come down to women pleasing men instead of the other way around. 'I could be a nun,' I would yell after her accusing figure. I liked the idea of being a nun. All that silence, the hours of contemplation. And the singing! How I love singing. But as I grew older, entering churches made me flinch. So much gore, all that death and punishment. Fusty hymn books with browned edges where the gold had worn away. It all reeked of decay and death.

What makes one religion more right than another anyway? So many battles in the name of God, when what it was really about was greed.

Under my mother's influence, the word 'Spinster' assumed dire overtones until I was about eighteen years old, as though a life lived alone could result only in emotional poverty, loneliness and, at the core of it all, a kind of social unacceptability. And that, of course, was the real disgrace in my mother's eyes. That was why she hammered in the theory that living as a single woman was a shrivelled existence. Perhaps for her generation, it was. Or maybe she had a point. The compulsion to love, to share, to have a partner, is a driving force, even if the happiness doesn't always last.

I can't help feeling that the title 'Spinster' follows Mackellar like a menace and pigeonholes her – which is what titles are all about. Titles cut out the need for explanations. Mackellar, despite her wealth, education and privilege, seems to have fulfilled the 'Spinster' myth. She became a lonely alcoholic and died in a Randwick nursing home. Her household staff – the housekeeper, the nurses, the chauffeur – were her only close family in the end.

When I read the small print of the Certificate of Title closely, I see that Fanny Elizabeth Pickering of Balmain, too, was a 'Spinster', so she must have been Henry Bartholomew's sister. And because old documents make me curious about the long-dead people they refer to, I cannot help wondering whether she found happiness in a life uncomplicated by passion, love and family. Or did she feel she led a life unfulfilled? As my mother would insist, she must have. I can never know, of course. Three or four generations have come and gone since Fanny Elizabeth lived. It is astonishing how quickly we mislay the details of the past.

4

The phone rings.

'I think we have a problem,' says Bella. 'The tide's coming in and Obea* is lying on the mudflats. He hasn't moved for a couple of hours.'

Obea is a golden labrador who wanders the bays like a feudal landlord. He's also a rogue, a swindler and louche with his affections. He seduces easily and without qualm, lured, more often than not, by the luscious smell of roasting lamb − or sizzling steak. Doesn't understand the meaning of remorse.

Bob's in his shed. Which I suspect he sometimes uses as an escape. I stick my head inside. 'Obea's on the mudflats. The tide's coming in and he hasn't moved.'

Bob puts down his drill. 'It's got to be a bloody tick.'

We cut through Lover's Lane dodging overhanging branches. The kind ticks drop from with military precision, landing on a neck, shoulder or head. They're ghastly little beasts with eight legs

*I spelled Obea's name incorrectly as Obi in my earlier memoir, *Salvation Creek*; he is named after the US sprinter, Obea Moore.

53

and pointy heads that run hell for leather into the warmest, moistest spot on your body. When they bite there's a quick sting, which is when you reach for the tweezers to pull them out. A day later, the bite itches or burns or throbs with pain. They can cause paralysis in children, although it's rare. Dogs are their more constant victims.

On the mudflats, Obea sees us coming towards him and wags his tail as though he's just stumbled across his oldest and best friends. He tosses his head, scrabbles in the mud with his front paws, slowly drags his body to face us.

'He's gone in the back legs,' Bob says.

The tide is about twenty feet from the dog. The channels are already calf deep with water. We wade through sea grass that winds around our ankles with a slimy caress, watching for stingrays buried in sand in the shallows. Disturb them and their frying-pan flat satellite bodies glide smoothly away. Step on them and they flick their tail, serrated as sharply as a bread knife, and pierce your skin like a poisoned arrowhead. The pain is excruciating and the sting is deadly if it's not treated quickly.

'Obea,' says Bob, man to man. 'What's up, old boy?' He squats, thumps the dog's rib cage in a heavy pat, runs his hands along his body to his back legs. 'Let's see if we can get you up.'

Bob puts his arms under Obea's roly-poly tummy and lifts him until he's standing on all fours. When he takes his arms away, Obea collapses. The dog looks vaguely ashamed and embarrassed. Mr Suave no longer.

'Bloody ticks,' Bob mutters. He looks from the dog to the shore, then back at the dog. Sighs. Bends and picks him up. He's the same weight as a ten-year-old child.

'Heaviest bloody dog in the bays,' Bob says. 'Why couldn't it be a Shih Zhu?'

'Let me help!'

'No. More comfortable for him if one of us carries him.'

Bob makes it to the seawall and heaves the dog onto the grass. Obea bangs his tail on the earth in a mute thank-you. How come his tail is unaffected when his back legs are dead? Bob rests his head in his arms, getting his breath back. Then he turns and looks at me.

'S'pose you think we should take him home?'

'Who else will look after him?'

'Ok. But he's not coming in the house, and that's final!'

''Course not!'

Obea doesn't seem to have a home. He's always been a party boy, turning up on back decks for barbecues, inviting himself onto boats. His original owners, who seemed to have a very loose relationship with him, sold their home and moved away, and his new owners aren't sure they really *do* own him, because he's rarely there. If Obea were human, he might be called commitment phobic. And as with anyone who can't commit, when the chips are down, it's hard to know where to turn. Or maybe he simply has no idea where he really belongs anymore.

Bob sighs again. 'Stay with the dog,' he says, climbing the seawall. 'I'll get the truck and the boys in the boatshed can help me load him.'

Bella comes out of the house, apologising for not helping. She's been on a business call to her head office in Switzerland.

'Bella, if you hadn't spotted Obea he would have drowned,' I tell her. 'You've done your part and the boys from the boatshed are coming.'

In the courtyard at *Tarrangaua*, we lie Obea on a dog trampoline. It's a fraction too small and his nose hangs over the edge but it's off the ground at least, which means less pressure on his body.

I call our offshore vet, Ray. 'Obea's got tick poisoning,' I explain. 'Can you get here quickly?'

Ray the Vet is tall and bony with a huge smile. Looks like he's always been Mr Laidback, but it's not so. Once he had an overloaded suburban practice. Stress, pressure and then a divorce made him rethink his universe. 'Lived on a boat for a long time,' he explained during a visit for Chip Chop's annual kennel cough and heartworm shots. 'Teaches you what you need in life. No room for anything but essentials.'

He's a bit winded by the time he opens the back door and sticks his head in to say he's arrived, with his little boy Sebastian, in a pack, on his back and a huge medical kit in his hands.

'Come in. Do you want a cuppa before or after seeing Obea?'

He unclips the backpack and lowers Sebby to the floor. 'Let's look at Obea first.' He unfastens a million buckles and releases his boy, who roars down the long hallway that links the eastern and western ends of the house. All kids do that – and most dogs – like it's an indoor running track.

'This is such a beautiful house,' Ray says, instead of whingeing about the steps he's had to climb and the load he's had to carry up them. But complaining isn't in his nature, so he chucks a compliment instead.

In the courtyard, he runs his hands over the dog, searching through his thick fur for the tick. Eventually he finds it inside his top lip. Big, fat, blue and ugly. He pulls it out with tweezers, sprays Obea with so much insecticide he looks wet, and injects him with anti-tick venom serum, talking softly to the dog the whole time. He's comforting, I think. To the dog and me.

'Now it's just a matter of waiting,' he says, coming inside to wash his hands.

'He'll be ok, though, won't he?'

'He needs to be turned every couple of hours.'

I hand him a cup of tea and a slice of lemon cake. His little boy, wide-eyed and clumsy, tucks into his own slice of cake, poking torn-off bits way down deep into his mouth. Perhaps he's frightened they might drop out.

'Sebby likes the cake,' Ray says, laughing. He looks at his son and it's as though someone is shining a light on his face.

'What should I feed Obea?' I ask.

'Fluids. He won't be able to eat for a couple of days.'

'I've got a freezer full of chicken stock.'

'Perfect.' He drains his teacup and stands. 'Call me if he doesn't improve.'

'What then?'

He shrugs, loads Sebby into his carrier and swings him onto his back. Picks up his case. Says thank you for the tea.

When he's gone, I fill a bowl with warmed chicken stock and take it outside to Obea. He's slurps it everywhere, trying to drink it sideways because he can't lift his head. Most of it spills on the ground but he's lapping it up. A good sign. Worry when he stops eating, I tell myself. I set the timer on the kitchen windowsill for two hours. And so the routine begins. Grab his front and back paws, hold them together, swing him over. Talk to him to give him courage. Tell him he's loved. Bob and I share the shifts.

Two nights later, he's visibly better and we drop it back to every four hours. Two days after that, I take him for a wobbly walk on the front lawn, just to give him a different view. The next day, I call Ray.

'I think he's had a heart attack,' I explain, tearfully. 'He can't get up.'

'It's another tick,' Ray says flatly. He returns to the courtyard and we begin again.

Bob and I are due to travel to Melbourne for five days to visit his children, but Obea is still struggling. 'What am I going to do?' I ask Caro. Obea's into day four since the second injection.

'David and I will drop by twice a day. That should be enough.'

The phone rings later that night. 'Nick and I will drop by twice a day to see to Obea,' says his wife, Ann.

Later still: 'Therese and I will check on him a couple of times a day,' says John.

And finally: 'Stefano [Stef] and I will visit him regularly,' says Bella.

They feed him, talk to him and wash him down with a cloth soaked in warm water so he doesn't have to lie in his own piddle. They clean up his messes, make fresh chicken stock for him, and slip him his first solid food when he is well enough to lift his head.

Obea should have died. He came so close. The puckered skin around his mouth turned blue, his breathing came in short, shallow gasps. Without the kindness of strangers, it's unlikely he would have survived. Hard to give up, though, when you're surrounded by love and care.

By the time he can stand, Obea is rake thin, his fur worn bald in patches, and he's anything but handsome. There's still a whiff of the rogue about him, though, he's still an old lounge lizard charmer.

'We've got to find him a new home,' Bob says. 'We can't keep him.'

'I know.'

Two dogs and you've got a pack. We'd been down that path before, when I had a second Jack Russell terrier called Vita. She was the sister of Chip Chop, who was known as Dolce at the time. They became a pack and hunted in the bush, two tan and white streaks, noses to the ground, following the gamy scent of wallabies. Choosing which dog would stay and which would go was a terrible decision. We found a gentle bloke whose old mutt had died a couple of months earlier, and I decided that Vita, the fearless hunter, ringleader and prime troublemaker, must be the one to begin a new life in the city. Seemed a perfect solution. Until one morning about two weeks after she'd gone, when I got a call from a woman with a strong Eastern European accent.

'I haff Tiny,' she said.

'You have the wrong number, I think,' I replied.

'Tiny. I haff Tiny. Your dog,' she insisted.

'That's impossible. My dog is here.' And then I realised what must have happened. Tiny – or Vita – must have escaped from her new home. 'Where did you find her?'

'In park, hunting, I tink. She was so hard to catch.'

'Her name is Vita and I gave her away –'

'You geff away your baby? What kind off muzzer are you? I bathing her, feeding her. Now she sleep on bed wit my udder four babies. She happy. Why you giff away your baby?'

There was no way to explain, so I took her number and called the man who had adopted Vita. Turned out Vita had dug under the back garden gate and taken off, dodged the city traffic and made it to the park where he walked her four times a day. Then went on the rampage, the instinct to hunt too strong to be denied. It took her another month to settle into life as a café latte dog when she was returned to her owner. Now she lives in pampered splendour. I sometimes wonder, though, if she remembers the bad ol' days on the ran-tan with her sister. Or are her memories of another life more like a dream now, which is often what happens? So I know that to keep Obea would only lead to heartbreak once again.

The word goes out. A few days later, Ann says she may have a solution. 'Ric and Gill are back from England. They've always loved Obea. They might take him.'

'Can you ask?'

'Well, I've mentioned it. And Obea's circumstances. Now it's up to them.'

Ann is tall, slim, endlessly elegant, beautifully mannered, kind, smart, English and reserved. Rock strong in a quiet way. When Caro and I spend time with her, we walk away murmuring about how we want to grow into our sixties like her.

'She's an inspiration,' Caro says.

'Yeah. Good in the old-fashioned sense of the word, as in *good through and through.*'

Obea is still weak when I run into Gill at The Point. 'Will you take him?' I ask her.

'I'll have a go at getting Ric to agree. I'd really love to have him.'

I can't bear to think that she may not understand the commitment it takes to have an animal, and I am afraid Obea will be tossed from house to house again, so I am brutally honest: 'He's a handful. He's a wanderer. He's liable to get another tick. Treatment is extremely expensive and he might die anyway. He needs mountains of love. He needs to know where he belongs once and for all. And it's no good one of you wanting him if the other doesn't. He's a full-time commitment and you better be damn sure you know what you're doing.'

'Oh, Susan, don't worry. In England we had two dogs, and when they were old and incontinent, I used to carry them downstairs to the garden two or three times a night.'

She'll do, I thought.

The next morning, Gill calls. 'We'd like to have Obea, if you agree,' she says.

'Ric wants him?'

'We both want him.'

Obea is still far from looking his best when Gill arrives to take him home. He wobbles around the courtyard in little spurts, flopping and panting as though his heart can't pump oxygen fast enough. He's eating, but not a lot. Bob and I lift Obea (and Gill) into the back of the ute and bounce our way to Little Lovett Bay. Gill nurses him like a child, so his head doesn't bang on the steel truck bed as we bump along the fire track. In the rear-vision mirror Bob sees Gill pitching from side to side, holding on to Obea like he's sacred, and he starts to laugh. 'Think that dog's just kicked a goal,' he says.

At the top of the narrow track leading through the scrub to Gill's house in Little Lovett Bay, we unroll the dog stretcher. But after we lift him out of the truck Obea staggers for a moment and then saunters off. Unsteadily, hesitantly, but on his own four massive paws. We follow him single file to the back door, where Ric waits like the perfect host. 'Hello, Obea,' he says, ignoring us and patting the dog fondly. 'Been a bit crook, have you, old boy? Well, never mind. You'll be right. Let's go and have a bit of toast together, shall we?'

And they wander inside as though it has never been any other way.

Through the summer, Gill and Obea walk along the front lawn of *Tarrangaua* every morning. He gets stronger, Gill gets fitter and slimmer. They are good for each other.

'Obea would have made a good barge dog,' I tell Toby when he picks up Stef, Bob, Michael and me from the Lovett Bay ferry wharf on Clean-Up Australia Day.

'He would've been a shocker,' Toby responds. 'Gone visiting wherever we tied up.'

'Yeah. Probably,' I admit.

Less than ten years ago, Toby was a slick advertising executive with glossy suits, crackling white shirts and shiny shoes. He traded expensive lunches in five-star restaurants for bologna sandwiches out of a brown paper bag in the wheelhouse of his working barge, the *Laurel Mae*. He's never had a moment's regret, he says. The sight of the grey barge, broad and flat as a duck's bill, working in the bays is so familiar that if it's missing for a day or two, you ask if anything is wrong. Toby has become an essential anchor in this waterside community of ours. Since Bomber and Bea traded Pittwater and the *Trump* for vegie patches and dams on the Central Coast, Toby is the one you call if you need a barge for a volunteer community project.

'Ever get sick of it?' I ask, stacking our picnic baskets in the wheelhouse.

'No, mate, no. You gotta take care of your space.'

'Some people don't get it, Toby.'

'Yeah. It's a shame.' He looks at the baskets. 'What's the snack-ettes today?'

'Cheese and chili corn muffins. Vegetable frittata and an almond cake. Coffee, too.'

He lifts the tea towel from the muffins and reaches in for one. The chili bites him back. 'Shit. These'd wake up the dead,' he says, his eyes watering.

'Bit of a Sunday heart-starter,' I reply, grinning.

There are three other volunteers on board, including one of the Annettes from Scotland Island, who works indefatigably for the community.

'Marg not here?' asks Bob.

'No, mate. She reckons she's getting a bit long in the tooth for lifting.'

Marg is on the wrong side of seventy but not much slows her down.

'Not sick or anything, though?' Bob asks.

'Just age, mate. Just age.'

Toby points the barge east towards Coasters Retreat, where volunteers have filled bags with rubbish collected from the beaches and the bush. They're stacked head high at the ferry wharf, full of plastic bottles, broken glass, old rope, smashed timber, dead kettles, a rusted tinny. There are crates of empty wine bottles left hidden in the scrub for so long they're sprouting, and even a rubber owl that yachties fix to their masts to stop real birds from shitting on the boat. And the remains of a cast-iron bathtub that's so heavy Toby has to wrap it in strong canvas slings and crane it on board, over our heads until Stef, Michael and Bob can guide it safely on deck.

An unshaven, stringy-haired bloke who looks like he's rolled out of bed and straight into his banged up tinny rafts alongside. He has blue eyes and the faraway look of a dedicated seaman, and he won the annual Woody Point Yacht Club Put-Put Day Gentlemen's Launch race in a svelte wooden boat with the sheen of loving care. Toby, the out-going commodore, picks through the rubbish to the wheelhouse to reach for the winning trophy. A green glass ball, an ancient fishing net marker, is anchored to a block of wood. The trophy is as informal and laidback as the yacht club, created in 1987 by a group of *social drinkers with a boating problem – anything that floats can sail.*

'Good on you, mate,' Toby says, passing it to him carefully like it's worth a squillion. 'See you on the water.'

The Palm Beach water taxi idles alongside, looking for a place to offload a group of passengers carrying bags, ice-boxes, a pram (filled with food) and a case of wine. They're in a hurry so instead of waiting for us to finish stacking the rubbish on board, it ties up to the *Laurel Mae*. The passengers step from the taxi to the barge and pick their way through the growing piles of debris to reach the wharf. No-one says a word. They must be weekenders or someone's guests, we all think. Locals would stop and have a chat like the taxi driver, a slim young woman with long blonde hair who comes aboard for a chili muffin and a quick coffee poured from the thermos. Then her phone rings, and she leaps in her boat, turns the key, revs for a second and then spins away from the *Laurel Mae* with a cheery wave.

'Thanks,' say the Coasters mob when the rubbish is loaded. They hand Toby a chilled bottle of white wine. 'Have it with lunch!'

'Thanks. Very kind of you.'

And the barge slips away for Scotland Island like a dignified grande dame who refuses to be hurried. We cut thick slices of roasted vegetable frittata slick with cheese and eat from enamel plates. Annette hands around chicken and salad tightly wrapped in pita bread, which is a lot less messy to pick up.

At Cargo Wharf on Scotland Island, there are mountains of sharp-edged and bulky rubbish. Rusted water tanks, dead tinnies, stacks of timber pallets, a mishmash of discarded building materials. The *Laurel Mae*'s crane swings load after load onboard. Ryan, a young fella who's making a name for himself as a top builder, lifts a clapped-out boat engine like it's no heavier than a hat and chucks it on top of a pile.

'Got muscles in his eyebrows, that bloke,' says Toby, full of admiration.

At Bells Wharf we pick up two battered fibreglass dinghies destined for the dump and fill them with the last of the junk. On our way to off-load on the mainland Cargo Wharf we hear shouting. 'You've taken my boat!' yells an anxious young fella, frantically waving his arms.

Toby looks around the deck, sees it under a heap of crap. He turns the *Laurel Mae* back to Bells Wharf. 'You'll have to come with us, mate,' Toby tells him. 'Grab it when we get the rubbish off it.'

'Yeah. Right.'

'It's clapped out. What d'you want it for?'

'Might be able to save money by rowing instead of taking the ferry,' he replies.

Toby looks at the dinghy uncertainly. 'Yeah, well . . . you might live longer by using the ferry.'

When the dinghy is finally free, Toby eases it overboard. It lands in the water with a heartening splash. The kid, who only seems to have a single oar, jumps in. There's a sound like a burp and the dinghy starts to sink, water pouring in through a long, slim rip in the hull.

'Better get out, mate, before you get too wet,' Toby advises calmly. The kid, his face filled with disappointment, scrambles over more wrecked tinnies tied to the wharf, to the safety of the shore. 'We'll give you a lift back to Bells, mate,' Toby says, trying to ease the sting of a bargain gone belly-up.

'It's ok. I'll walk to The Point. Get a lift there.' He sets off, bare-foot, shoulders hunched. The hubris of youth and optimism flattened.

'We'll find you another boat,' Annette shouts encouragingly. 'There's got to be one hanging around that isn't being used. A safe one. I'll make some calls.'

He waves a thank-you without turning back.

At the end of the day, when everyone's too buggered to lift more than an icy cold beer, we chug across glittering blue water into the shelter of Lovett Bay. Michael lights a fire in a pit at the base of two smoke-stained boulders on his lawn. Toby cooks thin sausages and fries heaps of onions. We slap them between pieces of bread with some tomato sauce and it's better than five-star.

5

As THE DAYS GROW colder and night falls so early there's still a couple of hours before it's time to prepare dinner, I drift into my study and browse through Barbara's research and reference books. Drawn by the past, as though if I dwell on it for long enough, it will somehow find a way to talk to me and the bagged brick walls of this sometimes sombre house, where there could not have been much of a difference between the hopes and dreams of people then and now, will give up its secrets. It begins to feel like blasphemy to wander its corridors or blast through the waters of the bays or tramp the tracks without any understanding of the way it once was here.

Pittwater, I learn, was changing fast by the mid-1920s, when Mackellar bought her land. Rough slab huts were being demolished to build grand holiday homes for Sydney's elite. The farms and orchards of the 1800s that supplied food for an ambitious, young Sydney colony were slowly fading away under the pressure of development. Palm Beach established a golf club *with* a clubhouse. Cars were becoming common. The jazz era was in full swing. The Depression loomed but few people saw it coming. This was still the Roaring '20s!

There was a new ferry service from the city to Manly and then a regular coach to Mona Vale which made Pittwater easily accessible for daytrippers. They trekked here in crowds, beguiled by the bush, the wildflowers, the beaches and surf, and hikes along the stone pathways built in 1895 when there were ambitious plans to make Pittwater a wilderness playground like Yellowstone National Park. They picked pretty, soft flannel flowers and pink boronia in spring, picnicked in a cool, dark cave where it was fashionable to pause and boil a billy for tea. A few metres beyond the cave, on a flat rocky outcrop with a sheer drop on the water side, the same strong men who probably built the stairways cut a socket for a flagpole into the stone and hammered in four hooks for guy ropes. They named the walk Flagstaff. The socket and hooks are still there.

'You'd see a flag for miles around,' Bob says one day after we have walked to the top. We are puffed and sweating as we sit on the iron and wood seat at the lookout beyond the cave. Below us, Pittwater sprawls in shades of blue. Yachts look the size of bathtub toys, jetties are like teeth reaching out from the mouth of the shore. Beyond, the Pacific Ocean stretches in a thin misty streak, paler than the sky.

'Must have been emotional, seeing a flag flying in the wind,' I say, because the sight of an Australian flag when I am far from home can easily make me cry.

'We could bring a pole back here, you know. To hoist a flag on special days. Australia Day, Anzac Day. Could be our own community celebration. Wouldn't be too difficult.'

The idea takes hold.

'A little plaque, very small, with Barbara's name and dates,' we both agree, would be inoffensive. *Barbara Story 1943–2000*. No different from the graffitied initials and dates carved into the top of the table in the cave, each one a memorial of a kind.

A couple of days after Bob brings home the glossy white,

twenty foot long flagpole, we drag it through a tunnel of cabbage palms, around scratchy hairpin bends, up steep flights of hand-cut sandstone steps, across massive rocks folded on each other like thick lips. Then through the murky ancient cave to the pinnacle. Flagstaff. Bob rigs the pole with wire and rope clamps to hold it strong in even the most severe gales. Then we do a test run with a satin flag we've made for Bella's daughter's twenty-first birthday. *Happy b'day Simona*, painted in letters so large we ran out of space to spell *birthday* in its entirety.

The Australian flag is in the cupboard, waiting for Anzac Day. 'Thing is, with the flag, it's got to be raised in the morning and lowered at sunset,' Bob says. 'That's protocol. Who's gonna do a sunset run to Flagstaff on Anzac Day?'

'I will,' says Stef, when we ask around for a volunteer. 'Our house is closest.'

It is a tradition for the offshore community to attend an Anzac Day service at The Point. At close to eleven in the morning, we float from Scotland Island and the bays like a small naval invasion. Engines are cut and our tinnies slide noiselessly onto the beach for the final few yards. Children, dogs, teenagers and adults crawl over the sides and wade to the water's edge – although the little kids stop to splash if the day is warm enough.

Old-timers Stacky and Jake, so frail they seem hardly to exist, arrive in wheelchairs from local nursing homes. They wear brass-buttoned navy jackets that their bony shoulders no longer fill. Marg from Little Lovett Bay pins a sprig of rosemary to their lapels and cannot resist kissing their foreheads, running a fond hand through their wispy white hair. They are not long for this world, anyone can see that.

Each year someone is elected to give a speech. Once, Di Watts from Scotland Island talked about her father, Charles Hume Baldwin, who was a tall, handsome 21-year-old boy from the bush with a larrikin smile and laughing eyes when World War II broke out. He worked on his parents' property in Queensland, but he dreamed of flying like a bird over the land where he rode horses and mustered brumbies. He joined the Royal Australian Air Force in 1941 and trained as a fighter pilot in Manitoba, Canada. From early 1943 to July 1945 he completed thirty-three bombing missions over Germany, France and Italy with one of the many RAF Lancaster flying crews which included Britons, Canadians, New Zealanders and Australians. The average life expectancy of the men in these crews was five missions.

Although my father spoke of his missions quite rarely, we came to hear of some of his most vivid memories . . . Late on the night of August 15, 1943, 214 Lancasters set out from England carrying both incendiary and explosive bombs which they dropped on the cities of Milan and Turin in Italy. We believe that on that particular night, my father's duty was that of bomb aimer. The bombs were dropped. They flew home. Eight Lancasters and their crew didn't make it back.

. . . Dad also spoke of the agony of waiting on the ground to see who came back and who didn't – and the horror of seeing aircraft shot down over the channel and even on approach – when they were so very close to home.

For his own part, Dad was badly burned in two crashes and sustained a number of other physical injuries, although it was his psychological scars that proved to be the most enduring.

He returned at last to Australia and was discharged on March 18, after four years and 102 days of service. In his post-war life he worked for the Agricultural Bank in Innisfail, Northern Queensland, helping new European immigrant farmers establish their properties. A few years later he bought a dairy farm on the Atherton Tableland.

Life on our farm was quite normal and yet we all felt the effects of the war. As a small child, I had difficulty understanding why Dad was so sad so often, and later, why violent nightmares would always follow a war movie or whenever the smell of smoke was in the air.

. . . On what can truly be described as a fateful day, Dad met an Italian family south of Cairns. They had come to Australia after the war . . . They had lived in Northern Italy until a terrible bombing raid occurred on the night of August 15, 1943.

When my father realised it was his raid, and quite possibly his bombs, that had wiped out this man's family, a sense of remorse and guilt overwhelmed him. Something inside him came unstuck, his grip on reality was lost, and he spent the best part of a year in a psychiatric ward in a Brisbane hospital.

When he eventually recovered enough to come home, he and this man spent many hours together. The friendship . . . grew and grew. As my sister said, our two families became as one. Although I was only five years old, the huge spaghetti meals we shared on their verandah in the cool of the afternoon are crystal clear in my mind. In fact, this man came up with a plan for our two families to intermarry — the only minor complication being three boys on their side and only two girls on ours!

. . . That they could be friends at all seemed like a miracle under the circumstances, but somehow, in each other's company they found healing and comfort. Not only did the friendship help my father make a full recovery but it lasted for the rest of their lives.

. . . My father discovered first hand that the horror and the dreadful tragedies of war can only truly be overcome by love, forgiveness and compassion — and that we can, if we so choose, share these gifts with each other.

. . . I am proud to be here in my father's place, a little more than a year after his passing and his eighty-fifth birthday, to tell his story on Anzac Day.

Di folds her notes and steps back from the microphone, her head bowed. We stand for a full minute, silent. It is impossible not to remember everyone we've loved who has died, soldiers or civilians. How can we not?

The bugler, Di's husband Duncan, begins the 'Last Post', which he's been practising at home for weeks. He reaches for the high note and wobbles up to it. All our hearts break. The

Australian flag is raised. Old Jake, tears streaming down his nursing-home-white face, tries to struggle to his feet from his wheel-chair. Two blokes move to his side, link their arms under his shoulders like comrades. They hold him upright and steady so he can raise his arm in a trembling salute. In the distance, looking no bigger than a handkerchief, our flag flies from the summit of Flagstaff.

Within a week, we get a call from National Parks and Wildlife. There have been complaints. The flagpole, even though no flag is flying, is an eyesore.

'It's part of our history,' we argue. The rangers are polite, even sympathetic. But the pole must be removed.

'Where is the harm?' I want to know.

'It's not the point,' we are told.

Nick and Ann, Caro, Stef and Bella, and Bob and I make a pilgrimage to retrieve the pole. On the way back, Ann, an energetic and committed grandmother, picks a branch of dried baby gumnuts.

'What are you going to do with those?' I ask.

'Use them as tips on knitting needles.'

'Bit rough, aren't they?'

'For you, perhaps, but not for little children. Give them a couple of pieces of dowel and some sandpaper, and then the gumnuts, and they can make a good strong pair of knitting needles. Then you teach them to knit. That's the hardest part.' And her words take the sting out of the day.

Bob erects the flagpole on the front lawn at *Tarrangaua*.

'Even more appropriate than Flagstaff, I reckon.'

'Why?' he asks.

'Because this was Barbara's home and where she was happiest. Let the plaque rest here.'

A couple of years later, a friend visits from the US. It is her first time at *Tarrangaua* and I show her Barbara's pottery, the photograph of her laughing with Bob, the plaque on the flagpole.

'How can you have all these reminders of his first wife? I would be jealous. I'd get rid of them,' she says.

'How can you be jealous of someone who is dead?' I ask. It is the moment I understand that I have settled comfortably with the past. And accepted the house.

One morning after a phone call from my mother triggers the usual guilt, an unseasonably frigid southerly wind cuts bone deep. Bob sees me layering on sweaters and thick trousers. Less than an hour later, I throw everything off as a dreaded hot flush pounds in. When my teeth start to chatter, I retrieve the clothes.

'I'm going for a walk,' I mutter crossly, loathing and infuriated by the indignity of a disobedient body. How glibly I lived in my young flesh.

I grab Chip Chop and slip her into her harness. She raises a paw to help, like a baby lifting an arm to slip into a sleeve. On the upper track, not far beyond the youth hostel, five male lyrebirds, their tails fanned like exotic dancers, are wooing a hen. Five! Their performance lasts for only a moment, then they dash away. One bird flies to a branch, the others scurry off, though not far. I stand still, watching, hoping for more. None wants to be the first to flee and perhaps lose points with the hen, but then they all move further into the scrub and I lose sight of them.

At home, I rave about the lyrebirds.

'You're so elated,' Bob says, remembering the surly woman who set off less than an hour earlier.

'It was such a privilege to see,' I reply. 'One of those moments that will always stay with me.'

'Got a phone call while you were out. I've been asked to look at a project for a brickworks north of Brisbane. We could spend some time, if you like. Maybe go and see Pia,' Bob suggests, his eyebrows raised in query.

'Sounds great and when we get back, I'd better start searching for a closer home for my mother. She told me she has the flu but not to come and visit. She's always been like an old dog when she's crook, going off into a corner and lying low until she's better. But it's not good. She can't go on and on forever without help.'

'How about we have her to stay when we get back?'

'We could try. But I doubt she'll come.' I turn into my study where I'm writing a story for *The Weekly*: 'Don't know about this retirement business. Seem to work harder than ever.'

'But you get to pick and choose what you do. That's the bonus.'

Pia and I shared a house when she was newly divorced and I was newly a widow and neither of us had the faintest idea what to do next. We had a great time living together and what had been acquaintanceship turned into abiding friendship – with only the usual number of glitches. Looking back, I wonder how I could've been petty enough to bicker about whose turn it was to do the vacuuming. This is a woman who searched the streets for me when I was drunk and hysterical and unable to find my way home. All night she sat and quietly listened while I ranted about a man who was unable to be faithful even to his mistress. She never said a word, either, when the next morning I slipped back on the face of denial and continued with the affair.

Not long after I found Lovett Bay and went my own way, she discovered Brunswick Heads. It's an unspoiled little town on the far north coast of New South Wales, close to crowded and colourful Byron Bay. She bought a rundown weatherboard shack on the main street with draughty gaps between the floorboards and only a shapely poinciana tree to recommend it. I thought she'd lost the plot. To be fair, she thought the same thing when I bought the *Tin Shed*. She has the knack, though, of finding beauty in the rough. Says she looks at a house as though it's a movie set and every corner has to be a perfect little picture. In less than a year she transformed it into an airy, light-filled palace with a master bedroom and bathroom separated from the main part of the house by a covered walkway. The bridal suite, I call it. It's blinding white with diaphanous curtains that float down to the black-stained floorboards, a couple of white-covered, swan-like antique chairs and an oval table with turned wooden legs. Elegant. Like she is.

She had a scare not long after the hammering and painting subsided and the neighbourhood began stretching its neck over the fence to see what she'd built. And whether she'd broken any local council codes. 'Tired as, most days,' she said during a telephone call.

'Renovating is exhausting,' I soothed her. I didn't think any more about it. I should have known better. A few weeks later, she phoned to say she was having blood tests. The tiredness was unshakable, no matter how many hours she spent in bed. When she turned out to be anaemic, the sirens started flashing. Bowel cancer. They plonked her in Lismore Hospital so fast she barely had time to buy a new nightie. I drove up to try to help her switch off the doomsday monkey that props in your head when a doctor diagnoses cancer. Hard to shift, that damn monkey.

Two days after the operation, though, she sat in bed looking incredibly rosy-cheeked and fresh and said she wasn't worried. 'I know I'll be ok,' she said in a way that left no room for doubt. 'I'm a lucky woman. Got it early. I'm a lucky, lucky woman.'

The day before I began the long drive home, a good-looking fella in a bright red vintage Mercedes pulled up. He jumped out and wandered over to where I was sipping a cup of tea on the new deck. He carried a giant bunch of strelitzias, their orange and purple heads sticking out of tissue paper like fierce tropical birds.

'Hello. I'm John. I'm the *other* style queen of Brunswick Heads,' he said, full of humour. And bravado.

'Good to meet you, John. But I'm not Pia. She's in hospital. She'll be home in a couple of days.'

He went beetroot red, stammered a little. 'I've just spilled my guts,' he spluttered, 'to a total stranger!'

I laughed and told him to come in for tea. Took his phone number for Pia who called him a while later. He helped her to build a lush and sumptuous tropical garden full of colour and texture and they've been friends ever since.

It's been almost a year since her surgery. Although we stay in touch by phone, it's not the same as sitting down for a good, cosy yarn.

'How long do you reckon we'll be away from home?' I ask Bob when we've set a date for our visit.

'Five days. A little longer if you feel like it. We can take Chip Chop so we don't have to rush back.'

It's a mind-numbing twelve-hour drive along the erratic Pacific Highway. Lanes swing from double to single, speed limits switch from fast to slow and then slower. There are roadworks every-where. Concentrate or pay the price. Chip Chop refuses to stay in the back seat and sleeps on my knees. She feels like a hot loaf of bread. We make our first stop three hours after leaving so she can have a run. She sniffs around, pees but stays close, checking regu-larly to make sure we haven't left her behind. Maybe she's smarter than we think. Lose her here and she's lost forever.

I pull out the picnic basket, set out morning tea on a lawn alongside a sandy river estuary. The last slices of dark Christmas fruit cake, fragrant with brandy, are wrapped in tinfoil. There are a couple of bananas, and two thermoses of coffee made almost completely with milk and heavily sugared. For wake-up hits. Leftover roast lamb – which we'll have with spicy tamarind chutney, cucumber and lettuce on sourdough bread – is thawing for lunch as we drive.

This is how we used to travel when I was a kid. Only the tartan blanket is missing. There weren't many roadside cafés then. Travellers stopped for picnics in a paddock by the side of the road. Inhospitable farmers hung signs saying *Trespassers Will Be Prosecuted* where you couldn't miss them, if you weren't welcome. My mother once broke her ankle on one of our picnic stops. Slipped on a riverbank at Tambo Crossing in north eastern Victoria when she wandered off searching for wildflowers. 'You'd just had scarlet fever,' she reminisced one day during a phone call. 'I was looking after you like you were a heart patient. Which is what you did for people with scarlet fever back then.'

My mother didn't watch where she put her foot and slipped on wet grass. 'The people at the hotel were so kind. Brought a mattress to carry me up to the car. We drove to Bairnsdale Hospital where it took a long time to get treated because of the school holidays. There were kids with broken bones everywhere.'

Not far away on the coast where the Brodribb River flows into the Pacific Ocean near Marlo, Nan, Pa, Uncle Frank and Auntie Belle were fishing their hearts out when suddenly, Nan had a *flash*. 'Something's wrong with Jean. We've got to go home,' Nan insisted. (My mother was called Jean until her sixties, when for some reason – neither of us can remember why – my brother and I began calling her by her first name, Esther.)

Everyone snorted and told her not to be an idiot, but Nan was a tiny, long-chested woman who knew how to *put her foot down*, as she was fond of saying. So they gave in and packed up the camp.

'On the way home, they drove past the hospital. You and your brother were playing on the front lawn. Uncle Frank noticed you so they stopped and came to see what was happening. Best *flash* Nan ever had. No-one ever forgot it. Nan's flashes were always spot-on. Mine are, too. It's just that nobody believes me. You should, you know. Second sight is always passed from generation to generation.'

'Not to me,' I retort, unable to believe my mother's story is true. Although I do remember the mattress, the broken ankle, even the grassy slopes of the river.

'No, of course not. You're too much of a bull at a gate. But your cousin Jayne [Uncle Frank and Auntie Belle's daughter], she's got it. Remember that trip so clearly,' my mother continues. 'The car broke down on the way home. The car was always breaking down. Dad couldn't use a screwdriver without asking which end was up. We all scrambled out. I was struggling with crutches. There were cows everywhere. Wild cows! I was terrified but I didn't want you kids to know so I started singing. Those stupid cows followed us. Apparently cows love music. But they didn't charge.

'You and your brother picked wildflowers. Dad walked ahead, hoping to find help. At the top of the hill, he looked back at his little family. "I'm not just an ordinary man," he shouted down at us. "I'm the luckiest man alive!" Never forget that,' my mother says. 'My great big bear of a husband who couldn't get his head around saying "I love you" unless he had a few grogs in him, erupted with joy. Stuck with me all these years, that memory.'

I check the story with Uncle Frank because my mother has a tendency to embroider the past beyond recognition and Barbara's research is teaching me the necessity of establishing the facts if we're ever to truly understand the past. When I think about it, my mother's stories mostly end in a grating one-liner that leaves you nowhere to go. I wonder, sometimes, if that is her goal. To kill the queries before they pierce the shell and the past comes oozing out.

Because my mother has secrets, I know she does. One day, she may tell me what they are. Maybe.

'Not quite right,' Uncle Frank says. 'Your brother saw us driving along. When he couldn't catch us, he ran inside. Your father jumped in the car and followed until he caught up.'

Later, I admit to Esther that I ran the story past Uncle Frank to make sure it was true. She's not even shocked or angry. It is appalling to realise we have so little faith in each other.

'And?' she asks, with a hint of smugness in her voice.

'Yeah. Close enough to the truth,' I grudgingly reply.

'You might want to listen more carefully in future, you might learn a few things. Your old mother's not as silly as you think she is.'

'I have never, not for a single moment, thought you were silly,' I tell her. 'Frivolous. But not silly.'

My mother prepared the most glorious food for our picnics. Cold roast chicken salads, new baby potatoes, chocolate cake – made from *newfangled* cake mix, but we didn't know the difference. Food we kids would eat. It was the best part of any trip. By the time I grew up, roadside cafés were epidemic and picnics faded out of fashion. But I have drifted back to them since I married Bob. I like the quietness of stopping by a country roadside instead of a busy café. Of eating food that I know is fresh. And we can give Chip Chop a run.

Bob and I drink our coffee, eat a slice of cake. Put down a bowl of water for the dog, which she ignores. Then I take over the driving. The black tarmac is smooth under our wheels, like licorice. There's not much traffic and fewer hulking great trucks than usual. Further north the heat builds. We move the thermostat from warm to cool air in the car. By late morning, the sun bounces off the rear windows of cars ahead of us like a pickaxe of light and my head hurts.

'I need a break. How about an early lunch?' I say.

Bob nods, but I can't find a good spot to pull over so I keep going. About an hour later, it begins to rain. Lightly at first.

'Wish we'd get some of this at home,' Bob says, shaking his head at the futility of rain that falls where it isn't needed.

By the time we reach Grafton, the windscreen wipers are going at full strength and on-coming cars loom out of the blur with their headlights blazing. We tune in to the local radio station, listening for the weather. The host is interviewing a country singer, Troy Cassar-Daly. There's no weather report. We pull into a rest stop, leave the radio on, eat our sandwiches and drink our coffee in the car. Brush crumbs from our laps onto the floor.

'Vaccum, Chippy,' I tell her, pointing at the crumbs. 'Off you go.'

We give her a tiny bit of cake to make up for not giving her a run. Bob gets out of the car and races around to the driver's side. I slide across and he jumps in, smelling wet, and wipes his face with his hands.

'Are you cold?' I ask.

'Nah. It's tropical rain. Warm as bathwater.'

Near the turn-off to Evans Head, water falls in black blankets. Bob pulls over. 'Might give Pia a call, see what's happening,' he says, reaching for his mobile.

She picks up immediately. 'Where are you? There are floods everywhere. The Pacific Highway is closed from Ballina. You'd better head for Lismore and come the back way.'

We wait a while for the rain to lighten, but it only gets heavier. Still no talk of floods on the local radio station. We ease slowly back onto the road and travel at forty kilometres. It's too hairy to go any faster. Visibility is mostly guesswork. By the time we reach Lismore, it's early evening. The streets are so empty, it's eerie, as though the whole world has hunkered down. When we reach the river on the far side of town, we find out why. It's flooded and the road to Brunswick Heads is under water.

'I'll get out and see how deep it is,' I say, rolling up my trousers. I look at Bob's face and expect to see tired resignation, but he looks like an excited teenager with greying hair and waves of deep wrinkles chiselled into his forehead and fanning from the corners of his eyes. The drive has become an adventure.

I sigh. The rain has finally stopped. Another car arrives on the other side of what looks like a small lake. People get out, walk to the water as though they might be able to find a way to part it. They wave to us. We all wait a minute or two to see who'll be first to have a go at crossing. No-one moves so I start wading in the headlights of the car. The water is tepid, the colour of tea. The noise of frogs is deafening and mozzies zoom in like choppers. When I'm knee deep, I turn back. There's no way we're going to get through.

'Call Pia. We're stuck here for the night,' I say.

We have dinner in a Chinese restaurant where we're the only customers and stay in an upstairs room of a motel that doesn't allow dogs. Chip Chop is irate. She barks incessantly making Bob so cranky he jumps out of bed to drive the car a block away to an empty city street. No-one there to keep awake. She's euchred.

Overnight the flood waters drop as quickly as they've risen. The Pacific Highway is clear so we retrace our tracks and follow it to Brunswick Heads. By the time we reach the Byron Bay turn-off, it's as though it was all a dream. Only the frogs keep up their torrid chant long after the deluge ends. No rain at home, though. Not a drop. For us, the drought goes on and on.

'Thought we'd never make it,' we tell Pia when we pull into the driveway.

'You need webbed feet to live here sometimes,' she replies.

Bob grabs our bags. Chippy leaps all over Pia, who babysits her occasionally when Bob and I go away.

'I've put you in the bridal suite,' she says.

'No way! We don't want to turf you out of your bed!'

'The spare bed is too small for two,' she replies. 'You'll be more comfortable in the big bed.'

Bob drops our bags inside the door. On the deck there's an old blue and white Chinese pot filled with water plants.

'Tony's?' I ask.

She nods. 'Still miss him, the silly old bugger. Why'd he have to go and die on us?'

'Yeah. Some holes never fill.'

She goes into the kitchen to put on the kettle. 'S'pose you want a cup of tea?'

'Do we ever!'

The next day, Bob is ready to leave for the brickworks before the sun is up. Pia is awake and gives him tea, toast and marmalade. Then she and I spend the day together. Catching up. Going out for coffee and cake. Playing Scrabble. Being silent.

'You look so well,' I tell her.

'We are lucky gels, you and I,' she says a bit tearily. She gives me a hug and I hug her back.

'That's a first,' Pia says, laughing. 'You used to stand stiff as a board if I tried to give you a hug. Like it was an assault of some sort. Bob's good for you.'

'Must be going soft in my old age,' I retort.

'Aren't we lucky gels,' Pia says again, 'to think we're going to *have* an old age!'

Bob walks in on our tears. 'Thought you girls would be enjoying yourselves,' he says, concerned.

'We are!' we reply, wiping our eyes and grinning like idiots.

6

ONE DAY WHEN THE wind blows in from the south east so hard the sound of branches crashing to the ground is like distant gunshots, I delay Chip Chop's morning walk. 'Don't want to get donged on the head,' I explain when Bob asks me when I'm going to put the dog out of her misery. 'I'll wait till it eases.'

'That's when the biggest branches fall,' he says, grinning and heading for his shed.

'Ok, ok,' I mutter. Because I know he's telling me fear cannot drive life. But there's nothing wrong with being sensible.

Chip Chop jumps on the daybed in my study, sighs heavily and accusingly and falls asleep. I pull out Barbara's files and go travelling into the past. The most detailed and personal document from Mackellar's time at *Tarrangaua* is the inventory. It is formally set out and reeks of gentility and an era when whatever the wealthy touched assumed an importance, even provenance, of its own, regardless of its tangible worth.

The front page begins:

INVENTORY AND VALUATION

(For Insurance Purposes)

of

HOUSEHOLD FURNITURE
APPOINTMENTS AND EFFECTS

Contained throughout the residence

'TARRANGURA'

LOVETT-BAY

VIA CHURCH POINT

The property of

MISS DOROTHEA MACKELLAR

Under instructions from

THE TRUSTEES EXECUTORS & AGENCY COMPANY
LIMITED,
1 BLIGH STREET, SYDNEY

JAMES R. LAWSON PTY LTD

Valuers and Licensed Auctioneers

234/6 CASTLEREAGH STREET

SYDNEY

9th June, 1953

It is typed on an old Remington in the Times New Roman type-face, the kind I used when I was a cadet journalist on the *Sun News Pictorial* in Melbourne. The machines were heavy and black with round keys rimmed in cool steel. Words always came out mottled because the ribbon was used over and over and wore out unevenly.

The paper carriage, when you flicked the steel arm at the end, slid back with a satisfying thump followed by the sound of a bell. Thump! Ping! Thump! Ping! Two more lines done. One paragraph per sheet. And a final full stop banged with such relief it punched a hole in the paper big enough to let daylight through. Then all the pages of a story were clipped together loosely enough to fan and slipped into the copy box. From there, it took on a life of its own. Corrected, subbed, given a headline, typeset . . . until the words came fully alive on the page of the newspaper the next day. Printed and therefore part of posterity. I had no idea, then, of the responsibility of it all – how much trust is involved when someone gives you his or her life story.

The name of the house is spelled wrongly – 'Tarrangura' – on the inventory and valuation document. The typist was probably unable to read the handwritten notes of the valuer who also signed it. His writing is almost illegible, if his signature is anything to go by. And Lovett Bay has been given a hyphen, Lovett-Bay, perhaps to make it sound grandiose. People were big on hyphens, and grandiosity in general, in the fifties.

The list begins with the *Living Room*. In a quiet way, it reveals much about the poet. There is a 'Library of General Literature comprising some 500 Volumes', valued at a whopping two hundred pounds. A 'Mah Jong set in Blackwood Case' (eight pounds). A 'Fumed Oak Small Writing Desk fitted 1 Drawer' (four pounds). 'A Remington No. 10" Standard Typewriter' (seventeen pounds ten shillings). There was an ' "Orchestrola" Cabinet Talking Machine and Quantity Classical Records' (fifteen pounds), too, as well as dining chairs, a 'Brazillian [sic] Rosewood Circular Dining Table with Pillar Support and Shaped Base with Carved Lion Paw Feet' (thirty-one pounds) and various chairs, blue willow pattern china, electroplated silver trays and two Australian cigarette boxes.

Books, clearly, were a passion. Adrienne, the Buddhist nun, told me Mackellar once tried to give her a complete, signed set of Joseph Conrad's work. 'I was touched by the offer but I turned it down,' Adrienne said. 'Taking gifts from vulnerable people is somehow ghoulish. I wanted no part of it.'

I told her, then, about another of George Bennett's stories.

'After Miss Mackellar died,' he said, 'the trustees for the estate hired about ten schoolkids to pack up the house. Cheap labour, I suppose. But they had no idea what they were doing and were rough as guts. Threw stuff into tea-chests, breaking the spines of books and tearing pages. They had a bonfire going, too, near where the generator was kept at the back of the house. They burned photographs without understanding they were part of history. Her papers, too. It's impossible to guess what went up in smoke. Nothing personal seemed to have any value to them. Only crockery, silver, paintings and ornaments. All the furniture was left in the house, though. Probably because it was too difficult to carry down the hill to a barge. It was auctioned with the house.

'Those books were precious, you know. They were first editions, signed by the authors. All with a bookplate on the front page. "Dorothea Mackellar", it said. So you always knew where to return a book. It broke my heart to see them ruined. Books were so expensive.'

'Why didn't you rescue some of them?' I asked. Because I knew if I'd been there, I would have grabbed the lot without the slightest qualm.

'Oh no,' he replied, quite shocked. 'That would have been stealing.'

'You could have asked if you could have them,' I said, still upset at the waste.

'Things have to be *given*, not asked for or taken,' he insisted, as if there could be no other way.

Then he told me that 'Miss Mackellar' often cooked a pot of soup or stew for the doctor who lived down the hill, carrying it to him in her finest blue and white china tureens.

'Dr Fraser, that was his name, well, he never returned a dish or even a plate,' George said, as though it was a form of theft.

'Legend has it that he was in love with her.'

'It was the other way around, if you ask me. But he wasn't interested.'

His wife, Thelma, disappeared into another room for a few minutes and returned carrying a small stack of thick, mildewed parchment tied together with black cotton tape threaded through roughly punched holes.

CALENDAR
For
1927
For Doctor Fraser
From Dorothea Mackellar.

There were five neatly typed pages in red and black ink with the days of the month and a collection of sayings that began in January with: ' "True happiness never flows into a man but always out of him. Heaven itself is more internal than external." NEWMAN'

' "Love is the net of truth," ' Mackellar typed for February. ' "Love is the noose of God." Arabian Proverb.'

Like a child's school project, there were cut-out pictures of ancient Greek and Roman statues and marble reliefs stuck on every page.

'All fairly deep and gloomy stuff,' I suggested to George and Thelma as I read more sayings from Plato, Marcus Aurelius, Florence Nightingale, Shelley and Walt Whitman. 'How did you come by it?'

'It was left in the doctor's house along with the crockery after he retired and stopped coming to Lovett Bay,' George explained.

'What made you keep it?' I asked, curious, because it had no real value.

'I took care of the house and property for Miss Mackellar after she was too old and ill to spend much time at Lovett Bay. So it was a link with the past.'

When I told Adrienne the story about the reckless damage of valuable books a few years later, a tear trickled down her pale cheek. 'Oh, how I wish I'd accepted the gift. First edition Conrads. Signed. Gifted to Dorothea Mackellar. A part of history.'

'Do you know why Conrad gave her the books?'

'They were friends,' Adrienne explained. 'Good friends. She

spent a lot of time with him and his wife when she visited England. Miss Mackellar had a way with older men, I think. They liked her mind and her conversation. She didn't play flirty games with them. Which would have appealed to someone like Conrad. They had Australia in common, too. Conrad came here many times when he belonged to the British Merchant Navy.'

And passion, I think. Conrad wrote about emotion until you felt the words in your heart. Mackellar channelled her passion into poetry, the only option for a woman who was closely chaperoned until she reached her thirties.

I flick through the rest of the inventory and stop at the contents for bedroom number one – her bedroom, which is where Bob and I now sleep. I read the list closely, intrigued, unable to stop myself from comparing now and then.

BEDROOM NO. 1

Pair Cotton Curtains and Fittings	1. 10. 0
Mirzapore Handwoven Carpet Square, about	
9' x 7'6	12. 10. 0
Walnut Oval Chess Top Table on Tripod	
Legs with Plate Glass Overtop	7. 7. 0
Pine Towel Rail and China Slop Bucket	1. 12. 6
Camphorwood Chest with Lift Top and Brass	
Handles	10. 10. 0
Rectangular Wall Mirror in English Lacquer	
Frame, decorated in the Chinese Taste	7. 10. 0
Camphorwood portable Chest with Escritoire	
and 4 drawers	30. 0. 0
Lacquer Small Tea Caddy	2. 12. 6
Pottery Jug Shape Vase and Pottery Jug and	
Basin	2. 0. 0
Walnut Finish Rocking Chair and Bedroom	
Chair with Cane Seats	5. 0. 0

Victorian Dressing Table in Mahogany with Oval Swing Mirror and Drawer to Frieze	21. 0. 0
Carlton Ware Covered Box, Silver Photo Frame and Hand Mirror	2. 15. 0
Walnut Davenport Writing Desk with Slope Top and Under Platforms	10. 10. 0
Engraving 'The Reading Magdalan'	2. 2. 0
Water Colour 'Trees' by Enid Cambridge	8. 8. 0
Lithograph 'Shags' by A.B. Webb	1. 11. 6
Coloured Aquatint Cloud Study	1. 11. 6
Large Coloured Print 'The Birth of Venus'	4. 4. 0
Coloured Print 'The Angel'	2. 2. 0

So much is essentially the same as it is now. Chairs, paintings, carpets, cotton curtains. Then it strikes me. There's no bed. And only one set of curtains in a two-window room.

'Which bedroom would you think of as number one?' I ask Bob when we're sitting down to dinner. Outside the evening is black. The wind still gusts in short, sharp bursts, growing stronger. It will be a fierce night.

'Ours,' he replies without hesitation.

Can't be, I think. 'Nope!'

The fire flickers, alive and warm. Wood fizzes tunelessly with burning sap. Norah Jones sings hauntingly, asking us to come away with her. There's a pot of lamb stew on the table, made with cinnamon, cloves and tomato. Dried figs on top. Quince works well, too.

'So why don't you think our bedroom is number one?' he asks, sipping a glass of red wine.

'Because bedroom number one has two windows and there is only one set of curtains listed on the inventory. It must be the room at the kitchen end of the house.'

'Do you want to put money on it?'

I am suddenly wary. Bob never bets unless he knows the outcome. I've missed something. Would Mackellar have put curtains on one window and not on another? Unlikely.

'I only bet on horses,' I reply primly.

'So what's really the secret with the bedroom?' I ask Bob grumpily over morning tea the next day. 'How come you're so sure it's bedroom number one?'

'Still don't want to put money on it?'

'You're too strutty. You know something.'

He picks up his tea, takes my hand and leads me along the hallway.

Inside the bedroom, he puts down his mug and opens the wardrobe door on the right side – my side – and slides my untidily hung clothes tightly to one end. Inside, in huge blue lettering on panels of wood, the carpenter has written: 'Return to cupboard in bedroom number one'. The carpenter's name is there too: 'J.G. Taylor, Lovett's Wharf Pittwater'. I must look in that cupboard almost every day, searching for a shirt, jacket, trousers. And yet I've never noticed the large, looping hand-writing.

'Ok, right. But! How come there's no bed on the inventory?'

'Beats me,' he shrugs, grabbing his tea and walking back to the kitchen.

'That's it, beats me? Nothing else to add, Einstein?' For some reason, I'm cranky. Not noticing details until it's too late is an old, bad habit of mine.

In the kitchen, I remind him about the missing set of curtains. He takes my hand again, saying nothing. We go into the courtyard at the back of the house, stepping around little hills of spongy green moss that creep along the flagstones like a living carpet.

'Barbara's camellia pots need turning,' I point out as we pass them. On the side where the sun doesn't reach, the branches are almost bare.

'Have to move them soon, anyway. Getting too big to fit under the eaves,' Bob says.

We round the corner where the old water tank used to be, and stand back to study the wall.

'See that?' He points at brickwork that is different from the rest, smoother and more lightly rendered. 'This whole area has been altered at some time. Perhaps the only window here in Mackellar's day belonged to the bathroom. When the bathroom was eventually split in two to make an ensuite, the original window was bricked in. A new bathroom window was built closer to the corner of the wall, leaving space for a second to be added to the bedroom. And that,' he finishes, 'is the best I can do?' He says it like a fanfare after a drum roll.

'Did you study every inch of this house when you bought it?'

'Just about.'

'Why?'

'Barbara wanted to know all the details so she could record them. It was her passion, really. She had me under the house, on the roof, scratching around the bush. To her, it was history. And she didn't want it to be lost.'

'Do you think anyone but us will ever care?'

'What does it matter?'

It does matter, I think, because when the past is destroyed, knowledge disappears with it and then we're free to invent anything that suits us. Regardless of the facts. When, later, we get a leak in the bathroom wall it bleeds through into the bedroom closet, rotting the panel with the carpenter's name on it. Bob fixes the leak and replaces the timber. And a small piece of history is gone in a flash. Never, ever to be restored.

Bob uses bedroom number two as his office. The closet is full of stationery, boxes of files, a couple of wet-weather jackets hanging neatly. The furniture – bookcases, a long narrow table he uses as a desk, a battered Chinese sideboard – is a mishmash of shelving and timberwork that fulfil a purpose, regardless of how it looks. With Bob, function comes first.

On the walls he has an aerial photograph of Lovett Bay taken after the 1994 fires changed the landscape forever, and some old, slightly rude pen-and-ink drawings of New York City I'd stored for years. Would Mackellar be shocked by images of breasts, bodies and penises amongst the skyscrapers?

Mackellar had opulent, silver and blue tapestry curtains and Mirzapore rugs in this room. What would it cost today, for a hand-woven Mirzapore rug? Where's Mirzapore anyway? India, probably, but I look it up on the internet. Bengal, India, on the west bank of the Houghly River. But there's nothing about carpets. What does a Mirzapore carpet look like? I ring the Mona Vale Library. They're amazingly kind and helpful but can't find any references beyond the name of a town. I call a rug dealer. 'Maybe,' she says, 'you'll find it in a book about dhurries.' Her words open a new door and in the end the Mona Vale Library finds a rare book in the Sydney Library and arranges a loan although I am not allowed to remove it from the building. It reveals a family fled Iran for undisclosed reasons and settled in Mirzapore in the early 1800s. To earn a living, they began making carpets in traditional Persian designs.

Much later, visiting Pia again, I wander into a rug shop in Bangalow and ask the owner, Milton Cater, if he knows anything about them.

'Yes, of course,' he says, correcting my pronunciation (*Meer*zapore, not *Mur*zapore). 'It was part of British India, then. Carpets from that area sort of took over from Axminster. They were mass-produced for the middle-classes. Like Ikea. Now the area is known as Bhadohi and there's a booming carpet industry there.'

'Blue and gold?' I ask.

'Known for red carpets back then, actually. With a bit of gold. Blue would have been unusual.'

'Thanks,' I tell him.

'Happy to help. You've got to keep contributing to knowledge. That's what life's all about.'

I add: 'It's stupid, really, but I assumed that the rugs would be rare because the woman who owned the house was enormously wealthy.'

'Yeah, lots of people make that mistake. That's why knowledge saves you.'

In Mackellar's day, bedroom number two also had a linen press, washstand, a couple of small tables and chairs, and a bed with a wire base and kapok mattress and pillows. Knick-knacks included an iron candlestick, a pair of 'art' plastic bookends and a copper inkstand. The mention of 'kapok bedding' brings back memories of holidays with my grandmother. Bedding so soft it felt like floating on clouds. Horsehair mattresses, too. Warmer, on wintry nights in country Victoria than any electric blanket.

A copper *inkstand*. I count the years since I sat at a wooden desk with a white pottery inkwell nestled in a hole in one corner, in a little state school at Bonegilla Migrant Camp . . . nearly fifty! Half a century! And yet I can still remember the tinny smell of the ink, and going home with stained fingers. I remember, too, when a new, *royal* blue ink replaced the old greenish-black and it seemed so beautiful we kids fought over it because there wasn't enough to go around.

We sang 'God Save the Queen' with our right hands over our heart every Monday morning in those days. I adored our teacher, whose name I cannot bring to mind, although I recall she had beautiful long blonde hair and wore very bright red lipstick and fluffy sweaters. And she was incredibly kind. Sometimes, I would knock on the door of her hut after school and she'd let me in for a while. She'd cook frankfurts on a bar radiator and we'd slam them between two slices of bread with a bucket of tomato sauce. Then she'd walk me home.

After a year, she married one of the ex-army blokes and moved into a hut a stone's throw from ours.

'She'll be so close, Mum,' I said, happily.

'You're not to go over there,' my mother instructed me. 'She's newly married.'

Unable to understand what marriage had to do with anything, I ignored my mother and knocked on the door three or four times a day after school, and on Saturdays and Sundays. Until she got completely exasperated one afternoon and told me firmly to *go home immediately!* I felt utterly betrayed and abandoned.

'You'll understand one day,' my mother told me. 'Nobody loves a pest.'

Which didn't help the hurt at all.

There are now two bathrooms, instead of one, in *Tarrangaua*. The smaller of them connects to the main bedroom. The third owner of the house, Eric Sime, an architect, told us he rebuilt one of the hallway cupboards so he could find space for the second bathroom. Originally, he said, each end of the hallway had mirror-image cupboards.

The kitchen is located at the western end of the house. It is an L-shaped room with three tall, paned windows overlooking Lovett Bay. Now, it's painted pale green with white wall tiles and a white ceiling. A faux Tiffany lamp hangs from the ceiling in green, pink and red and a glass-paned door leads onto the verandah where we keep a table and some comfy old cane chairs.

From each window, rugged escarpments stare back unblinking, tens of thousands of years old and still intact. A miracle, of a kind. The only history, perhaps, that really survives truthfully, no matter how diligent we are. Through the window next to the stove, bare rocks look like giant, rusted stepping stones where the waterfall runs. When there's a deluge, they disappear behind a swathe of white and furious foam, glacier-smooth in the distance like a lustrous, long white ponytail. From the sink you can look out at Bob's saucy-bottomed yacht, *Larrikin*, swinging on its mooring. If her rear end, which sits high in the water, suddenly drops, we sprint down the steps in a panic. It means the bilge pump isn't working. Leave her too long and she'll go under.

A cluster of mop-topped spotted gums screens the waterfall from the third window. Every November and December, their salmon pink bark rips like fabric from the trunk. When the wind blows hard, pieces hurtle through the air until they shred and fall on the lawn like litter in the aftermath of a frenzied party. The underbelly of the trees is silky. Lime green. Renewed and youthful every season as though it's no effort at all.

A bench with sliding drawers for kitchen equipment sits in front of this window. The food processor stands on it, and bowls of fruit. When I make cakes, I gaze at busy bush life. Noisy miners get sexy in spring. A scruffy old kookaburra lands on the same dead bough at almost the same time every day as though it's part of a personal training program. Magnificent but skittish king parrots, bright crimson and vivid forest green, drop in when the magpies fly away. On hushed summer evenings, flocks of snowy-white sulphur-crested cockatoos pace the lawn with long strides or stare down at us from the trees. Subdued for a while, but still an arrogant army.

When Bob lived here with Barbara, the kitchen had a table and eight chairs with kangaroos and koalas pressed into the wood on the backs. Bob wanted his daughter, Nicole, to have the table. 'She has her own children now,' he explained. 'Nice for them to carve their initials into the top alongside their mother's.' To take its place he built a large island bench with a top made from Tasmanian oak and sliding drawers to store spices, little white dishes of all shapes and sizes, mixing bowls and platters. He might have been hoping the extra storage space would free another hallway cupboard for his files. It didn't.

'You can never have too much cooking equipment,' I told him when he suggested getting rid of the least used stuff. When he looked doubtful, I added: 'The kitchen is my version of your shed.'

Understanding flooded his face.

'And books,' I added, because I was on a roll, 'are my version of your tools.'

'Ah!'

Only a built-in cupboard with glass panes that can be opened from the kitchen or the living room has survived intact. Visiting French friends were intrigued by the design. 'So modern,' said Helene. 'And so clever!'

Her husband Marc, a farmer from Normandy, checked the workmanship. 'It's good,' he announced. 'Very useful.'

'Praise from the French,' I said to Bob after they'd gone. 'It *must* be good!' And I look at it with fresh eyes. The caretaker's grandson told us there were wooden plate racks along one wall, too, but they are long gone, replaced by glass-doored cabinets.

Next to the kitchen, the pantry is a small, self-contained room with a window for light. Not like the dark built-in cupboards of so many new houses, where shelves are short and deep and anything shoved to the back gets lost forever. Each wall has shelves reaching almost to the ceiling. There's a wooden ladder that looks like it's as old as the house. Which it is – the inventory lists it in the broom closet and notes it is worth two pounds and ten shillings. A sinister black house spider has lived here since we moved in, and his web mats the window. Every time I brush it away, it's back the next day, thicker than ever. I could poison him or squish him, although he moves like lightning into a protective crevice when I come too close, but I opt to let him die of old age. He's not doing any harm.

'Can you tell if the pantry has changed much?' I ask Bob.

'Yeah, it's changed, but not a lot,' Bob replies. 'A couple of shelves have been pulled out. A couple put in. The original doorway is where the fridge is now.'

The kitchen and pantry seem to have been austere spaces in Mackellar's day, perhaps because they were mainly the domain of servants:

KITCHEN INVENTORY

Seagrass Matting Mat	3. 3. 0
2 Kitchen Chairs and Stool	2. 10. 0
Utility China and Glass	5. 0. 0
Burmese Silver Tea Caddy	3. 13. 6
2 E.P. Toast Racks	2. 10. 0
3 Various Tea Trays and Cane Newspaper Holder	2. 10. 0
Set Scales and Weights	1. 10. 0
Copper Kettle and Copper Hot Water Jug	3. 10. 0
Mixing Bowls, Moulds and Pyrex Dishes	3. 12. 6
Aluminium, Tin and Enamel Ware	7. 10. 0
3-Burner Kerosene Stove	12. 10. 0
'Prefect' Kerosene Refrigerator in Cream Enamel Cabinet	70. 0. 0
2 Colored Woodcuts by Margaret Preston	4. 4. 0

PANTRY

Galvanised Flour Bin	1. 5. 0
3 Various Baskets	1. 15. 0
Sundry Kitchen Utensils	1. 10. 0

I close Barbara's file and put it back in its box, wondering how the assessor must have felt as he catalogued the contents of the house from east to west. Did he close doors after he'd finished with each room, the way removalists do? Did he covet? Or was the house simply full of *things*?

How about seventy pounds for a kerosene refrigerator? A monumental sum in those days. And two woodcuts by Margaret Preston on the kitchen walls! Two in the bathroom, too. Now they'd hang over the fireplace. It's a thought that sends me rushing back to the file. The art! I've completely overlooked the art. Art tells you so much about a person's taste and even, sometimes, hints at inner desires. I write out a list of the artists' names: Margaret Preston, Percy Leason, Kenneth Macqueen, Thea Proctor, Violet Teague, Lionel Lindsay, Arthur Murch, AB Webb, Gladys Owen, J Richard Ashton, B Mansell, Frank Payne and a few others, including C Fossi, who I discover is probably C Rossi.

Randomly I pick out Violet Teague and research her on the internet to find that at the turn of the nineteenth century she was one of Australia's most internationally recognised artists. Yet she is almost forgotten now, when you think of her in the context of Preston, Lindsay and Ashton. She is credited with introducing Aboriginal artist Albert Namatjira to painting when she visited the Hermannsburg Mission in Central Australia in 1933. At the time, the community was suffering from a long drought so when she returned to Melbourne, she organised an exhibition to raise funds to set up a permanent water supply. It was hugely successful. Hermannsburg today has a thriving Aboriginal art colony and I can't help wishing she was alive to see how a single compassionate act made such a difference.

And what about Preston? 'Hard to believe you could buy a Margaret Preston woodcut for two guineas,' I say to Bob. 'Last time I looked, they were about $25 000.'

'Tough, being an artist. You rarely make a living until after you're dead.'

'It's all wrong, isn't it? It's like we never appreciate talent until we lose it.'

Bob shrugs. 'Human nature. You always want most what you can't have.'

'Not me. Not anymore.'

Preston was diagnosed with breast cancer in the 1930s and it's generally thought she moved to Berowra, on the Hawkesbury River, not far from Pittwater, to recover. Or perhaps to die. She fell passionately in love with the crackling bush and lost interest in what she scathingly referred to as *garden flowers*. Each year she waited impatiently for the beginning of the native flower season and she had the rare gift of seeing power where others saw only ugliness. She turned that power into art. Even the dead-looking grey cobs on banksia trees had a primeval beauty in her eyes. Preston, who never had the luxury – or curse – of inherited wealth like Mackellar, knew what it is like to have your back to the wall. In her, it brought out the best, as it so often does.

7

SUMMER UNFURLS AFTER a hot, dry spring. A luscious lipstick red flower blooms alongside the pathway from the shore to the house, throbbing with colour in a bush seared yellow by the drought. A few days later, more blooms erupt like spot fires.

'There must have been a garden here once. A formal garden, I mean,' I say to Bob. 'Filled with flowers for vases.'

'Maybe. Hard to know how, though, with wallabies that eat almost everything,' Bob replies.

'Well, they don't eat these plants. We know that. And they seem to be drought resistant.'

I discover they are called fire lilies (*cyrtanthus*). And they are not native but come from South Africa, so I put aside ideas of filling the garden with them. With regret.

During the next few weeks, Bob clears bracken further back from the edge of the stairway. It is part of a plan to drive ticks as far away as possible from where we walk. Each day, he finds little treasures under the matted bush. Stone steps. A clump of rock orchids. A pebble pathway. Some exotic palms chewed so low by wallabies they're hard to see. At some time, someone has attempted to build a structured garden. Could they have succeeded? Or have we stumbled over the remnants of failed dreams?

Late one afternoon when Bob is pulling out clumps of agapanthus (also from South Africa) to stop them spreading, I take him a cup of tea and a slice of fruit cake. The kind where you boil the fruit and then tip a cup of brandy over as soon you take it from the oven. It sizzles and soaks up the alcohol, then stays moist for months. He is sweating from the effort, covered in dirt. He sees me and grins. And I want to tell him how the sight of him makes me weak. And strong. But I say nothing. There's really no need to.

We sit together on the steps to drink our tea. A halyard knocks the mast of a boat, making a soft sound, like a cowbell. The sky and water are matching shades of peach.

'Why don't we go to Mt Annan Botanic Gardens and talk to some native plant experts, see what might go well at *Tarrangaua*?' I ask. 'There is such careful planning to the paths and garden beds. Shame to let it sink into the soil until it completely disappears. To let all that hard work of long ago amount to nothing.'

Bob sighs. He feels a noose tightening around his neck. Gardens are ruthless. They bleed your strength and your bank account. And revert to wilderness the moment you turn your back. But he cannot bring himself to say no.

'Could shift a few projects around, make some time,' he says, handing me his empty mug. 'But it might be a waste. This is a tough environment. Anything that will grow is here already.'

'Maybe you're right but we'll never know unless we have a go.'

Mt Annan is located in the seared heartlands of Sydney's south west. A bloke called Peter, who seems to run the place, gives us a tour, makes suggestions. I buy a couple of flannel flowers in pots and a couple of glossy native gardening books, but I'm disheartened. Everything that blooms prolifically needs full sun and *Tarrangaua* lies in the dappled shade of spotted gums.

As we leave the car park, one of the gardeners runs towards us. 'Heard you want to start a garden?'

We nod.

'Heard you live near Bayview.'

We nod again, puzzled.

'There's a garden open there this weekend. One of the most beautiful gardens I've ever seen. Go and have a look at it. It's your area. Maybe what grows there will grow for you. Hang on, I've got the newspaper where it's listed.'

He darts off, a little man with grey hair and a bowling ball tummy under his gardening overalls. Dives into the back of his car and waves the newspaper at us as he rushes back.

'Here it is! Waterfall Cottage. Open Saturday and Sunday from ten am to four thirty pm. Cabbage Tree Road. There's tea. And the cakes are fantastic! A woman owns the place. What's her name? Ah, here it is. Jeanne Villani.'

Bob shakes his hand. 'Thank you.'

'Be lovely to have a wander around,' I tell Bob when we're driving home. 'Good gardens inspire you. Wonder what kind of cakes?'

On Saturday morning, we find the name of the house chipped into a large sandstone block at the top of a steep, potholed driveway: *Waterfall Cottage. 90 Cabbage Tree Road.*

'We're early. It's not even nine thirty. Might still be closed,' Bob says, half hopefully.

'Let's go down anyway. You never know,' I reply.

Closer, we see a trampoline and an old restored ute parked on a bare patch of ground.

'Sure we're in the right place?' Bob asks. Around us, the brittle drought-stricken bush is both melancholy and menacing.

'Hang on. There's a sign. Next to those green gates. We're looking at the wrong house.'

We pick our way down the track and then stand and stare: 'Oh.'

There's a long, straight gravel drive bordered by a lawn of baby-fine grass lolling loose and unkempt. Thick stands of bamboo loom above us. Deep blue wisteria crosses the driveway like a wedding arch. Rainbow-coloured carp glide in a pond. There are cliveas in orange swathes, azaleas in bloom like bridesmaids' dresses and, in the midst of it all, a sandstone house with chimneys and peaks, like something out of a fairytale.

'This is . . . extraordinary,' Bob says, looking around.

'Yes. Not quite real.'

We pay a small fee and wander along secret pathways softened by drifts of flowers, mostly blue and pink. Bromeliads sit lightly on rocks at the bottom of what must be a waterfall when it rains. Hundreds of doves in dovecotes as big as cubbyhouses coo in a muffled chorus. The air is steamy, not thin and stringy like the parched world outside the gates.

'Feels like we've stepped into another country,' I say. 'Looks like it was a stony, barren gully once. Wonder how long it took to build?'

'It must take a team of gardeners to keep it going.'

'We're a team,' I respond.

'Not the kind it takes to do this,' he replies flatly.

We return to the house and find a table on the porch set for tea. There's a steaming urn, white mugs, a wooden caddy filled with every flavour of teabag Twinings makes. Slices of cake are perfectly arranged on small blue and white china plates. Chocolate and carrot, six slices of each. Six muffins, too, lightly dusted in icing sugar. We throw some money into a basket, choose a cake and sit down.

Bob sees desire plastered across my face. I hunger for a garden. A real one, where you can pick flowers for vases and wait each season to see what will happen. As a kid, our garden was one of the best at Bonegilla Migrant Camp, where we lived while my father worked as the supply officer. A stunningly vivid collection of trees, shrubs and flowers planted and tended by my Uncle Ted, who came to stay for two weeks and didn't leave until he died almost two decades later.

Uncle Ted was practical, but my mother had the ideas. She brought home cuttings snipped ruthlessly from other gardens. She always had huge vases of flowers at home. Later, when she and my father ran a pub, people came from miles away to see the arrangement in the front lobby. It was vast and voluptuous, like something you'd find in Windsor Castle before a formal dinner. And she'd pick most of it from roadsides or by leaning into front yards. Other people's front yards, of course. She would get caught occasionally, but she always charmed her way out of trouble. Beautiful women have that knack. No, it's not a knack. It's confidence.

When my first husband and I lived in the white house on the banks of the Nepean River, I planted fruit trees, herbaceous borders, and massive beds of sunflowers that were so damn beautiful I'd stand and stare until my legs began to ache. I built stone retaining walls, rock by rock, and covered them with roses. I grew vegetables for the table and herbs that made even the dullest meat taste luscious. My friend Pat, who stayed in the house when Paul and I were away, taught me about preparing soil and *watering in* new plants. She laughed herself silly the day I rushed out with all the umbrellas I could find to protect the baby tomatoes from hail. In the end my husband, who thought gardening was a lot of toil that frequently culminated in disappointment, grudgingly admitted it was worth the effort.

My mother was fit enough then to fetch and carry gardening tools all day without a break. I never hesitated to send her off to find the secateurs I'd casually left somewhere in a five acre garden. She grumbled a bit but she always found them. One day

I rented a ditch witch to dig trenches to lay irrigation hoses. It was so powerful it took two of us to swing it around at the end of a line. My mother took one handle, I took the other, and we pooled our strength and beat the machine, laughing our heads off when we let go for a second and it took off crookedly on its own.

'Straight lines are boring,' my mother said, still laughing as we grabbed it again.

'Anyone can do "straight",' I agreed. 'We're creative!' Remembering that silly day makes me wonder if she realises she is barely coping at home. She boasted a few weeks ago that the local grocery store now delivers her shopping to her kitchen. I thought she meant services in her small town were getting swish but a few days later, I realised she was telling me she no longer has the strength to carry her groceries up the steps. I promise myself that Christmas will be the deadline for insisting we make major changes in her lifestyle.

When Paul and my brother died, I couldn't see the point of gardens because you have to believe in the future to be a gardener. Breast cancer made me even more suspicious of planning ahead, so it is a stirring of old passions, this desire for flowers and shrubs, born out of contentment, or perhaps a new ability to relish the process instead of yearning for the result.

'Let's see if we can find the owner,' Bob suggests with a sigh. 'She might be able to give us some advice.'

Two women, one old and one young, are wiping dishes in a kitchen with gleaming wooden benches.

'Which one of you two old tarts owns this place?' I ask. I have no idea why I've been so rude. Overcoming shyness? It's still inexcusable.

The elder of the two women looks up. She puts her hands on her hips, tea towel still clasped in one of them. '*This* old tart,' she says, unoffended and with a grin on her face.

'We want to build a garden. A small one,' I explain.

'Good,' she says. 'Everyone should have a garden. Any size.'

'Would you come to lunch one day, and have a look around?' I ask.

'Why not?' she says. 'I'm really busy next weekend but leave your number and I'll give you a call.'

'The thing is, you'll have to get in a boat to get to us. Is that ok? We're "water access only", in Lovett Bay.'

She's smart enough to ask what *kind* of boat.

'Stable. Like a tennis court. And it's only about five minutes from shore to shore.'

'I'll give you a call,' she says. 'It might take a couple of weeks but I *will* call you.'

On the way home, Bob is quiet. 'We can never have a garden like that, not where we live.'

'I like the bush the way it is,' I reply, although it's not entirely true. I just want to ease his mind. Stress slides off him like soapy water.

Jeanne Villani does call to make a date for lunch. I'm delighted. Bob is noncommittal.

'Relax. This isn't really about a garden,' I tell him. 'This is fun. I like her. Don't know why. Didn't spend more than five minutes with her. She's . . . engaging.'

'You like her because she's the same as you. Likes gardens and cooking.'

'Yeah. Maybe.'

I fluff around working out the menu. For once I am restrained. Jeanne, it turns out, is a partner in two restaurants called City Extra, one at Circular Quay, the other in Parramatta. Best to keep it simple. I settle on spatchcocks served with a Thai noodle salad.

The spatchcocks have been a favourite since the Melbourne Cup lunch. They're easy cooking. A white chocolate tart for dessert, with raspberry coulis. Make it all ahead. Nothing to begin with. It's lunch. Keep it light.

About half an hour before Jeanne's due, I have a panic attack. *There's not enough food. People will go home hungry.* It's the same old same old. I don't know why I'm like this, but if I don't over-cater to a ridiculous extent, I break into a cold, nervous, stomach-churning sweat about running out of food. I had a more than sufficient childhood and the only time I've ever come close to feeling hungry was when I was twenty-one years old and living in London. I earned so little I couldn't afford to pay the rent *and* eat. But I got a night job as a barmaid in a local pub and the chef took pity on me. Ate well from then on. Sophia, my Buddhist friend, would probably suggest my paranoia stems from memories of a former life. Can't think how to test that theory, though.

I yank a side of smoked salmon out of the freezer and turn the hairdryer on it to thaw. Dice some tomatoes, cucumbers and red onions. Drizzle oil and vinegar over them, chuck in a few capers. When the phone rings, the salmon is still solid. I whack it in a sunny spot on the bench.

'I'm at the ferry wharf,' Jeanne says. 'Is it the right place?'

'Yep. Don't move. I'll come over in the tinny and get you. Be about five minutes, maybe ten. No longer. Hope you're wearing sensible shoes.'

'The only time I dump my orthotics is to go to the opera,' she says. 'I'll be fine.'

The tinny starts first go. It's another godzilla of a day. I consider throwing a line off the back to trawl for fish. Decide to skip it. Don't want to keep Jeanne waiting. And if I caught one I wouldn't know what to do with it. Bob does the gory stuff.

The second year after I moved to Lovett Bay, there were so many fish you could almost lean over the edge of the boat and catch them in your hands. That year, the heavens emptied over and over. Rain, thick and black, banging on the tin roof like rapturous applause. A yell would go out, usually from Jack: 'Get your rods! The fish are on!' We'd rush for our boats and set off trawling. We caught twelve tailor in less than ten minutes one day, elegant silver fish with downturned mouths and sharp teeth. Could have hooked hundreds but what would we have done with them? That night we lit a fire in an old washing machine drum at the bottom of the garden and everyone came around. Cooked fillets in a blackened cast iron frying pan and smoked a few in Stewart's tin smoker that I borrowed and kept forgetting to return. Used brown rice and tea as a base. The fried fish was much better. Simple stuff usually is.

It was so fecund that year, it was surreal. Gluts make me uneasy, though. They feel like a last gasp, fattening us before the famine. The drought started after that. Slowly at first, with rain here and there so we couldn't guess what lay ahead. Then the fish stopped running. Jack went out over and over, searching for kingfish to slice into slivers of sashimi. Nothing. Bob put out crab pots, trapping one or two blue swimmers at the most, more often none, whereas before he'd get four, five, six and, once, an astonishing eight. It's a cycle, I tell myself, but sometimes it's hard to believe the lean times won't go on forever.

'Hello!' I yell. Jeanne stands at the end of the ferry wharf. She's in cotton trousers with a lime green shirt over a white T-shirt. Her skin is pale and flawless. Her baby-fine blonde hair stands up in the breeze. She wears sturdy black shoes and lifts an arm in a wave.

'You'll have to help me climb aboard. I've got a bad hip,' she explains when I get the boat alongside without more than a bump or two. She walks down the yellow steps to water level, looking slightly hesitant. The step into the boat is about eighteen inches.

'No worries, the boat's stable. You'll be right.' But I have to hold on to the steps to keep the boat from drifting. I can only help her with one hand. I look around. It's the weekend and the wharf is awash with tourists. No-one familiar. No-one to help. Before I can tell her to step straight onto the floor of the boat, she plonks a foot on the gunnel. For a horrible moment she sways precariously. I let go of the wharf and grab her with both hands. She staggers into the boat, dragging her second leg along just in time, clutching the roof for balance.

'See. Easy,' she says.

'Right,' I reply. 'Next time, though, you might find it even easier to put your foot into the boat first up. Steadier than the gunnel. Lots of stability.' No need to tell her how close she came to a swim.

'No, no, it was pretty easy,' Jeanne replies obliviously.

'Oh. Right then.'

The tinny idles slowly away from the ferry wharf.

'That's McCarrs Creek,' I tell her as we pass a flotilla of expensive yachts moored from the mouth of the bay to as far as the eye can see. 'On the southern side, houses have road access. Lot of people prefer that.'

Outside the eight-knot zone I consider speeding up then change my mind. Yachts under sail glide in a gentle breeze. Resting seagulls float in small groups, bobbing like corks, waiting for a school of baitfish to zoom past. Hills roll like gentle waves. It's too glorious to rush. And the salmon needs time to thaw.

At lunch, we begin with polite questions. Where are you from? How did you come to be at Bayview? Do you have children? Probing, in a way, to discover enough without prying too deeply. Turns out Jeanne is English. Her father ran a plant nursery at Hastings, in Sussex: Gower's Silverhill Nursery. She helped him after school and at weekends. Learned how to nurture seedlings until they grew strong, how to plan a garden for colour, texture and effect. She migrated to Australia in 1955 when she was twenty-one years old and took a job as a nanny in Goulburn. She was expected to look after the children, take care of a hypochondriac wife and even scratch her employer's head if it was itchy. After a year, she quit and hitchhiked to Surfers Paradise.

'Got a job working as a nanny for the baby son of a bookmaker and his wife,' Jeanne says. 'When he found her in bed with another man, he flattened them both. I walked away from that job the next day. He couldn't understand why!'

She laughs. Australians, she'd begun to think, were a strange lot. 'But they knew how to have fun and I loved the freedom, the lack of formality. Anything seemed possible if you were prepared to work hard and take risks.'

Back in Sydney, she worked nights in a Kings Cross café and days in an advertising agency. Two years later, she met Matt, and they started their own art studio. In 1960 they married and moved into the fast lane. She bought a Porsche, he drove an Alfa Romeo. They entertained lavishly. So we can measure her success, she adds: 'Haven't done my own cleaning since I was twenty-three years old. And I'm nearly seventy!'

In 1982, two years after her husband died from a heart attack, Jeanne bought *Waterfall Cottage* as a weekender. Back then, it was a flimsy fibro cottage with pythons living in the roof. 'Matt's was a lesser life than it could have been,' she says. 'He wanted to be a painter but didn't have the courage to do it full time. I told him I'd take care of the business, that we'd be alright. He didn't believe me.'

'Maybe he didn't think he was good enough?' I suggest.

'He wasn't a genius, if that's what you mean. But people loved his paintings. He would have done quite well.'

'Do you still miss him?'

She is silent for a long while. 'I wish he'd been happier, that's all. Wish he'd been able to see joy instead of bleakness. I used to love cooking delicious dinners for the two of us or for dinner parties. Food is such a pleasure if you let it be. But he saw it as fodder. "Let's get dinner over and done with," he'd say. Told me my love of cooking came from a desire to show off. Perhaps it did, but what does it matter? As long as it's fun.'

Showing off? Is that what I do?

As we talk, the sun falls lower in the sky. Jeanne cups a hand over one eye.

'Is it too bright, would you like to go inside?'

'No! Not at all. I only have one eye and the sun seems to concentrate on it sometimes and makes it hard to see.'

It takes a minute or two to absorb the words. Then it all makes sense. The eye that never quite turns with the other one. The way she moves to be on a particular side of you. The angle of her head looking at the drop from the wharf to the boat.

'How did you lose it?'

'Cancer. Melanoma.' It's hard not to sigh out loud. Cancer. Is it ever anything else?

'How long ago?'

She smiles and her face is girlish for a moment. She is a good-looking woman now. She must have been a knockout in her youth. 'Years! Too many to remember.'

And she begins another story that is full of mystery and leaves us reeling. It began in 1980 as it turned out, the same year Matt died. 'I'd been having trouble seeing out of my left eye,' she explains. 'When the doctors checked it out, they found a tumour. Diagnosed melanoma.' She would lose her eye, they told her. She had no choice. 'One eye, I told myself, wasn't too hard to handle. I could still see.'

After surgery, with a wadge of bandages over where she'd once had an eye bluer than the sky, she was feeling 'pretty damn fine!'

'I was bouncing around, happily waiting to go home, when I picked up my chart at the end of the bed,' she continues. '"Metastasised to the liver", I read. I'd never heard the word before, wondered what it meant. I casually asked a nurse.

'It means to spread,' the nurse replied. 'Why?'

'Just curious,' Jeanne said. She felt so well, though, she still didn't worry. But when the eye specialist swept in for the daily check-up, she asked him about it.

'You have secondary tumours in your liver,' he replied matter-of-factly. 'When you're through here, I suggest you see a specialist.'

Two weeks later, one of Sydney's top cancer specialists told her to go home and get her affairs in order. She asked how much time she had to do that.

'Twelve months. If you're lucky,' he told her.

'Not much of a bedside manner,' I say.

'Facts are facts. Doesn't matter how you dress them up.'

As she left his surgery, she told herself she was pleased she'd led such an interesting life and that no-one escaped death – she was just like everyone else. And that's how she coped.

'That night I went to a concert at the Opera House. I looked around at the audience and thought, you're all going to die one day. That's what happens. There's nothing different about any of us. Nothing different about you, Jeanne. You are ordinary. We are *all* ordinary.'

Another fortnight later, she was racing to meet a deadline with some artwork when she sighed in frustration. 'I'm too busy to die, I thought. I'm just too busy.'

'Sounds like one of those defining moments,' I suggest, getting up from the table to put on the kettle for coffee.

'Maybe. But I also thought that if modern medicine had written me off, I'd try something else. What did I have to lose?'

She'd heard about a faith healer in the Philippines who allegedly performed miracles and she booked an airline ticket to go to see him. 'I needed a miracle. That's what I was told.'

I bring a tray to the table, pour our coffees. Perhaps I look scep-tical, although I don't mean to. Miracles exist, I know they do. I see them outside my window every day.

Jeanne looks straight into my eyes and smiles. 'It's impossible to explain this to anyone who hasn't seen what a faith healer does,' Jeanne says, 'so I don't expect you either to understand or believe it. Sit down and I'll just tell you what happened.

'Essentially, this skinny little man wearing nothing but tattered drawstring trousers and a singlet brought his hands together like he was about to pray and blew on his fingertips. His eyes were closed. Then he dived into my stomach with his hands. There was a little blood. No pain. A few minutes later, he ran his hands over my stomach and pulled away from me. He told to me go. It was all over. There wasn't a mark on me. The same thing happened every day for a week. To this day, I can't figure it out.'

Back at Sydney airport, she bumped into Marcus Blackmore, the vitamin king, who was a friend of a friend. He asked her where she'd been, what she was up to. When she told him, he suggested she see someone he knew who was experimenting with the effects of vitamin C on cancer. 'Within a week,' Jeanne says, 'I was buying one-kilo bags of vitamin C. I now know where the saying "goes through you like a dose of salts" comes from!'

I am intrigued, though, by the faith healer. Blood but no wounds? Hands disappearing into flesh but no pain? 'So the faith healer dived in metaphorically?' I ask.

Jeanne smiles, like I'm an innocent child. 'No,' she replies. 'The only way I can explain what he did is to tell you another story.' She looks around. 'I'm not boring you, am I?'

'No way,' we chorus.

'Good.' She takes a breath and continues. 'A while after I returned, I was talking to my neighbour about his holiday in India. He told me about seeing an exquisite statue in a street parade. He told his Indian companion that he was overwhelmed by its beauty. "Would you like a statue of your own?" his friend asked.

'My neighbour was embarrassed by the offer and didn't know what to say. Finally, not wanting to be rude, he said "Yes, that would be wonderful." He expected his friend would go to a market and buy a small replica. But instead, he stepped into a park filled with roses, and plucked one. He peeled back the petals to reveal a perfect miniature of the statue. My neighbour couldn't figure it out. He asked his friend to do it again and again. Everytime he peeled back the petals, the statue appeared like magic.'

Jeanne continues, 'A few weeks later, I was telling a group of friends about the faith healer and the statue and the rose. Everyone was amazed, except one couple. "Dematerialisation," they said, as though it was no big deal. They travelled to India often, it turned out, and had seen it happen over and over. For the first time, though, I felt I could make sense of what the faith healer did for me,' Jeanne says. 'But I don't know if any of that makes sense to *you* . . .'

I watch Bob's face as Jeanne tells her story. It's rubbery with disbelief and he wriggles in his chair uncomfortably. He's an engineer who deals in science – facts and figures, or don't go there. And Barbara died from secondary cancer in her liver. No miracles for her, just an irrevocable fact.

'So you were cured? You went back to the doctor and had a check-up and the tumours were gone?' I ask.

'No, nothing like that! About eight years later, when I was thinking it was taking a long time to die, I was at a dinner party in Newtown. Just before we sat down at the table, I got the most excruciating stomach pains. To this day, I have never felt as ill as I did then. I drove myself to Royal Prince Alfred Hospital, abandoned my car in the driveway and insisted on being admitted. I cannot tell you how terrible I felt. They took my medical history and I was put on a drip. About six hours later, I felt much better. I thought I'd had food poisoning and was about to be discharged when the doctor on duty marched in and ordered me to get back into bed. I had a history of cancer, she told me, and she wanted more tests done.'

Jeanne pauses, sips her coffee. She smiles a little, as though only she understands the joke, before continuing: 'When my liver was checked, there wasn't a tumour anywhere. It was perfectly healthy.'

We're silent. No-one knows what to say.

'And here I am, more than twenty years later!' She adds: 'I really don't care how weird all that sounds. I've just told you what happened.'

It's late afternoon when we rise from the table. Lovett Bay is deep grey, blistered with pools of pale blue light. Soon it will turn pink. Or maybe gold. Impossible to guess. We wander around the property, showing her the land. Jeanne looks behind the house towards the laundry.

'I'd get rid of the clothesline before I did anything else to the garden,' she advises.

Bob and I look at each other, aghast. 'I love the clothesline, Jeanne. It's a Hills Hoist and a truly Australian statement. Nearly every backyard had one when I was a kid. Most of them still do. It's got to stay.'

She looks at me as though I'm mad.

'You're English,' I say. 'It's impossible to explain.'

She is thoughtful for a moment. 'Well then, plant something big and bushy to hide it.'

We walk on, following the front lawn along the verandah. A kookaburra sits on the back gate. Roguish. Head tilted cheekily, eyes bold and challenging. He flies to his favourite broken bough on the spotted gum and his light-throated chuckle crescendoes into maniacal laughter. A private joke.

'We've kind of rethought trying to build a garden,' I begin when the song ends and we're walking back to the house.

Jeanne stops suddenly, as though she's been whacked on the chest. 'Why?'

I shrug, trying to find the right words . . . 'Too many wallabies, bandicoots, brush turkeys and lyrebirds. To garden formally would mean going to war with them, and we sort of like it the way it is. Although I did think spathiphyllums would look lovely along the walls of the house.'

The words are out before I can stop them. Bob's shoulders slump. I feel I've betrayed a trust. 'But wallabies eat everything so there's no point in even trying,' I add hastily.

Jeanne looks at the two of us standing with our backs to Lovett Bay. Before us, the house looks both powerful and restrained. Shadows dance on windows, enigmatic, inscrutable . . . the closed, other-world feel of the place. I shrug off a sudden wave of pessimism.

'You cannot live in a house like this without at least having a good go,' Jeanne insists. 'It doesn't have to cost much. I'll call you every time we prune at *Waterfall Cottage*. Nearly anything will grow from a cutting.'

Bob relents on the spathiphyllums and Jeanne and I roar off to a nursery to pick up a swag.

'I'll choose the plants for you,' she says. 'My father taught me how to pick healthy specimens.'

'Fine by me.'

The nursery spreads over a couple of acres in the backblocks of Sydney's west. Rows of trees, shrubs, hedge plants, weeping plants, frothy plants, water plants, scratchy plants and fragrant plants. Thick plants, skinny plants, silver ones and emerald green. And every shade in between, even purple and brown. But the brown foliage looks dead and depressing and I walk straight past it. Pots of flowers – pink, red, white, yellow, blue – beckon seductively, but they are meant for cottage gardens with a permanent water supply and chocolate soil, not hard-packed clay, seams of sandstone and voracious wallabies. It would be futile to succumb.

The spathiphyllums are under shadecloth, a surging sea of

massive, rippling green leaves. Jeanne picks up a pot, stares at the base, puts it back. 'It always amazes me when people walk into a nursery and pick up a plant without checking it out. Nurseries sell seasonally, so you'll look at hundreds of azaleas at one time. But each of them is different. Don't just pick up the closest or the one with the most flowers. Look carefully for new growth, healthy leaves and stems. Check for vigorous roots, although I don't worry if they're pot-bound. You're going to loosen the roots anyway when you put them in the ground. And check the leaves for diseases. You don't want to take a problem home to a healthy garden.'

Jeanne lifts each spathiphyllum and searches for new growth, gently pushing aside leaves to look into the soil. 'Three for the price of one!' she announces cheerfully when she finds plants that have begun multiplying in the pot.

We fill the car with fifty vigorous spathiphyllums glossy with health, and a few potted flowers I know won't live beyond a few weeks. But they give such joy that in the end I cannot resist. Once, when I was three-quarters of the way through chemo treatment, I felt too tired and ill to move beyond the house so I sat next to a gardenia in a pot on the deck, with my little dog lying comfortingly on my feet like a furry guardian. The first flowers of the season were out, pure and white and so fragrant that if I closed my eyes I could imagine myself in some faraway exotic garden. It gave me an intensity of pleasure I can hardly describe, like my body and soul had been briefly flung into a rapturous universe. It was the moment I understood why the very old and ill refuse to let go of life.

I load the last spathiphyllum into the car. Jeanne eases the leaves down gently so they won't be damaged when I slam shut the rear door.

'You're so careful, Jeanne.'

'Because it takes time for plants to grow and when you are old, you never know whether you'll be around to see if what you carelessly hurt recovers.'

'When they flower, it will look like white sails floating in the garden,' I murmur dreamily.

'Lovely,' Jeanne sighs.

We celebrate our vision of the years ahead by stopping on the way home for a creamy yellow tart with slivers of ruby baked quince on top. Coffee, fragrant and steaming. With sugar. What is coffee without the sweetness to balance the bitterness?

There was a time when I would have reached for a glass of champagne or, at the very least, wine, and I would have lost the rest of the day and most of the desire. I am so glad, so very, very glad, I have found richer ways to celebrate. In the evenings, when the habit of a drink is strongest, I pick up my knitting. I'm a terrible knitter, but I keep going, square after square, right through what used to be the cocktail hour. When I have enough squares, I sew them into blankets. The last blanket I knitted is on our bed. Pale blue, cream and light brown. It's knitted in 20-ply wool, so the squares are huge and heavy. Bob says it's like sleeping under a flock of sheep. I'm not sure he means it kindly.

'How are you going to wash it?' he asked when I sewed the last of the border with a giant aluminium needle he made in his shed because I couldn't buy one with an eye big enough to thread the wool through.

'I had no idea how *big* squares get when you use 20-ply wool,' I replied, trying not to sound defensive.

Bob warned me when we bought the wool on a weekend jaunt to the country. He knows much more about knitting than I do. His mother, he told me, could read, knit and watch television at the same time. But I refused to listen to him. I was seduced by the creamy feel of the thick yarn, the huge hanks ready to roll into balls. My grand-mother and my Auntie Belle knitted nearly everything the family wore and their hands were never idle. 'Busy hands' was the biggest compliment you could pay a woman in those days. Auntie Belle knitted my brother an absolutely magnificent white tennis sweater in the finest yarn. It took her weeks. She loved my brother – we all did – and my brother loved clothes. When our mother accidentally threw the jumper into the copper and boiled it, my brother went silent with rage. Then he took the matted, shrunken little garment and buried it in a drawer. He held on to it for years.

'Every time I hear the click of knitting needles I see my mother,' Bob says. 'It was the drumbeat of my childhood. Click. Click. Click.'

'Does it annoy you, my knitting?'

He takes a while to reply. 'No. The knitting is good,' he says finally.

It takes all day to prepare the garden beds and tuck the plants into their new home. They look full of promise as the sun goes down, standing straight and tall, with deep-veined leaves so glossy they catch the light and bounce it back in your face.

'I think they bloom in late January,' I tell Bob happily. 'Can't wait.'

He doesn't reply immediately, just leans the shovel against the shed wall and presses down the lid on the blood and bone container. 'Cuppa would be good,' he finally says, wearily, because he has done all the work.

The next morning, instead of lingering in bed I rush out onto the verandah to look at the new garden. It takes me a moment or two to understand that our tall, elegant spathiphyllums have been reduced to ratty little nubs about two inches high. Chewed to the ground.

'Bastards!'

'You can't change the bush,' Bob says, coming to stand beside me. 'It's a losing battle.'

'The next person who tries to tell me a wallaby won't cross a dog's scent is going to get an earful,' I rant. 'Must have been a whole herd here to do this. There's not a single leaf left.'

I storm inside, slam down a mug on the kitchen bench. The phone rings.

'Hi, it's Caro.'

'Can you believe those bastard wallabies have eaten fifty spathiphyllums! FIFTY!'

Her laughter echoes down the phone line. 'Did they look gorgeous for an hour or two at least?' she asks.

'Yeah,' I reply as my frustration slips away. When will I ever learn I have to adapt to the bush? It is never going to adapt to me. Not unless I kill it first, and that would be heinous. 'Enjoyed them for a couple of hours. Should have taken a photograph. Would have been a nice memento.'

Bob has one last go at saving them. He installs an electric fence which is effective for a few weeks. Then we come home late one night and see three wallabies feasting on the other side of it. They have learned to jump the wires. When Bob pulls out the wooden stakes, they are riddled with termites. The fence would have toppled anyway.

'Must have been heartbreaking in the early days,' I say to Bob. 'Wonder how they ever kept going. Everything's against you here.'

Gill strides through the back gate a few days after the spathiphyllum disaster, looking nautical in a white shirt and navy shorts. She holds a hairbrush in one hand, like a small club. Obea lumbers along not far behind her.

'Want a cup of tea?' I call from the verandah.

She waves and nods and I go into the kitchen to put on the kettle. Obea waddles up the front steps, panting with the effort, swinging his hips. He's massively overweight. The good life might be killing him.

'What's the hairbrush for?' I ask, pouring tea as we sit on the verandah.

'I brush Obea on the track,' Gill explains. 'Keeps the house cleaner. And the birds collect the fur for their nests.'

'Ah! Saw the piles of blond hair when I walked Chippy. Bit mysterious at first.'

I take a sip. Look again at Obea. Chip Chop lies alongside him, her head almost in his mouth like she's still the little puppy that first fell in love with the boofy golden labrador from across the bay. Her hips, too, are spreading. If only, I think to myself, we were like spotted gums. We could shed the old skin each year and begin again.

'Obea seems to have put on a bit of weight,' I say, although he is as golden as ever.

'Found a way to get into the cupboard where we keep the dog food,' Gill replies ruefully. 'Ate a whole bag. Our grandson, Adam, was looking after him while we were away. Obea just lay on the deck, groaning. Adam called Ray the Vet, who said he might die and that he needed X-rays. So Adam heaved him into the water taxi, then the car, and took him to Mona Vale. Just as the vet was getting ready to examine him, Obea threw up all over the surgery. Had to starve him for three days. Obea, that is. Ray's so skinny he can't afford to miss a meal.'

'Always loved his tucker. Still, that's another one of his lives used up.'

'He's using up those lives quite quickly,' Gill says. 'Did you hear about his solo voyage?' She leans her elbows on the table, mug in her hands.

'Is this another cuppa with a cake story?' I ask.

'Oh, do you have any cake? That would be quite nice, and it's a long tale.'

Gill follows me into the kitchen. I have finally moved on from lemon cakes. I found a simple little recipe for a cake made from coconut and almonds that only needs stirring before baking. It comes out of the tin almost wet with moistness and you can double the ingredients without compromising the end result. Freezes well, too, and makes lovely cupcakes which are delicious served with poached plums and thick cream. I cut us a couple of slices.

'Cream?'

'Why not? Obea keeps me fit enough.'

We move back to the verandah, carrying our cake and tea.

'Ric and I were away in London,' Gill begins, settling comfortably into her chair. 'Marion and Michael kindly agreed to house-sit and look after Obea. We felt it was better than sending him somewhere strange. He's had too many homes, that dog, and he was just starting to really understand that he's with us for good.'

Marion is a generous-spirited artist with curly brown hair and angel's skin. She is also a librarian, and sometimes works on Scotland Island for Paul Smith, a gangly master printmaker with such a passion for colour and perfection that his clients, artists such as David Boyd and Margaret Olley, say he reveals layers to their work they weren't even aware were there. Her own art, which is bold and abstract, is all about Pittwater's hues and textures. It hangs on walls all over the bays.

Marion's partner, Michael, is a documentary film maker and photographer. Like her, he is multi-talented and also works on wooden boats, restoring beautiful timbers left uncared-for. His passion is film, though. He made a short documentary about the much-loved ballet dancer Trudi, who lives at the top of Scotland Island. Tiny enough to be a child herself, Trudi is in her late eighties. She teaches The Island children to dance, inspiring them, as gifted teachers always do, to give their best. She explains carefully, and in a way that even preschoolers understand, that fulfilment comes from struggle and discipline, and talents hard-won are of the most value. The film is a gem.

On the day Gill is talking about, Obea accompanied Marion when she went to work at Paul's studio. 'She took him nearly everywhere, really. She's got such a soft heart and Obea has a way of looking at you . . . he doesn't exactly plead, it's more like he expects to always be part of the group,' Gill says. 'The funny thing is that after a lifetime of wandering, he never strayed far from Marion.'

Marion worked all day with Paul and his offsider, Dimitri, a passionate Russian who also creates exquisitely detailed religious icons and powerful portraits. Marion and the two men were making prints for painter Tim Storrier, of a starry sky in the dusty glow of late dusk. They all quit work as the winter light faded. Without the sun beating through the windows, it was numbingly cold.

'Time to go home,' Marion told Obea, who thumped his tail in mute agreement.

She and Obea wandered along the jetty to wait for Michael, who'd been in meetings all day. He saw her as he roared around the bend and waved, looking incongruous in his best city clothes as he rode the choppy water in the tinny, holding tight to the bow line for balance. Accountants, though, don't understand salt-stained boat shoes and mouldy wet-weather gear in their multistorey, air-conditioned offices. They think you might've lost the plot.

'Too windy for Tennis Wharf,' Michael yelled. 'I'll meet you at Greg's pontoon.'

He rounded the tinny and sped to the pontoon, anxious to get out of the freezing wind and inside a warm house.

'Get in the boat, Obea. Come on. Get in the boat,' he pleaded, holding the tinny steady.

The big dog hesitated. Shuffled in a kind of tango, unsure of himself. Michael turned off the engine. Obea isn't a dog that likes to rush.

'Let's go, Obea. Now!' he encouraged. Obea finally leapt and landed safely.

He lay flat, a smart tactic in high winds and choppy seas. Michael rubbed Obea's ears. 'Good boy.'

'Wait till I start the engine,' he told Marion. 'Then get in.'

He grabbed the bow rope to hold steady while he pulled the engine cord. Pull. Cough. Nothing. He pulled again and again. Nothing. Then he gave a final mighty heave and the engine kicked into a furious roar. It also slipped into low gear, and took off. Michael toppled straight over the stern while Obea sped off into the distance, a puzzled look on his handsome face.

'What have you done to Obea!' Marion moaned.

Michael, hanging by his arms from the pontoon, looked at her in amazement. 'Obea? What about me?'

'Oh, you'll be alright,' she said not unkindly as she bent to help him. 'But Obea's in danger!'

Michael, soaked and shivering, judged the boat would arc straight back to Tennis Wharf.

'He'll be ok. Really,' he reassured Marion.

'He could hit a boat on a mooring, Michael. He could be killed.' She ran along the shoreline towards Tennis with Michael trailing behind her, his good city shoes oozing water with every step. In the distance, Obea plodded unsteadily forward in the tinny but his massive weight made the bow dip so that waves flooded the hull. Obea staggered nervously back to the stern. The boat lurched, wobbled, teetered. Completely out of control.

Then the ferry came in sight. The driver, Alan, a quiet sort of fellow who wears a black Greek fisherman's cap, took a minute or two to figure out there was an empty tinny coming towards him on a collision course.

'First he thought someone must have fallen overboard,' Gill said. 'Which was right, in a way. Then he saw Obea.'

'I could see he was having trouble steering the tinny,' Alan said later. Deadpan.

The passengers twigged that something was up and ran to the boarding area near the captain's cabin.

'It's Obea! And he's alone. Oh, poor Obea!'

Alan slowed the ferry and swung round to come alongside the tinny. One of the passengers leaned over and grabbed a rope then tied the tinny securely to the ferry.

Alan pushed the throttle forward. 'I can see Michael and Marion at Tennis,' he told his passengers. 'We'll go and drop Obea and the tinny off.'

'From all accounts, Obea wasn't too anxious,' Gill says. 'Think he's been saved so many times he just expects the miracles to keep rolling in.'

Marion fell on Obea, crying with relief. 'Oh, poor, poor Obea,' she said, her arms around his neck.

Michael stood behind her. The passengers turned to him, shaking their heads. 'Could've been a disaster,' they told him, as if he didn't already know. 'Poor bloody dog. Take him a while to get over it, probably.'

Gill pressed a finger to her plate to tidy up a few slivers of almond. 'Thing is, not a single person asked Michael why he was standing there, dripping wet, in his best city clothes,' she said. 'He waited and waited for a hint of curiosity. No-one even noticed.'

In the end, he looked around and pointed at his chest. 'I'm wet,' he said. 'I'm cold. And I've ruined my best clothes.'

'Yeah, mate,' someone replied. 'But you want to be a bit more careful with Obea. He's not a young dog anymore.'

Gill finishes her tea and gets up to leave. Obea lurches to his feet with a grunt. He gives a drooly goodbye, wags his tail, performs a little front-footed jig in the same spot. He is still his own man plodding to an unhurried song. But he is wearing out and we all know it.

8

SEASONS FOLLOW THEIR INNER drumbeat, shifting gently from one rhythm to the next. One day, the luscious spring scents on the back track, which follows the shoreline from Lovett to Towlers Bay, fade away under the heat of the sun. The snowy flowers on the blueberry ash wither until they clench tightly into small green berries. Later, they ripen to deep purple. The twisted trunks of the angophoras turn tan, like skin. An oleander, a rogue exotic in the place we all know as The Secret Garden, erupts in hot pink flowers. There's a cumquat tree there, too, a relic of a European style garden where a house once stood. Only the chimney remains, and the mauve crazy-tiled floor of what was once the back porch. Each year, whoever has time picks the fruit. When Ann, who is more diligent than the rest of us, makes a deliciously gold and bitter marmalade, she gives us a jar labelled 'Secret Garden Marm. March'. We bring it out on special occasions.

Once I tramped this track to the point of collapse, trying to still the yammering of grief and despair. The bush was foreign and disturbing to me at first. Sharp-edged, lacerating, like the life I was leading. Sinister, too, as almost anything is when you have no understanding of it. I was used to crowded city pavements. Streetlights, cars, keys and office boltholes where we all huddled without question, tapping at a keyboard while the years pirouetted away from us. Believing that what we were doing mattered. But not much of it did – although it paid the bills, which is certainly important. Now the back track is as familiar as family, a hugely diverse, engaging landscape, far more fascinating than the city stage I once thought was the only world worth knowing.

Once morning a while ago, I met a weekender walking her dog. 'I am so bored,' she confessed unhappily, drawing lines with her shoe in the dust.

'With Pittwater?' I asked, aghast.

'No. With my life.'

'Why?'

She shrugged. If she knew why, she said, she would fix it.

We moved on in different directions, but her words stayed with me. When was the last time I felt bored? So long ago, I cannot even pinpoint the occasion. Certainly *Before Pittwater*, as I refer to the years of my other life. So why not now? Because there was a time I was too ill to do anything much, and now, even the worst chores feel like a privilege. And no matter how small, I try to do each job to the best of my ability. It is a way of life I learned from my Buddhist friend Sophia, when she came and stayed with me during the dark days of chemo. When death loomed closer than it ever had, and each day I played black and white reruns of my life in my head, searching for moments of nobility and finding only helter-skelter.

Each job, Sophia told me as we sat on facing sofas sipping honeyed tea in the final winter of the second millennium, must be done with care. At the time, I thought she meant that if you demean your work you demean yourself. But she meant much more. Although I didn't really understand that until I put aside a natural instinct to get to the finish as quickly and haphazardly as possible, and instead found reward enough in the process itself.

Neighbours meet randomly on the back track and walk and talk together for a while. If it suits. With our dogs: Chip Chop, Louie, Gadgie, Ziggy, Lizzie, Blonde, Bailey, Ferdie . . . Obea, of course, and others who arrive with the weekend influx.

Ferdie is a Jack Russell and Staffordshire terrier cross (we think), who lives in Little Lovett Bay with Chris and Tessa. Bob calls him the Bowling Ball. He's big-chested and hard-muscled, with one ear that sticks straight up and another that flops as though it's missing some sort of wiring. He passionately detests goannas. Tim and Leisa, who also live in Little Lovett Bay, have a couple of chooks. Although they're good layers, Leisa rarely gets an egg. In the early hours of the morning, a goanna sneaks in and steals them. The goanna raided the eggs late the day Ferdie furiously rounded him up in the chook shed. The noise was horrific – yapping dog, hissing goanna, hysterical chooks, feathers flying, fangs flashing. Tim says it sounded like war and he rushed up from his boatshed office to find Ferdie locked in combat.

'Get out of here, both of you!' Tim yelled, but the little dog held on, demented with rage. So did the goanna, his eyes filled with glittering black fury. Tim finally shoved them both out of the chookhouse with a rake. They rolled down the hill, still fiercely locked together.

'Bloody hell,' Tim said, trying to settle the flapping chooks.

Then he looked up. Ferdie and the goanna were rolling straight through the open kitchen door. Leisa yelped, their own dog, Gadgie, hid.

'Get that goanna out of here, Tim,' she screamed. 'Now!'

'Jesus!'

Chris and Tessa, hearing the ruckus, raced across the lawn separating the houses. 'Ferdie! Ferdie!' called Tessa, her voice high-pitched – the little dog's special sound. And finally, Ferdie looked up and let go. At that precise moment, the goanna vomited two perfectly intact, stinking eggs. Then he slowly, and with as much dignity as he could muster, lumbered out of the kitchen, blending into the bush like a chameleon. Unbeaten and undamaged.

Ferdie, who needed Ray the Vet to stitch up a wound, hates goannas even more now, but he steers clear of them. Mostly. 'That wretched goanna is still scaring the chooks. Haven't had an egg this year,' Leisa says. And we part, going in different directions.

'The brush turkeys have returned, building a mound in the backyard,' says Maureen, further along.

'Gotta get the pulse rate up. See ya!' says Kirstie, semi-jogging past.

'Seen all the lantana Nick and Ann have cleared? They're miracles, those two,' says Caro when we meet, as we do most days unless our schedules don't fit.

Some mornings – and there is no pattern or season – lyrebirds tiptoe around the track like pale brown feathered ghosts: plain hens and showier males with long tails stretched out behind them. They flee at the slightest disturbance, blending into the scrub in seconds. Often, we stop and squint into the bush, hoping to see the beautiful fanned tail of a courting male.

Caro lives above Frog Hollow, near a somnolent little creek and a deep green rainforest where, in a light wind, cabbage palms rustle like taffeta skirts.

One day she and her husband, David, were returning home in the boat. As they neared their house the sound of someone playing Space Invaders – *Kachink. Kachink. Kachewwww* – was so loud, they could hear it over the whine of the outboard engine. They looked up to see, high above in a large, deep cave just below their house, a lyrebird singing his lovestruck heart out: *Kachink. Kachink. Kachewwww. Kachink. Kachink. Kachewwww.* Some people say they have heard lyrebirds imitating chainsaws, sirens, the opening bars of a symphony, a kid practising on his violin . . . which can get on people's nerves. A bit. But when they sing for themselves, it is soft and full of melodies that rise and fall like laughter set to music.

Towards the end of October, glossy black cockatoos, with splashes of red under their wings and tails, lurk high in the casuarinas, invisible in the needle-like foliage. But we know they're there by the sound, like fingernails lightly tapping a table, of cracking seeds. Under our feet, the discarded pods are hard round balls through the soles of our shoes.

'Saw some yellow-tails the other day,' Caro says. 'Unusual. Perhaps their habitats are changing.' They are rare, quiet and self-possessed birds, so much more gentle than their prodigious and destructive white cousins, the sulphur-crested cockatoos – bad-tempered thugs with yellow crests who live to create chaos. Airborne terrorists with an uncanny ability to wreck what you most cherish, they fling lemons to the ground to rot. A whole crop can be wasted in minutes. Not content with shredding one window frame, they rip hunks out of all of them in a sudden frenzy. Is it the pleasure of destruction? Or an instinctive attempt at a territorial grab-back? *We were here first* – is that it?

At dusk, their discordant screeching is deafening, like blasts of electronic feedback from a bad rock band. What makes them so angry? And yet, when they stride across the lawn, swinging their legs and shoulders arrogantly, they look pure and beautiful. Blindingly white. But their eyes are full of madness. They are a ruthless, winged mafia.

Caro thinks I am being hard on them: 'They are more like cartoon characters than thugs. Cheeky. Irreverent.' Which makes me wonder if my antagonism is tied up with their destruction of my lemons. Hard to feel kindly towards anything that knows no respect for the efforts of others.

In the very early morning or late afternoon, wallabies linger on the slope that slips towards to the worn cliff of Woody Point. They stand and stare as I walk past, some so innocently beautiful they trigger a dull ache. Occasionally, skinny back legs and a ratty tail will dive into a pouch. The joey somersaults and a moment or two later, a pointy face with wide, curious eyes pops out. In the flat light of noon the lush brown pelts blend into the landscape, as still as a log or large rock. Impossible to see if you don't know they're there.

One day just before noon, two stumps, mottled grey with age, stand like bookends in the middle of the track. Where have they come from? They are so out of context I hold the dog close and tiptoe. When I am five feet from them, they explode. Wings flapping with a whooshing sound, two birds lift off like heavy-bellied freight planes painted in camouflage colours. They land on a bough, lightly for such large creatures, and stare down, frowning like schoolteachers who expected more from me. They are tawny frogmouth owls. Did I interrupt some still, silent courtship? 'I'm sorry,' I call, because true love should never be thwarted. But I am excited. I've never seen them before.

At the turn where the spotted gum stands bleeding from the drought, cabbage palms in full warrior headdress muster in a gully like troops. Vines creep sinuously over low-lying shrubs, like breaking green waves. Impenetrable. Mysterious. Beyond, the sea meets the sky in shimmering blue.

These, I know as I march along in a softer rhythm, are my most wondrous years. If anyone had told me, even a decade ago, that all this calm lay ahead, I would have laughed. Bitterly, I suspect. What is so great, after all, about a body screaming through the rites of menopause and the narrowing gap between now and the end? And yet somehow, it *is* great. Because one day, no matter how carefully and correctly I try to live, no matter how many silent pacts I make with the bigger universe, it will all end.

≈

Someone, we're not sure who, built a magnificent henhouse at *Tarrangaua*. It's a large space, braced by timber poles and wrapped, roof and all, in sturdy wire. When Bob and I disagree, we threaten each other with a *night in the chook shed*, in the same way my mother used to tell my father he was *in the dog house*, when he came home in a state of disrepair.

The chookhouse overlooks the bay, Scotland Island and even as far as the shores of Newport and Avalon, which gives it some of the best views around Pittwater. Inside the wire cage, there's a sheltered, steel shed with a concrete floor where beautifully crafted plywood laying boxes are stacked in two tiers, considerately scooped at the front for easier access for chubby-chested hens. The boxes are so appealing, I remove one to use in my study for files.

Bob chucks weeds in here, the kind you don't want spreading through the bush, which keeps them contained while they rot. He throws in agapanthus, too, when they pop up outside the house boundaries. They are plants that rampage if you let them, multiplying from their roots or from seed heads. There are thousands of them, matted in clumps so deep it takes a pick to dig them out. For some reason, wallabies won't touch the leaves, although they munch happily on the new buds each Christmas. If we end up with one or two flowers, it's only because they've been overlooked.

When Sophia phones to say her son, TY, is looking for work to fund his trip around Australia, we sigh happily. TY, short for Tupten Yeshe, is named after Sophia's great Buddhist mentor, Lama Yeshe. She's spent more than twelve years meticulously researching and writing his biography. It is a labour of great love, respect and intellect. TY is tall, with lion-like strength and a gentle nature. He reminds me of my father, who was also a giant of a man – six foot five in his bare feet. Little blokes fuelled by a few grogs would often target Dad, aching for a fight. My father always turned away. One day, my mother called him a coward. He shambled up to her, very close, told her that if he hit a little man, he'd probably kill him. Better to be called a coward than a killer, he said.

Unlike my father, TY is not afraid of his strength because in him it comes with a beautiful, gentle calmness. Perhaps because he has nothing to prove. He sometimes works as a bouncer outside the front door of clubs. In the early hours when drink and drugs play havoc with reason, the sight of him, placid but firm, stops most brawls.

'Fancy digging out a few plants?' I ask him when I pick him up from the bus stop at Church Point. He shrugs and smiles. 'Oh yeah. Sounds good and healthy work.'

'Agapanthus. There's plenty of them. Keep you going for a few days. But the ticks can be fierce if you don't spray yourself with insect repellent. Still interested? The alternative,' I add, 'is a bit of walking, fishing, a kayak or two . . . and three meals a day. Holiday stuff.'

'Think I could manage the lot,' he says. 'Not the fishing, though. Not into fishing.'

Of course not, he's Sophia's son and a Buddhist.

I hand him a pair of old sky-blue overalls and a blinding yellow T-shirt left behind by goodness knows who or what. 'Begin at the bottom,' I suggest, following him down the steps to the shore. 'Work your way up. Easier, I think.' He looks full of purpose as he sets off with his pick slung over his shoulder, like a handsome fairytale character.

At the foot of the property, massive sandstone boulders surround a bowl of bare bush that spills towards a sandy red beach. Further along, loose stones tumble chaotically along the shoreline. Oyster shells bleached white by the sun look like giant bird droppings. A clump of plants obscures a charred, rough plank between two low stumps that announces *Tarrangaua*. Not a single bushfire in nearly one hundred years has done more than lick its edges. TY braces a leg against a sandstone step, leans down, grabs some leaves and pulls. There's the sound of ripping fabric and thick roots, like masses of white worms, come away with a pop. When I first moved into the *Tin Shed*, Bob often brought me agapanthus plants to start my garden, because it was easy to keep them contained around the *Tin Shed*. I've always loved agapanthus. My mother called them *Star* of Bethlehem, and we cherished them because they'd flower abundantly even in droughts.

TY throws the agapanthus onto the sandstone track. 'I'll come back and tidy those later,' he explains. 'I'll need a wheelbarrow.'

'No, we'll chuck 'em in the back of the ute, drive them up to the house. You'll need a barrow to get them into the old chook pen, though.' I leave him to it.

The V-shaped ragged mess of bush between the car track and the steps is full of native grasses flowering in vicious yellow spikes that draw blood if they catch you. Like an old bull, a coastal banksia has thrown its seed all around to sire a small plantation. There are scrappy wattles, sharp-edged native holly, flannel leaf, muttonwood, kangaroo apple and a few geebungs. Names I know from Barbara's reference books, neatly titled 'Plants Native and Weed at Lovett Bay' and dated 15 March 1995. I often pick a leaf from a tree as I pass, then flick through the binder with its faux marble cover to check shapes, veins, descriptions and size until I can identify it. Anxious not to pass through this landscape in ignorance.

The plants are full of secrets. Umbrella clusters of red leaves when tree heath shoots newly. Four petals for boronia, five for wax flowers. The delicate charm of the flowers of the blueberry ash, like miniature fringed bells. The wickedly heady perfume of pittosporum, which floats on warm breezes in spring. Barbara filed notes on herbs, climbers, shrubs and trees alongside simple line drawings photocopied from a reference book – a legacy for all of us who come to live here.

'Learning much about the bush?' I ask TY when I take him his lunch. I hand him a box filled with vegetable frittata, salad, buttered baguette, a slice of almond cake.

'Mostly just getting attacked by it,' he responds, not unhappily.

On his third and last day, exhausted but still quietly patient and persistent, he fills the barrow and wheels it to the back of the ute. He throws a handful of limp plants in then sighs. Grabs both sides of the overfilled barrow, picks it up and swings it into the ute tray upside down. It is a feat of Herculean strength.

'Sorry. That was a bit rough,' he says. 'But I only had enough energy for one last go.' He smiles sheepishly.

'Fine by me,' I reply, still dumbfounded. Touched, too, that he didn't want me to think he was showing off. 'No ticks?'

'No ticks.'

Three days working in the bush and not a single tick. Perhaps they sensed he was a Buddhist and left him alone.

Bob and I pin notices advertising free agapanthus from Church Point to Scotland Island. People come over and grab armfuls for the next couple of weeks but there's still a mountain in the empty chook pen a month later when I murmur longingly about fresh eggs: 'Be nice to have fresh eggs, don't you think? They taste different, you know. Eggier. Velvety too, instead of rubbery. The white should sit up in a contained little puddle when you break the shell. The yolk should hold like a firm breast. Most eggs you buy splash like water. They're not fresh. Not fresh at all.'

Bob is silent, stuffing the last of the unclaimed agapanthus into two giant drums. He'll fill them with water, wait a year until the plants have rotted, then use the liquid as fertiliser. Like my Uncle Frank used to, though he added chicken and cow manure to the brew, too. Once a week he'd fill the watering can over and over and hand-water the vegetables with what we all called his *liquid gold*. His garden was an Eden: beans, cauliflowers, lettuce, beetroot, the sweetest tomatoes that we'd pick and eat warm from the sun when we visited on school holidays. Peas, too, which we shelled each night. It kept us busy between dusk and dinner and stopped us running amok. No capsicums, eggplant, zucchini or radicchio in those pre-gourmet days. But Uncle Frank is almost eighty and no doctor or dentist has ever made enough out of him to buy even a cheap bottle of wine.

He never had the slightest interest in flowers, though. And the garden around the house was meagre and roughly tended. To him, flowers were decorative, not useful, although he did look after a tree here and there because it provided shade. To be fair, though, everyone was on tank water in those days, and there was never enough for a lawn or flowerbeds. If they ever meet, I reckon he and Jeanne will spit fire, because Jeanne thinks the greatest use of all is beauty. It nourishes the soul. My Uncle Frank believes in nourishing the body. The rest follows.

He and my Auntie Belle, who made the most wonderful apple pies with cloves that scented the house long after we'd scoffed the pie, had chooks roaming everywhere. They scratched around the yard and kept the insects under control. There were a couple of cows, too, usually with calves at foot. My Uncle Frank was a child of *The Depression*. He understood early that the only way to survive was to be self-sufficient.

He made it look so easy. I remember thinking, even as a kid, that he managed to touch the universe lightly but effectively, and in my childish imagination, I gave him superhuman powers. '*My* Uncle Frank,' I'd tell anyone who would listen, 'can do anything!' Now I am older and have tried to create my own gardens, I understand there was nothing magical about his success. All it took was hard work from first light until the moon came up. It's an ethic he still holds dear even now.

'Gets up at five thirty every bloody morning and expects us to do the same,' moans my cousin, Jayne. ' "Frank, it's still dark," I tell him. "We can't start work until the sun comes up." ' But he clanks around the house making such a racket we end up nursing a cuppa at the kitchen table until it's light. 'Been married thirty-one years,' she adds, 'and he's lived with us for twenty-eight of them. Miracle we're all still speaking to each other. Most days, that is.'

'Build him a separate house close by,' I suggested when Bob and I called in to the orchard to say hello on one of our trips to Melbourne.

'Don't be ridiculous. We'd miss the old bugger terribly. Have nothing to complain about.'

When Bob jams the lids on the weed containers, I launch back into my nag: 'Cakes are better when they're made with fresh eggs,' I say. 'Lighter and more moist. As for frittata . . .'

'How many?'

'How many what?' I ask.

'Chooks. How many chooks?'

'Ten, do you think? The chook pen is big enough.'

'Not even *you* could use ten eggs a day.'

'They won't all lay every day, will they?'

'Do you know anything about raising chooks?' he asks.

'Not much, but there's sure to be a book about it.'

We call friends, Bruce and Lesley, who once lived on Scotland Island but now have a small property at Pindimar on the Central Coast, across the road from Bomber and Bea. They have black chooks, white chooks, big chooks and small chooks. Calm chooks, hysterical chooks, baby chicks and a rooster or two that, like my Uncle Frank, rouses everyone at five thirty every morning.

One weekend when we visited for Bruce's birthday party, Bob stumbled over a pile of eggs hidden in the garden, so many of them lying neatly on top of each other, that they looked like turtle eggs. 'Omelets,' we all shouted. But nearly every one of them floated in a bowl of water. They were rotten as. Lesley placed them in the compost bin one by one so she didn't break them. 'Nothing worse than the smell of a rotten egg,' she said. 'Hangs around for days and makes you think something's died.'

'What kind of chooks would you recommend?' I asked her when we decided to have a few hens of our own.

'You need Isa Browns,' she replied. 'They're great layers. I'll get Bruce to organise a couple for you.'

'We want ten,' I tell her, firmly.

'Ten! What are you starting, a cake shop?'

Three weeks later, Bob and I drive north along the crowded Pacific Highway blasted, like a canyon, out of Sydney's famous sandstone rock. We reach Bulahdelah, a sleepy little town on the edge of the millpond smooth Myall Lakes at lunchtime and find the produce store at the far end of town. A salesgirl with long blonde hair and eyelashes weighed down with clumps of black mascara can't find our chickens. It's her first day on the job, she tells us, and she's still learning.

Bob goes searching on his own and finds two cardboard boxes with air holes punched in them. His name is written on the boxes in large black letters. 'Think these are ours,' he calls to the girl, who comes over, stares at them, then quickly lifts one and, before we can stop her, turns it upside down.

'Yep,' she says. 'Sounds like chickens in there.'

'You could've just opened the box,' Bob suggests. 'Not sure it's a good thing to turn chooks on their heads.'

'They'll be right,' she says, so carelessly I have to make a conscious effort not to slap her.

'Shall we open the boxes for a second, to check they're ok?' I ask instead. She jiggles each box, again so quickly that we can't stop her. We hear the sound of flapping chooks muttering crossly.

'They're fine,' she insists, refusing to open the boxes because she reckons the birds will take off and never be seen again.

Unconvinced and silently raging, we gently place the boxes into the back of the car. It's more than a three-hour drive home and a cool day has turned hot. I've just read Jackie French's *Chook Book* and I know chickens are fragile. Too hot and they die. Too cold, same thing. Thirsty? Yep, they die. Packed too tightly? Death. We switch the air-conditioning to max and hit the road. By the time we pull into Commuter Dock at Church Point, neither of us wants to lift the lids. We lower the boxes into the boat like precious cargo, heartened by the sound of scratching feet.

'You take them to the chook pen. I'll come up later. I can't look.'

Bob nods. We both know there'll be some kind of mortality rate. It's just a question of how many. Then I go with him anyway. We're a team.

There are two dead chickens in the first box. Two almost dead in the second, heads lolling, yellow eyes closed to thin slits, red cockscombs limp. Six birds are fit and charge out of the darkness ready to do battle. Bob shows them the water tray. Then we sit in the dirt, each of us holding an almost dead chook, drizzling water down their throats.

The tough chooks are already scratching, bizarrely uninterested in the ailing and dead hens. It's as though they can't see them or they don't exist. Chip Chop was the same when Obea was sick. She ignored him as he lay in the courtyard, not even bothering to look his way as she marched past with her bone. I thought she was heartless – Obea was her hero, after all – but perhaps detachment is how animals cope with death. The instinct to survive is overriding and grief can bring you down.

Our two sick little chooks finally raise their heads. We place them tenderly in a couple of laying boxes cushioned with straw, a nook for them to rest and recover. Hopefully. The other chooks keep their distance, pecking at the ground. Bob scatters a few handfuls of grain and we leave them, closing the door after us. They'll be safe. The pen is completely enclosed. No chance of any marauding goannas getting in here. 'It's as good as the Hilton,' I say.

Around us, dusk turns the sky rosy pink, the water too. Yachts point westwards but they are still now. The west wind has glided away. Bob grabs a spade and walks into the bush, the two dead chooks in a box under his arm. I head for the kitchen to start dinner. About ten minutes later, there's frenzied yelling, like someone's being brutally attacked.

Outside, Bob's dancing like a madman, yelling incoherently . . . well, a few words are clear enough. 'What are you doing?' I say, rushing up to him. 'What's the matter, for God's sake?'

He jumps, leaps, yells again. Roars. 'Ants!' he finally gets out. 'Fucking ants. I dug up an ants' nest.'

'Well take your clothes off, you idiot!'

'I'm OUTSIDE!'

'You're in the middle of the BUSH! Who cares?'

He rips off his clothes and stands there starkers, brushing furious black ants with angry red heads off his body, dancing up and down until there are none left. I shake his clothes vigorously and hand them back to him. He puts on his shirt, his jeans. And the roaring begins again. Didn't quite shake out all the ants. Determined little buggers, ants, when they're mad as hell.

'We'll need names for the chooks,' I tell Bob later that night when we're eating a quickly grilled steak and a salad with red onion and a few bits of blue cheese crumbled into it. There won't be chicken on our plates for quite a long time, I suspect. Bob's covered in chalky pink spots of calamine lotion but the heat has gone out of the stings. Amazing what a solid glass of whisky can do.

'How about Edline and Evangeline? Maybe Elizabeth, Emily and Esther. The Esther is for my mother. She loves chooks. Nice to name one after her. Maybe they should all start with "E". Edna and Ethel. Good country names. Strong. Need one more. Knew a woman called Eglantine once. Had a long neck, like a chook. How about that?'

And so the E-chicks bed in. The next day, it's impossible to pick the crook chooks. Two days later, Bob calls me. In one of the boxes, a single, small, smooth brown egg lies like a gift. 'Go on,' he says, 'collect it and take it into the kitchen. We better get a good-size basket. These girls are going to be prolific. By the way, which one's Esther?'

I look at the girls. Already one is the leader. She's bigger, tougher, bossier and the best looking of the lot. 'That one,' I say, pointing. 'That's Esther.'

Within a couple of weeks, even though *the girls* are still adjusting to their new life, we're getting three eggs a week. Bob does the figures. Reckons we're running at a baseline cost of $50 an egg.

One lunchtime, I make an omelet instead of a sandwich. The eggs are dense with freshness, saffron gold when they're cooked.

'Worth fifty dollars an egg?'

He looks at me. 'Almost.' But I think he's being diplomatic.

Not long after *the girls* take up residence in the Hen Hilton, a male brush turkey with a canary yellow scarf and gristly red head begins swaggering across the top of the retaining wall behind the house at the same time as the sun hits the bedroom window every morning. He is an ugly, comical bird, a florid pinhead on a black football of a body with a tail stuck on the end like a dowager's fan.

'That turkey reckons the chooks are his personal harem,' Bob says one morning. 'He circles the pen all day with a lusty glitter in his beady little eyes. Must be the mating season.'

'What do the girls think?'

'Not much. They try to peck his eyes out through the fence.'

'Bit rough, aren't they?'

A few weeks later, Bob finds the turkey scratching bush litter into a huge mound behind the water tanks. 'He's there all day,' Bob says, 'scratching away like a machine. He's building a home for his new bride to lay her eggs in. Except he hasn't got a new bride.' The mound, a great big pile of scratched-up grass, rots slowly and gives off enough heat to incubate a female's eggs.

Because once she's laid, she leaves. No maternal instinct in the brush turkey femme at all.

Bluto, as we've named the turkey, won't give up on the chooks no matter how often Bob chases him off. Then one morning, at his usual time, he struts past the bedroom window. Not far behind him there's a dowdy-looking female turkey.

'Bluto has finally found true love,' I tell Bob later.

'Yeah, I know. They've been in the tomato patch scratching out the plants. Had to chase them off.'

Makes me wonder, again, how the early settlers ever managed to survive. Sheer hard work, probably. Like my Uncle Frank.

About two months later, a little black chick with a jerky head, skinny legs and a fluffy black body bolts in front of Bob, neck stretched forward, shoulders hunched. Dashing like a demented roadrunner. It runs flat-out into the chook pen and refuses to leave. Looking for mother love? We let it stay for about a week but when the chooks start to attack it, Bob shoos it out. Then the baby turkey falls in love with Bob, searches for him every day and shadows him around the yard, looking heartbroken whenever Bob comes inside for a cuppa. Guess when you've been dumped early, any surrogate will do.

By the time the baby turkey is old enough to go and build a mound of his own, the chooks are laying prolifically and I have begun looking for cake recipes that call for a minimum of ten eggs. *Before* doubling the recipe. Then, as Christmas looms, Stewart calls to ask if we can manage another chook: 'There's one in Towlers that's getting raped by a brush turkey and she's not happy.'

So Chrissie joins *the girls*. She's bigger, tougher and feistier than even Esther. For some reason, though, despite being a brown chook, all her eggs are white, so we can tell which ones are hers. She lays prolifically too, with more double-yolkers than should be physically possible. But she never forgets the trauma of her past and every time Bluto wanders near the chook shed, she goes ballistic and all the other chooks keep out of her way until she regains her composure.

Jeanne wants to know if she can bring a group from the Garden History Society to visit *Tarrangaua*.

'There's no garden, Jeanne, you know that,' I tell her.

'Doesn't matter. The bush is great. And it's a lovely thing to do. Ride the ferry around the bays, go for a walk, look at native plants. The area's rich with flowers and trees you won't find in any nursery.'

'Could give you all a cuppa and a slice of cake. To make the eighty-eight steps worthwhile?'

'I'll bring the cake.'

'No you won't.'

'Yes I will.'

'My house. My cake.'

And we laugh. Because we both know she will *bring* a cake and I will *make* one.

A while ago, when Jeanne and I went to a cooking class, someone asked her if I was her daughter. Instead of being offended, because it would have made her a teenage mother, Jeanne was thrilled. 'There's something utterly wondrous about choosing family instead of being lumbered with the accident of birth,' she said.

'Reckon I could manage you for a mother. No law that says you can only have one, is there?' I replied, feeling a sudden twinge of disloyalty. 'Prefer you as a friend, though.'

'Yeah. Fewer fights.'

I like our relationship. Our shared passions, the density of our chats, passing on what we learn from one to the other. Jeanne doesn't let her world shrink. No matter how much her hip hurts, how tired she is at the end of the day, she refuses to let her body set limitations, and she uses her passion to wipe out pain and over-come physical hurdles. She, like Ann from Little Lovett Bay, is a model for how to grow older in a way that is stimulating and useful instead of passive and reduced. How lucky I was to wander down that pitted driveway and tumble into her expansive world.

I write a quick little history of the house for the Garden Society's newsletter, based on information in the Sotheby's auction notice and material from Barbara's files. Quite innocuous, I think. Until the emails from two of Sydney's leading heritage architects rocket back to Jeanne, accusing me of fraudulently claiming Hardy Wilson as the architect of the house. I didn't keep the emails, but I wish I had. They went something like this: '*Tarrangaua* was *not* designed by the architect Hardy Wilson. The owners should be told. And asked to stop making the claim.'

Jeanne calls, worried. 'Sorry to have opened a can of worms.'

'Don't be silly. We don't care if a plumber designed it,' I reply.

The moon is high and full, the light mottled like blue cheese. Outside, the night is silent. The scream is so short and sharp, I am not sure whether it is real or a product of my imagination. I listen, heart thumping. Nothing. A dream? A few minutes go by. I drift back into sleep . . . dull, heavy, the satisfying kind . . . Until a ragged screech curdles the night again.

'Bob!' I shake him gently because he has lived with serious illness when a sudden grab means emergency.

'Someone is outside, screaming. Should we call the police?' I whisper.

Bob listens. Nothing.

'Maybe she's lying dead somewhere?'

Another single, chilling screech cuts the night. The tension drains from Bob's body. He closes his eyes. 'It's a barking owl,' he mumbles.

'But it sounds so . . . human.'

'It's sometimes called a murderbird.'

His sinks into sleep again. The wretched screams rend the stillness once or twice more. Bob doesn't stir. Then they stop, and the bush is quiet again.

I'm too unsettled to go back to sleep. I slip out of bed and fling a blanket around my shoulders. Open the door onto the verandah. Lights are on in three houses across the bay. They look like yellow satellites hovering in the blackness. Did they wake, too, to those so-mortal sounds? I pull the weatherproof covers off the sofa at the eastern end and prop a pillow behind my head. Moonlight ribs the water, yachts are alert, waiting for the sun to rise. White pylons bead the shore like soldiers. At night, there's no whiff of eucalyptus. The air is dank, salty, damp. The night is a silent performance. And the house – no matter who designed it – is superbly sited to embrace it all.

9

CHRISTMAS. HAS ANOTHER YEAR really slithered past so quickly? The drought goes on, and it's hotter than ever. When did temperatures soar so high so early in the summer? My Uncle Frank, cousin Jayne and her husband, Edward, are battling to save their stone fruit orchard at Wangaratta in central Victoria, where their giant dams are cracked and barren with only dirty pools in the bottom like dregs in a teacup. If there's no rain soon, a lifetime of hard slog will be bulldozed into the ground – along with dreams of a comfortable retirement and an inheritance for their two children.

'Are you worried, Frank?' I ask when we call in on our way to visit Bob's children in Melbourne.

'Not much point in that. Worrying doesn't change anything. Just wears you out.'

When he needs a break from work, he visits my mother. The two of them sit like ancient parrots in her back room where the television blares from dawn onwards. They have been friends for nearly seventy years, ever since Frank married my mother's sister. They yabber away in what sounds like code because their history is implicit. They do not need to fill in the gaps: they fling around names, occasions, births and deaths, and the moment immediately slots into place. Their sense of humour, too, is from another era, sometimes so corny it makes me cringe. But they laugh and laugh, until I have to join in. Uncle Frank rocks back and forth, incongruous in the baby pink chintz recliner. Nut-brown face, muscled arms, jet black hair like a young man.

On one of my rare visits, my mother sits forward on the edge of the sofa instead of lying on it, like she usually does. Her elbows rest on her knees. She fiddles with bits and pieces on the coffee table – some earrings, a necklace, an old letter that she opens and closes without reading. But try to scoop any papers to throw in the rubbish and she snatches them back. 'I haven't sorted it all yet,' she insists. As each pile reaches toppling point, she begins another. *Nests*, I call them. They are all over her house. When I check the pile on the kitchen table, the dates go back a decade or more. I know it is time, no, it is past the time, for her to find a new home.

One day soon the two women at the local post office who have known her for nearly twenty years will retire, and when she asks the new manager to fill in her forms to pay her bills, he may say no. She will have no idea what to do then. The electronic world beyond the television remote control is a confusing, foreign universe to her.

'I've lined up a couple of retirement units for Esther to look at when she's here,' I say to Bob when I get home. 'I should have done it long ago.'

'Take it one step at a time,' he advises. 'Your mother will fight the idea. So would you in her place.' It's not in my character to go slow once I've set a course of action, but I know he is right.

The drought puts an end to dinners at the water's edge, sitting around a blazing fire in an old washing machine drum with a battered black camp oven hung over it. Cooking an old-fashioned stew, filling the bay with the smell of onions, carrots and celery. Fire bans are a way of life, now. On the rare days a fire is permitted, we still hold back. Who could live with the horror of being the one who lit the match that got away?

When I first came here, we spent many late summer and early autumn evenings at the waterside. The whole neighbourhood came by, with folding chairs, fishing rods and whatever they could find in their fridges to contribute to dinner: pasta, salad, cheese, chorizo, salami . . . Often we caught fish. They were plentiful, then. Crabs, too. Now they are so scarce, it is disturbing. Why have they run off? The water hasn't been cleaner for years. Highly toxic anti-foul boat paints are banned. Until the drought, even the oysters were coming back. Is it something we've done?

At Church Point Commuter Dock one day, lugging groceries and petrol – the staples of offshore life – Lisa mentions there's a new weed, *caulerpa taxifolia*, that's killing our sea grass. 'It's bad,' she says, loading a box of shiny red capsicums into her tinny. 'Sea grasses are fish nurseries where baby fish hide from predators. No grass – no fish.' It's already infested the water under the Elvina Bay public jetty and the east side of Scotland Island, she adds. 'Encourage people not to anchor in sea grass beds, if you can. It makes a difference.'

Sometimes, because our waterside barbecues are impossible, Jack sails his wooden boat, *Birrah Lee*, to Brooklyn, a haphazard little town on the great Hawkesbury River where most of Sydney's famous rock oysters are farmed. He buys a bulging hessian bag full and sails back the same day.

'Oysters are on! Seven o'clock, in front of the boatshed,' Brigitte calls to tell us.

Jack slings the bag on one of the trestle tables that Bob built for the tourist lunches and that now lives at the boatshed. Then he puts a folded towel in the palm of his left hand, slaps an oyster into it and stabs the lips of the shell with a pointed knife. He cuts through the muscle and removes the top shell, throwing it over his shoulder into the bay. It lands with a tiny splash, like a jumping fish. 'Look at that,' he grins, holding out the oyster. 'Plump and filled with liquor. You don't even need a squeeze of lime juice.' He tips back his head and lets the oyster slip into his mouth . . . and sighs. In the sky, a fingernail moon rises above Salvation Creek.

Each Friday, no matter how wet, cold, hot or windy, Michael, Bob and Stef gather in front of the open roller door of the boat-shed workshop for a *board meeting* amongst the sanders, grinders, workbenches and on a concrete floor that holds the heat and cold. John comes by, too, but not as religiously. Secret men's business, we call it − although if the evening is irresistible, Mary Beth, Bella, Therese and I join them.

'Can't get the pump on the boat going,' Stef says.

'I'll have a look at it,' Michael replies.

'Got a bit of a bulge in the retaining wall, Stef. What d'you reckon?' Bob asks.

'I'll have a look tomorrow,' Stef offers.

'Can't find a way to get a bloke to pay his bill,' Michael says.

'Here's what you do . . .' Bob and Stef leap in simultaneously, because they are both seasoned businessmen and Michael is soft-hearted. Perhaps because he comes from a large family where it was always a battle to make ends meet.

One night when we're all gathered for dinner at *Tarrangaua* after a twilight Woody Point yacht race, I leave the bowl of fruit for the Christmas pudding on the kitchen bench. It's soaked in Grand Marnier and the whole room smells of boozy oranges.

'Stir and make a wish,' I tell everyone who walks through the door, as I have done for decades now, wherever I've been living.

'Not like that!' Bella says, grabbing the wooden spoon from Fleury. 'My friend Pat reckons you can only stir one way if you want to make a wish and have it come true,' she says.

Fleury gives her a hard look. 'Clockwise or anti?' she asks, testing her. 'And does everyone have to stir the same way, or just one person at a time?'

Bella thinks. 'Oh, do it anyway you like,' she says finally. 'But I think it's clockwise. I'll call Pat to check.'

Bob sees me watching as he makes his wish. He deliberately blanks the expression on his face.

'Bet you don't know what *I* wished,' I mutter grumpily.

'Of course I do. Health. For everyone.'

He's right, of course.

MAKING CHRISTMAS PUDDING AT LOVETT BAY
Serves 10–12 people.
(*A recipe from* The Australian Women's Weekly)

CITRUS PEEL
2 large oranges (600 g)
1 medium lemon (140 g)
water for simmering
250 ml water, extra
440 g sugar

250 g seeded dates, chopped
250 g dried currants
120 g sultanas
120 g raisins, chopped
80 ml Cointreau
½ teaspoon bicarbonate of soda
1 tablespoon boiling water
250 g butter, softened
500 g firmly packed dark brown sugar
4 eggs
150 g plain flour, sifted

1 teaspoon ground ginger
280 g stale breadcrumbs (make them from a loaf of good sourdough)

Prepare the citrus peel a couple of days before the rest of the pudding. Peel the rind thickly from the oranges and lemon, including the pith. Add the rind to a pan of boiling water and simmer, uncovered, for 10 minutes. Drain, add fresh water and repeat.

Combine 250 ml water with the sugar in a medium pan and stir over the heat, without boiling, until the sugar dissolves. Add the rind and simmer, uncovered, for 10 minutes. Remove from the heat, stand 10 minutes. Transfer mixture to a heatproof bowl and stand overnight.

Return the rind and syrup to a clean pan and simmer, uncovered, for 20 minutes. Remove from heat and stand until cool.

Drain the rind from the pan, reserving 2 tablespoons of the syrup. Chop the rind into pieces about the size of a currant. (The original recipe suggests a citrus butter made from the remaining syrup. I made it once but felt it was overkill.)

Combine the dates, currants, sultanas, raisins and Cointreau in a large bowl. Combine the soda and boiling water, add to the bowl and mix well. Cover and stand overnight at room temperature.

Beat together the butter and sugar in a medium bowl until just combined (do not overbeat). Add the eggs one at a time, beating only until just combined after each addition. Stir the butter mixture into the fruit mixture and add the citrus peel and 2 tablespoons of reserved syrup from the peel. Stir in the sifted flour and ginger, then the breadcrumbs. If you have (clean) old threepences and sixpences, stir them in now.

Wrap the mixture in a prepared calico cloth* or pile into a heavily greased and floured pudding basin. Place in a saucepan of boiling water and boil or steam, covered, for 4 hours.

(*To prepare the calico cloth, boil a large square for 20 minutes. Remove it from the water and wring out. Using fresh water, boil it for a further 10 minutes. Wring it out and then lay it flat. Sprinkle hot calico with plain flour to form a skin on the pudding when cooked.)

A few days before picking up my mother to bring her to Pittwater, Bob and I decide to spend a couple of days touring the wineries of the Hunter Valley with his son, Scott, who is visiting from Pittsburgh. Ten minutes after we check into our motel, Bob's phone rings.

'Where?' Bob asks, sinking into a chair. 'How long ago?'

A moment or so later, he asks: 'Which way is the wind blowing?'

He looks at me, his face serious. 'Fires. Don't know whether to stay or go home.'

'Bloody bushfires,' I mutter darkly, picking up our bags because I know there is no choice. 'More traditional than Christmas turkey.'

None of us speaks on the return trip, silenced by dread and dismay. At Terrey Hills, fire trucks line the roadside like a massive ground battalion. Impossibly young men in yellow and navy uniforms lean against them, styrofoam cups in hand, waiting. The car radio flicks to the news. Firestorms north of us. Then the weather report.

'Wind's in our favour right now,' Bob says. 'Nothing to worry about.'

We pick up Chinese takeaway in Mona Vale and head home. The neighbours have already set up our hoses and pumps. It is ten o'clock, too late to thank them, so we climb the steps with our baggage and takeaway and eat barbecue pork and satay chicken watching the orange glow behind the hills of Salvation Creek. So far, the air in Lovett Bay is crystal clear. The wind is being kind to us. Once again, we wait.

'Might as well go to bed,' Bob says at about midnight. 'Nothing's going to happen tonight.'

At two am the phone rings. Scott answers it. Bob and I don't even wake.

'Scott. Scott, we're all on alert,' Brigitte tells him. 'Elvina Bay is burning. Anything could happen. I've called everyone. Be ready.'

Scott, a tall, quiet man, doesn't panic. He walks onto the verandah. There are flames on the other side of the bay. The sky is burnt orange but the air is still clear. The wind remains in our favour. He decides not to wake us. He sits for another two hours, watching. Then he, too, returns to bed and sleeps soundly.

The next morning, the wind is still our way and there's no threat, so we have tea and toast and amble down Lover's Lane to check on our neighbours. We stomp on John and Therese's back deck. 'Hello?'

The silence is unnerving. Nothing stirs. No smell of coffee, toast, bacon.

'Where is everyone?' I ask Bob.

He shrugs. We call out again. Nothing.

Next door, at Stef and Bella's, all is still, too. We look up to Jack and Brigitte's house. Not a sign of life. Not a single larrikin kid playing war games or cricket.

'Did the whole world change overnight? Have we missed the siren call?' I ask.

Bob doesn't answer. He goes back to John and Therese's house.

'John!' he calls.

There's a grunt: 'Yo!'

'Are you there?'

'Hold on!'

He comes up the stairs from the bedroom in white overalls, bleary-eyed. Therese follows on her backside, dragging a broken ankle. She flew into the air when they rode a wave over a sandbar out of a harbour, then crashed, harder than a coconut on cement, when their boat landed. John helps her into a wheelchair. Both of them look drunk with exhaustion.

'You're up early, boy,' John says to Bob.

'It's almost ten o'clock!'

'Yeah, but that's early when you didn't get to bed until eight in the morning,' he replies, though not as a complaint.

Stef and Bella stagger across from their house. They've been up all night too. 'What's happening?' Stef asks. 'What's going on? Heard shouting.'

'Nothing,' Bob says. 'Just came down to see you were all ok and to say thanks for setting up the pumps.'

'Well, we were ok. Until you woke us,' Stef says. 'Hard to get a good night's sleep around here when you've got noisy neighbours. Never dull, though, I'll give you that.'

And we all grin, because our bonds are like family and there's nowhere else we'd rather be. John puts on the kettle. We look out the window and see a helicopter scooping water from the bay and then dropping it like a sudden deluge on the smouldering bush. Technology triumphing over nature. Good or bad? Either way, to survive is the most basic instinct.

Bob's daughters, Meg and Kelly, arrive to celebrate Christmas bringing their partners . . . and dogs, Tali and Bear. Tali is a handsome black and white border collie with a baby pink lipstick smile and a ton of charm. He shadows Meg like her keeper. Bear is the ugliest dog ever born: too tall, skinny in the rump, big-chested. Not even her ears match. One sticks straight up. The other flops flatly. Her coat looks like it's been attacked by moths. Kelly adores her.

The floors of rooms all over the house are littered with clothing, mattresses and bedding for dogs and humans, strewn like the aftermath of gale-force winds. Lulu, my stepdaughter from my first marriage, comes with her partner and her border collie, Bella. Bella's muzzle is greyer than ever, although she still never stops dropping sticks in your lap and begging you to throw them. The sticks are more like toothpicks now, though. The floor space is chockers. Lulu will sleep in a tent on the lawn. She is kind enough to tell me she likes camping. Chip Chop is overwhelmed, but she cheers up at the sight of food.

Christmas dinner unfolds in chaos. The charcoal in the barbecue won't catch alight. The turkey, covered in the skin from the ham to keep it moist, is cooking too slowly. Dogs, stinky wet from a swim, hover politely at my feet in the kitchen, hoping a morsel will drop from the bench. When nothing does, they wander off, heads sagging with disappointment, pausing only to shake. The walls are sprayed with water. The salad, too. Chip Chop finds the ham skin after we take it off to brown the turkey. She eats it to the point of explosion. We call Ray the Vet who tells us she might die but there's not a damn thing we can do. We lock her away from even the smell of food.

My mother, resplendent in fire-engine red with strobing red reindeer earrings and a Santa Claus brooch that flashes like a light-house, tells me the Christmas decorations are a disgrace. 'I'll do them next year,' she huffs.

'I've gone minimalist,' I snap back. Truth is, with bushfires and getting beds and tents sorted, I ran out of time and energy for more than a few baubles and a small old flashing Christmas tree I've had for years.

'Minimalist and Christmas don't work,' she replies. And she has a point.

When we finally sit down to eat, I am sweating from a barrage of hot flushes. I whack down two glasses of champagne in rapid succession, then I look around. Smiling faces. Tanned arms reaching for a prawn, smoked trout, some mango salad.

'Ah bugger,' I shout. 'Put down your knives and forks. We haven't sung the carols yet.'

Everyone groans. Lulu hands around the words to six carols we sing every year before we eat. She's been sitting on them, hoping I'll forget. Not a chance! Is there an exploding point for happiness? There can't be.

Late in the afternoon, Stewart and Fleury and their two daughters, drop in. Lisa and Roy and the two Alans, too. At the sound of Lisa's voice my mother wanders into the kitchen, her red skirt a thousand thin pleats. Like the Chinese, she believes that red is lucky.

'Hello, Esther,' Lisa coos, folding my mother into her arms for a hug and a kiss. 'My, you do look gorgeous. What a stunning outfit!'

My mother smiles girlishly, holds her hand to her face in a mock 1920s pout, pats her hair softly, using a thumb to roll a curl more tidily. She pulls up a kitchen stool and the two of them chat away like old cronies. Lisa admires her necklace, her rings, her flashing earrings and brooch. She makes her feel beautiful.

'How do you do it?' I whisper to Lisa later.

'You get in first. Tell her she looks fabulous — and she does, as a matter of fact — then there's nowhere to go with a complaint. Works every time.'

'Told you that years ago,' Bob says, catching the tail end of our conversation. 'Used to tell my mother she looked great before she had a chance to say a word. Stopped her in her tracks.'

By midnight, we're all in bed, even the youngies. Bob grabs me tightly. 'Thank you,' he says, with a sigh.

'Oh no, thank *you*!'

And we both fall into a dead sleep. Holding hands.

On Boxing Day, lunch is set out in the kitchen. Leftover ham, turkey, baguettes, lettuce, mustard, cranberry sauce. 'Make your own sandwiches,' I suggest. 'Then, if you like, we'll watch the beginning of the Sydney to Hobart yacht race on television.'

A few minutes before the start, there's an almighty crash from the kitchen. We all look around, count . . . Everyone's present. Dogs, too. Except Tali. He's in the kitchen, looking sheepish. The ham is on the floor.

'Tali fancied the ham,' I call out to Meg. 'Pulled it off the bench.'

'Tali would never do anything like that,' Meg says, running in to defend him.

Tali hangs his head. It's covered with the stringy bits of fat we cut off to make our sandwiches.

'Oh, Tali,' Meg says, pulling it off his coat. Then she turns to me. 'It really isn't his fault,' she says. 'He's on cortisone for his rash. Makes him hungry all the time.'

'Yes, Meg.'

And I rush outside so she can't hear me laughing.

On New Year's Eve I help my mother into the tinny to drive her back to her home at the foot of the Blue Mountains. She's not a fan of ushering in the future. Or perhaps it's just that when you're in your eighties, it's more prudent to look back than forward.

'I'm going to swing past a place I want you to see,' I tell her. Suspicion fills her eyes. She twists her rings round and round, draws her lips into a smile. Red lipstick splatters her front teeth. The smile is full of fright. Her vulnerability is heartbreaking.

'What kind of place?' She cannot quite make her voice sound firm.

'It's a retirement *village*, not a *home*,' I tell her.

'I like my own house,' she insists, stubbornness creeping into her voice. 'Nothing wrong with it. And it suits me. I know where everything is.'

Gut-churning fear floods her eyes. Will I put her away somewhere and forget about her? She's read newspaper stories about foul nursing homes crammed with confused old people medicated to oblivion until, eventually, oblivion claimed them forever. She's heard about kids who never visit, who snap up cash and property and take off in search of the good life, leaving their parents for almost dead. As though it's their right and their parents, because they are old, have none. It is quite shocking to realise she doesn't trust me. I must have failed her badly in ways I don't even know – and, to be truthful, some that I do – for her to be so afraid.

'Let's just look. If it makes you feel uncomfortable, we'll turn around and drive straight out.'

At the village she hesitantly steps inside a sparkling white one bedroom apartment with views of a rainforest garden and the slushing sound of a creek. An eastern water dragon stands statue-still on the balcony, and she sighs at its beauty. 'It's like being in the bush,' she says. Which is where she grew up. The reptile stares at her. She moves closer, her hand outstretched to pat him. He flicks his tail, takes off.

'I want to be settled here within two weeks,' she announces.

It is so easy I panic. 'She'll be right next door,' I tell Bob. 'That's good in one way, but it could be disastrous in another.'

Bob, pragmatic as ever, smiles. 'Don't worry,' he says, 'remember the moat!' He pauses. 'You are *absolutely* sure she's not a good swimmer, aren't you?'

On moving day, she's still in her underwear when I arrive at noon to pick her up. Wandering, as though she's forgotten who she is and what she's doing. *Two steps. Sit. Two steps. Sit.* Change is always stressful. At my mother's age, it is addling. *Two steps. Sit.* She looks around her home, already emptied of the furniture she is taking to her new home. There is no recognition in her eyes. Her hands are shaky. Her hair, carefully coiffed at the local hairdresser's the day before, is flattened at the back from too many hours stretched out on the sofa. *Old lady hair*, we used to call it. But neither my mother nor I ever thought we'd let it happen to us.

'Here's your dress,' I say, handing her a garment I've found in the closet. 'Might as well get going.'

But she looks exhausted. Grey-skinned, with sweat on her upper lip. I am frightened that she might die. That beginning again, instead of saving her, might kill her.

We pack the bare necessities. In the bathroom, there's an unopened bottle of expensive moisturiser I bought her as a gift more than twenty years earlier, on display because she'd rather let people think she can afford mindless luxuries than use them. Appearances. Her whole life has been about keeping up appearances, like the rest of her generation. I want to weep.

I open the car door to help her inside. She is still dithery but trying to look brave. Her own car, *Mavis*, stays in the garage. More dented than whole, the round, small white 1984 Datsun is up for sale.

'I'll get a scooter,' my mother says, looking at me with a flicker of challenge in her rabbit-scared eyes. 'I'll fling a long scarf around my neck, toss my bag over my shoulder and hit the accelerator on the main street. I'll be unstoppable!'

I know she is thinking about Audrey Hepburn burning up the roads of Rome, her arms wrapped around Gregory Peck, her face snuggled into his shoulder. And I know, I just know, she'll do it if we let her get anywhere near a scooter. Dead in a week, I think, and mentally shove the scooter idea into the never-go-there basket. It is the moment I understand my mother has become my child. And I want to cry, again – loud and hard – for all the good times and the wobbly ones. Once we believed life went on forever and if we made mistakes there was plenty of time to do it again and get it right. And now we know better.

Her old dog, Wally, a slobbery Rottweiler with Marilyn Monroe hips and a grey snout, is heaved into the back of the car. He is coming to live with Bob and me – his own *retirement home*, I told my mother when I said we were taking him. Just like hers.

We slide onto the super-smooth motorway from an entrance road and she never looks back, focuses straight ahead with her purse held firmly on her lap. But her hands are still trembling and her face is sheet white. She must be scared as hell. No upside except hanging out in a retirement village, the kind of place we both used to call 'the last resort' when it seemed like we'd never have to go near one ourselves. I silently curse the frailty of old age: I don't want to be like her, I tell myself. But is there a choice? Do we slide slowly into infirmity without noticing the signs? Can't open a packet of sweets. Find it hard to turn on taps. Get up from sofas with a grunt of effort. Then the big signs: shortness of breath, footsteps that slide into the hesitant shuffle of the aged, the long naps at any time of the day, sleeplessness at night. The inevitable countdown because when you are more than eighty, you *know* time is running out. There are no miracles when you're old. And none of us is immune to the passage of time.

We swing into the driveway of the *village*, and wind through magnificent gardens of towering grey gums and rigid gymeas, of red hibiscus and fluffy bottle brush, to her new *villa*. She gives me the keys to her old house and I put them in my bag. Bob and I are going to prepare it for sale. Then I gently wrap her fingers around the keys of her new home. She gets out of the car, stiff-limbed, rocky on her feet. 'One, two, three,' she says, to urge herself on.

I take her arm, lead her to the front door. She fumbles with the lock until I take the keys back from her and open the door. Inside,

Bob and I have installed a new fridge, new washing machine and dryer, new pots and pans. There is a new electric jug, new toaster, new container filled with new cooking utensils. Spatula. Wooden spoon. Egg flip. Tongs. Like she is a new bride.

I've filled the freezer with homemade spaghetti bolognese, chicken curry and lamb stew. There's milk, bread, Vegemite, marmalade and all the staples. I've found a plastic bin small enough to place on the counter, so she doesn't have to bend to throw away her garbage, which she says hurts her back. The pink chintz granny couch and armchairs are in position. The heavy round table and Edwardian chairs with the green and gold brocade seats have been squeezed in. The single bed she wanted in place of her queen-size is made up with new bed linen and fat pillows. Her old pillows were flattened thinner than a slice of bread. It smells fresh, looks clean and new.

I let Wally out for a quick wander and piddle, fill a bowl with water. He flops onto the ground, as exhausted as my mother.

The water dragon turns up on the balcony on cue and for a moment her eyes light up. Then she sinks onto the sofa in a small, crumpled lump. And, again, I want to weep and weep. I thought she would be unstoppable forever.

Bob arrives to say hello, makes a cup of tea. 'You'll be fine, Esther,' he tells her reassuringly. 'You couldn't have continued where you were.' And it's true.

I try to show her how to work the washing machine but she can't find the strength to lift herself off the sofa.

'This is a new chapter,' I say, trying to be cheerful, to spur her on.

She looks at me and attempts the coquettish smile of old, but there is more confusion than flirtiness in her eyes, as though she can't quite work out what has happened. I feel suddenly afraid that something inside her has snapped and she'll never recover, wonder if we should have left her where she was, wonder if the struggle to survive is what kept her going this far. Now the pressure is off, will she collapse?

We finish our tea in the floral pink china mugs her local chemist gave her as a farewell gift and stand to leave. Bob wraps his arms around her.

'I'll call you in the morning,' I tell her, opening the screen door. 'We'll do a shop, get what you need.'

We load a reluctant Wally back in the car.

'We're going to Pittwater, Wally. You love Pittwater.'

But he doesn't perk up.

Bob and I meet at Commuter Dock. I am childishly angry and have flung compassion into an outgoing tide. 'She didn't even say thank you,' I hiss.

'She couldn't speak,' Bob replies. 'Give her time. She's old.'

Inside me, though, there's a seething, irrational anger. Fury, I suspect, because until today, every time I looked at my mother I saw a vibrant, energetic, good-looking woman in her fifties. I can no longer conveniently pretend that she can manage perfectly well if only she would make an effort, which is how I've excused my erratic care for years. She is old. Now it is my turn to repay getting me to adulthood with every advantage she could afford. *Duty* is such an old-fashioned word, but that's what it boils down to. Because love is taken for granted in family. Duty is the nuts and bolts.

'Yeah. Time. She'll be fine.' Anger rushes out of me like air out of a burst balloon. But will she cope? I'm not so sure.

Wally sees the water, sniffs the air. Lifts his leg at a post. He jumps into the boat like he was born in a tinny. There's a grin on his face and he tosses his age and exhaustion over the side. I swear he throws back his shoulders and braces for a final fling at youth. Perhaps he remembers the year I entered him in the annual Christmas Eve Scotland Island to Church Point Dog Race. Threw him off the start barge when he refused to jump and thought I'd drowned him – only dog in the history of the race that's ever had to be rescued.

'No more races for you, Wally,' I tell him. '*Them* days are over.'

At home, Wally settles in like he's never lived anywhere else, although Chip Chop's nose is out of joint for a few days. Then she relaxes. But she won't let him near the sofa. That's her territory and she's not going to budge.

The following week Bob and I move into my mother's house to prepare it for sale. We take the dogs with us. Wally is heartbroken because he thinks he's returning to a suburban backyard. He mopes all day, sighing like a doggie that's doomed. We let Chip Chop sleep on the bed so she feels superior. They only escape once, to go to the river for a swim. Can't blame them, really – it was on a day hotter than hell.

Bob and I strip faded wallpaper off walls and repaint the house, inside and out. On days when the temperature soars higher than thirty-five degrees, he mends cracked tiles in the laundry and fixes all the windows, broken by my mother when she locked herself out. Time after time.

We landscape a feral garden, dump all the old saucepans she's put at the back door to soak after burning their bums, and prepare for a garage sale. Bob even lays new carpet. It is hard, relentless physical work and we nearly have our first real argument when I return to Pittwater to borrow some giant cushions from Bella to make the place look current. Bob reckons good bones sell a house, not pretty cushions, and it's wasted effort. But it is my mother's last shot at a financial killing and I am pushing the limits to get every extra penny for her. Truth is, we are both knackered. Truth is, I am ashamed I let things get so rundown while she was living here, ashamed that I never looked closely at her life. Afraid that if I did, I would have to take some responsibility. I am ashamed that while I was partying inappropriately, her world was slipping into depressing decay.

After we've finished the repairs, my mother insists on returning to the house to see what we've done. I wait for a thank-you as she walks through rooms that echo with years that I suspect were mostly deeply unhappy. Although she never let on.

'Oh, you took down all the wallpaper,' she says. 'It was so beautiful.'

It was old, dirty and peeling, I want to scream, but I hold my tongue.

'Oh, what did you do with the hanging baskets? They used to look so pretty.'

The plants were all dead, I want to yell. But I stay silent.

'Where are all my important documents? I kept them in the kitchen drawer.'

I've thrown them out, of course, after checking them. Old receipts. Old bills stamped 'paid'. A couple of share certificates for companies that went belly-up in the sixties. But I don't say any of that. 'They must be in a box at your new place. Not unpacked yet.' Inside, I am smouldering.

She makes her way down the front steps to the garage. The detritus of more than eight decades is set out for sale. She moves through the trays like a canny buyer, picking up, putting down, as though it is all new to her. Then I catch her slipping odd pieces into her handbag. And I explode.

'If you put one more *thing* in your bag, I'll put you out on the freeway and make you walk home,' I snarl.

Cool as a cucumber, she looks me in the eye. 'That's right, take it out on your mother. That's what mothers are for.' And she plonks herself in the car on a stinking hot day and stays there until I finish with the real estate agent. I kick myself for lacking compassion. Again. Drive through a blur of tears because she hasn't bothered to say a single thank-you for all the backbreaking work. Not a grateful look, nothing. But when did I ever thank her during the long years of growing up? When she cooked, washed, ironed, supported, listened to the self-obsessed litanies of the young? Not once that I can remember. Because I assumed I had a right to all she could give. As she believes now, in reverse.

'If you look for praise from your mother,' Bob told me one day, 'you're doomed.' And yet I still do. Over and over. Are we always children around our parents? Even when we become the carers?

Twenty minutes later, as McDonald's looms on the side of the freeway, she speaks her first words: 'Let's have a hamburger and thick shake for old times' sake.'

It is a ritual. Every time I collected her to come to stay, we stopped there for a quick bite. The olive branch is down. I push aside anger, pick up where we left off. When I drop her back at her new home she sinks onto the sofa with a sigh, closing her eyes as though she will never feel rested again. I slip out the door without hugging her. Feigning haste when, really, there is none. I hold on to my hurt like a two-year-old.

'Tell me about Pittwater,' my mother says one morning when we are having coffee and cake at a café in Mona Vale.

'What do you want to know?'

'Start with the history. I'd like to know about the early days.'

'I'll take you for a drive when we've finished here. To look at the Aboriginal rock carvings at West Head Road. They're magnificent. You can see for miles, too. Right to the Pacific Ocean.'

It is the first time she's been curious beyond the wire door of her villa since the move a month earlier and I begin to hope that her inner geography is catching up with her new circumstances, that soon I will call in and instead of finding her asleep on the sofa with the breakfast dishes still soaking in the sink, she will be bright and alert, the garbage emptied, the bed made, the day ahead embraced.

'Join the pool group!' I tell her. 'Join the knitter-natters! Join the tai-chi class!' But she never stirs. Maybe showing her around her new landscape will break the paralysis.

Along winding McCarrs Creek Road, where Chip Chop and I always get queasy, the bush is tinder dry. The drought is annihilating. My mother closes her eyes to it all, refusing to open them at the waterfall, which is just a collection of rocks without rain to fill it, and where the creek is now no more than a trickle.

I turn into Ku-ring-gai Chase National Park and slide to a stop in a small area reserved for cars.

'What have you stopped for?'

'We're here.'

'Where are the rocks?'

'We have to walk a little. Not far. It's easy.'

Her face falls, panic flickering across it. I can see she doesn't want to move.

'Let's go. Can't sit here all day,' I say like a girl guide leader.

I move around to her door and open it. I take her hand – when did the bones get so light and frail? – and help her to her feet. She looks around as though she's memorising landmarks in case I dump her in the bush forever. I lead her into a serrated landscape of shrivelled grevilleas, drooping apple gums. When we're about to turn off the track for a rough pathway leading to the rock carvings, she stops and stands still.

'I need a toilet,' she says.

'Right now?'

She nods.

'Ok, there's a café at Akuna Bay. We'll go there. Maybe have lunch, if you feel like it.'

It's a start, I tell myself. We've made a start.

Over lunch, to fill in the silence, I tell her a story: 'In 1901, twenty-four years before Dorothea Mackellar made *Tarrangaua* her summer retreat, a woman named Maybanke Anderson bought a large waterfront block of land on Pittwater Road, at Bayview.'

She nods. Pokes at her fish and chips but doesn't eat anything.

'Maybanke's story is a bit of local history,' I explain, trying to engage her. 'It's quite interesting. Really.'

She puts down her knife and fork. She's not hungry. The morning tea was enough. I slam the lid on memories of my mother eating dozens of oysters at a time, of enjoying food with gusto and passion.

'Anyway . . . Maybanke came to Australia from England as a nine-year-old child and grew up to become a schoolteacher. She married unwisely. Had seven children and lost all but three boys to tuberculosis. Along the way, her husband became an alcoholic, a bankrupt and eventually deserted the family. But Maybanke had a lot of guts. And family support.

'With the help of her brother and mother, she worked and prospered only to find that, according to the law, her husband was entitled to custody of the children and control of her money. Nor could she be granted a divorce for desertion alone. The injustice of the system infuriated her, and she became a law reformer, a feminist and a campaigner for childcare and equal rights. She eventually divorced her husband for desertion, under a new amendment she helped to bring about. But she never forgot what it was like to be a single woman with young children and she helped to found the first free kindergarten at Woolloomooloo. When the press wrote about her, she was called "about the most intellectual woman in Australia". Love the about, don't you?'

The waitress comes over to clear our plates, my mother's food still almost untouched. Around us, boats costing more than a house are tied to pontoons. A young family is scrambling off one, kids in hats and shorts, a scruffy, tail-wagging, long-haired, black and tan dog. Parents red-faced from the sun, or maybe the wine, trying to keep control. My mother's eyes lock on them, then fill with tears. Oh God, how I hate seeing her like this. I race on with the story.

'Maybanke had just about every strike against her for the era. Divorced. A businesswoman. Politically active. A feminist,' I continue. 'Anyway, she met a bloke, they fell in love and married. Quite scandalous, it was. At the time, divorcees didn't usually get a second go because divorce was seen as an affliction, like the plague.'

My mother looks up. 'Remember Mary? She was divorced. That would have been fifty years after Maybanke, wouldn't it? And it was still scandalous.'

'Yeah, I remember her. Brought up two boys on her own. She was so beautiful. Must've been hard on her.'

'It was. We weren't a forgiving lot in those days. We were quick to judge and pass sentence, women as well as men, and we should've known better. Everyone makes mistakes and I reckon the way we hid them was nothing but cowardice.'

We're silent for a moment or two.

'Opportunities for women were scarce,' I say, 'and there wasn't any government financial support. My generation was the first to grow up understanding we'd survive whether we worked or not.' It was almost illicit to think you could go and line up at a window and get the dole for doing nothing. Anathema to everything we'd been taught. *Work hard. Reap the benefits. Save for your old age.* The mouse wheel went up in smoke with the dole, and parents, if they wanted, were off the hook. 'You could throw your kids out and know they wouldn't starve,' I add.

My mother sighs. 'I hope you don't think I threw you out when I pushed you to travel.'

'Of course not. You knew it was the only way you'd get to see the world. Dad couldn't say no when you said you wanted to join me to make sure I was alright.'

She looks at me, eyes wide, unsure whether to rebut or confirm.

But mostly shocked, I suspect, that I'd worked out the subplot. 'Oh, go on with your story,' she says when she figures out she's in a no-win situation. 'What happened to whatever her name was?'

'Maybanke Anderson. She built a house at Bayview, near where you live now. First, it was a weekender. They held lots of parties with delicious food. Students played games. Some wrote poems and stories.'

'When I was young,' my mother cuts in again, 'we had parties every Sunday night. People came from miles around, bringing flutes, harmonicas – any instrument they could play. We danced and danced. Your grandmother would sew late into the night so we girls always had a new dress. She made one from velvet, once. Midnight blue velvet. I put it on and thought I owned the world. Had a lace collar. God, it was beautiful.'

'Did you sing?' I ask, because my mother had a powerful soprano voice.

'Of course! Every new song that came out. We learned them in a flash. Songs were easier to remember in those days. They had a tune.'

'What was your favourite?'

'Oh, I don't know. Anyway, go on with your story.'

'You love all the old musicals,' I prompt.

'Are you going to tell this story or not?'

I try not to sigh, so I don't sound even more like a mother patronising her kid.

'Well. In 1920, Maybanke wrote *The Story of Pittwater*. She knew even then that one day people like you and me would want to know who lived here and how. Knew, too, that it only takes a single generation and history is either distorted or forgotten.

'Anyway . . . there was a farm on the other side of Lovett Bay – there's an old picture of it hanging in the hallway at home – where the Oliver family lived. One day, the blackfellas, as she called them, *bandicooted* a whole paddock of potatoes. *Bandicooted*? Isn't it a great word? Mrs Oliver kept a musket by her side after that. Sounds like a tough old girl. But . . . and this is the really interesting part, Maybanke wrote a little poem to be sung by schoolchildren.'

I couldn't remember the words on the day I lunched with my mother, so I managed only a vague description of them. But this is what Maybanke wrote.

Australia Fair

Australia fair, I love thee,
The dear land of my birth;
To me thou art the sweetest,
The brightest spot on earth.

I love thy golden sunshine,
The sky of peerless hue,
The soft greys of the distance,
The hills' faint tints of blue.

I love thy yellow beaches,
The clear waves tipped with foam,
The capes that stand like bulkwarks
To guard my native home.

I love the leafy gullies,
Where palm and ferntree hide,
The tall, grey gums that clamber
On every steep hill-side.

I love the ferny pathways,
Where wattle blossoms fall,
While in the leafy distance
The bell-bird rings his call.

I love the old slab homesteads,
Each peach and lemon tree,
The paddocks and the slip-rails,
They speak of home to me.

Dear Southern Land, Australia,
Wherever I may roam
My heart will turn forever
To thee, my native home.

'I can't help wondering,' I say to my mother as we get up to leave the restaurant, 'whether she and Dorothea knew each other, no matter how slightly. I wonder, too, how Maybanke felt when she heard, just six years after her own poem was published, Mackellar's "My Country" being read everywhere, over and over until it became iconic, as familiar as the national anthem. Do you think she smiled quietly, content that her passion for Australia had lodged like an arrow in a suitable heart? Or did the similarities rankle? What do you think?' I ask.

My mother has slumped again. She is barely interested. 'Everyone cribbed from each other in those days. There was no real way of checking. People with the most money were the most brazen.' She tells a story about her father being cheated out of his fruit shop when she was a very young girl that I don't know whether to believe or not. Wading back into the past brings her to life on the trip home. But not for long.

10

FLEURY HAS ANOTHER TOUR group and one of her guides has the flu. 'Could you come along and set out drinks and biscuits in the park? It will only take a couple of hours.'

'Easy. Took Esther there a few weeks ago so I don't even need a refresher course.'

'I don't need you to be a guide,' Fleury says hastily, recalling another day when I helped her out. I had a shocker attack of nerves, forgot all my words, mixed up Captain Cook and Governor Phillip and led my group around the track backwards, crashing into hers midway.

'Just set out the food and drink?'

'That's all,' she says, her voice firmer than usual.

They are a motley but well-heeled lot of men and women, mostly from the US. A hungover blonde. A woman with hair that matches her perfectly manicured and painted blood-red toenails. Men with dark brown hairpieces that clash with their grey stubble. Cheery matrons filling in time. None of them are much interested in Aboriginal rock carvings or delicate mauve grevilleas with their tendrils curled into a frail fist. Some of the boronias bloom, frothy and pretty pink. Native irises, so deeply purple they are almost black, jut up from the chalky white soil. But the tourists sniff. Not big or blowsy enough.

I first walked here when I stayed in Stewart and Fleury's house at Towlers Bay. On their deck with a full moon rising, I wondered if I'd finally found a place to belong. I had, as it turned out, only I was blind to it for a long time. I trudged the track, day after day, until I couldn't breathe. Looking for answers, hoping a deluge of wisdom would drop from a burning blue sky. I thought I learned nothing in the cacophony of those days. Despair, though, can be a great teacher.

'The thing about the Australian bush is that it's subtle. You have to work hard to see it,' I say, hoping to inspire the tourists.

The hungover blonde is unimpressed. 'I don't like to work hard at anything, honey,' she says. 'There was talk of champagne? Are we nearly to the bar?'

She's too young to be so desperate. I look into her eyes. Eyes tell you just about everything – anyone with secrets knows that. She flicks her head around, avoiding me. So young and so much to hide already.

A brown snake slithers quickly and silently across the path in front of us, gleaming like metal in the sun. Everyone screams and jumps. The woman with the blood-red toes confesses she hates all wildlife. As she speaks, a luminous blue march fly with an ugly bulbous head lands on her shoulder and sinks in its sting. She screeches and stumbles off in her impractical sandals to the enclosed safety of the bus. Once, I would have done the same.

The remaining tourists gather for cold drinks and snacks at the West Head lookout with its views across Barrenjoey and the Pacific Ocean. Dolphins, sharks and whales travel north or south along this route, according to the season. When the whales migrate, people line the shore for days at a time, entranced by their massive grace.

A six foot goanna lumbers towards us searching for scraps, black eyes scouring the scene. Its forked tongue flicks incessantly.

'It's not going to attack,' I explain to the more nervous members of the group. 'If it feels threatened, it runs up a tree with a whooshing sound. Out of our reach.'

They do attack, of course, if they're cornered. Bella found one in her kitchen once, when she came home from shopping. A hulking bastard in a foul mood. When she tried to shoo him out he turned on her. She threw oranges at him and then ran away to phone Stef. 'There's a giant goanna in the kitchen. Get rid of it. Now!' she insisted, all reason gone. Stef was in a meeting in the city.

'Throw a towel over its head and carry it out,' he suggested.

'That advice is grounds for divorce,' Bella replied, her voice colder than ice.

'Call the boys in the boatshed. They're closer.'

When Stef finally came home, Raoul told him the goanna was about six feet long: 'Big enough to run up a bloke's leg and rip his eyes out.' Not that anyone's ever had that happen. 'But this one was big enough!' he said. Stef's reconciliation dinner was *very* expensive.

The goanna in the park stops to rest. Some people edge closer, others shuffle further away. A man about fifty-five years old with very badly dyed hair stands his ground, staring. 'He's the same colour as the landscape,' he observes. 'The patterns on his skin could be a tree trunk.'

'You're not frightened?'

'Hell no!' He confesses it has always been his dream to visit Australia.

'Well, you've achieved it,' I say. 'So what's your next dream?' We are talking lightly, the way strangers can.

'I've given up on dreams, I guess. Now I have goals.'

'Goals are good. What kind of goals?'

He pauses then says: 'Youth. Youth is my goal.'

'Maybe you should put that into the dream department,' I say flippantly.

When I glance at his face, I see he is serious and my remark has hurt him. Before I can apologise, he wanders off. I stare at the back of his head. His hair distracts me. Maybe it's not dyed, maybe it's a wig? Whatever it is, it fails to deliver eternal youth.

When everyone has gone, I clear the picnic debris. The goanna ambles back, making wide swinging movements with his front legs. Up close, his faded, dusty old skin is peeling to reveal the new, beautifully marked pale green and beige striations underneath. For him, the illusion of youth is as easy as shedding his old skin.

'Doesn't matter what you do to the outside, old boy,' I say out loud. 'Only have to look into your eyes to know you've been around a long time.'

He stares for a moment, then folds his massive front legs over each other, heaves a weary sigh and drops to the ground where he falls asleep. I pack the car with the leftovers. When I return to check I've cleared everything, the goanna is gone. Then I catch sight of movement under the trees. He fixes me with his obsidian stare, his tongue still flicking hypnotically, his skin perfectly blended with the dead and dying leaves. I wave goodbye. He turns, his long tail swishing, and lumbers away.

A few weeks after our jaunt to (almost) see the rock carvings, I begin to fear that moving house has unhinged my mother's mind.

'The man next door has orgies every night,' she says. 'I can hear people through the walls. It's terrible. The screaming, then the arguments. Haven't been able to sleep since I moved in.'

At first I ignore her. The idea of sex orgies in a retirement village, where the average age is around eighty and everyone has a bad back, bad knees, a bad heart or uses a walking frame, is laughable. But my mother insists she's not dreaming. 'I've moved to the sofa to sleep,' she says in one of her daily early-morning phone calls. 'It's the furthest I can get from their noise. Thought the woman was being strangled last night.'

'Has anyone else said anything to you? I mean, you all live so close together, surely someone's made a complaint?'

'I haven't said a word. It's none of my business.'

A couple of days later, I run into one of the neighbours heading out for a game of golf. She's a tough, smart dame at the rear end of her seventies who doesn't suffer fools and who abhors laziness. She kindly took my mother shopping once a week until it wore her out.

'Who lives next door to Esther?' I ask, indicating the doorway of the unit alongside my mother's.

'That's Bertie, a lovely fellow. Quiet and gentle. He's in hospital right now. Been there for six weeks. His back is slowly crippling him. Don't think he'll be returning. His daughter wants him to move in with her so she can take proper care of him.'

'Ah, I wondered why I've never seen anyone around.'

When my mother gets into the car for our foray to the local supermarket where she buys cans of soup, truckloads of crème caramel and heaps of cakes and biscuits, I ask her if the orgies have quietened down.

'Worse than ever,' she responds gloomily.

'Have you seen these people come and go?'

'They arrive at about eleven pm and leave before five in the morning,' she says. And for the first time, I am absolutely sure it is pure fantasy, even though it is as real to her as the glittering rings jammed on every one of her fingers. Wraithlike figures in the dark hours, sounds that no-one else hears, a neighbour who doesn't even live there? Highly unlikely.

'Esther, Bertie's been in hospital for six weeks. There are

cobwebs across the front door. No-one's gone in the place for more than a month.'

'Yes they have,' she says sternly, looking me straight in the eye. 'It must be the staff then. Using the place while Bertie is away.'

It is madness, I know it, but she sounds so utterly plausible.

'What do you think?' I ask Bob.

'Tell her we're coming to spend a night. To check it out.'

When the stories escalate to two phone calls a day, I tell my mother we're going to sleep over.

'You can't,' she says. 'There's not enough space.'

For the following week, there's no mention of any next-door activities. Then she begins again. 'I'm going to have to move,' she says. 'I really can't take it anymore.'

'Esther, there is nowhere to go. This is it. The last stop. I'll talk to the front desk.'

But I cannot bring myself to say a word. What is there to say anyway? That my mother is going nutty? That moving tipped her into senility? And yet she sounds so completely rational and convincing that I am still not entirely sure she isn't telling the truth.

'Give her a bit more time to settle,' Bob advises. 'It will all probably fade away.'

'Got a spare bed for a few days?' Pia asks when she calls for one of our irregular check-ins.

'Few weeks if you can stand us that long.'

'No, don't think I could,' she says, laughing.

'Not coming for a check-up or anything, are you?' I ask, suddenly frightened she might be back in danger.

'Of course not. Just catching up with old buddies.'

She arrives in a cloud of style. Little round, leopard-skin-like

Gucci sunglasses perch on her nose. A beige linen skirt swishes around her calves, topped with a white linen shirt and a striped linen jacket. Perfect hair, glossy shoes. There's a gentle whiff of an exotic perfume. She is so un-Pittwater that for a disorienting moment she looks like another species. Then I think back to what it was like to lead a less feral life: the days of high heels, silk and hosiery, the flutter of excitement before a big night out, the thrill of believing that life was being lived on the edge. Do I miss it all? No, not for a moment. But in a way I am glad of the memories, as increasingly ephemeral as they are. Without the past, how would I be able to understand the richness of now?

'You look absolutely fabulous,' I tell her, because it is true. 'Quite beautiful. How come age leaves you alone?'

'I *am* quite pleased,' she replies, 'with the way I am wearing. Wish I'd covered up my décolletage when I was young, though. All those V-necked sweaters have left a weathered spot.'

'So what's the secret?'

She grins. 'Alcohol, I suspect!' And we laugh because there was a time when we thought wine seemed to hold all the answers. It doesn't, of course.

She makes it into the tinny without tripping on her skirts or getting a spot of dirt on her, clutching her swank little shoulder bag that I know, if I opened it, would be in perfect order. We load on her small suitcase that will be packed with a minimum of clothes for maximum impact. Style, for Pia, is instinctive and effortless. Once, I tried to be like her. Then I gave up. Even when I worked hard at it, I got it wrong.

'Want to go for a browse around Mona Vale tomorrow?' I ask.

'Hmm. It's a big ask, but I think I can manage.'

'Wouldn't mind if you had a chat to Esther. She's going on about all these orgies happening next door. Like to know what you think.'

'How is the old girl?'

'Bit worried she's losing her marbles.'

'The only thing your mother will ever lose is her keys. Don't worry, she's tougher than an old bull. There probably *are* funny things going on. I've read some amazing stories about life in retirement villages.'

'Maybe. But I don't think so.'

The next morning is still, bright, sunny. A few kayakers drift into Lovett Bay in lurid colours, like exotic birds. The only vibrant colour in a parched landscape. The drought goes on and on.

The next morning Bob offers to take Pia and me across in the tinny for a coffee and some food shopping in Mona Vale.

'Nah. Piece of cake,' I reply. He's working on a new engineering project and I don't want to interrupt.

'Learned how to drive that boat yet?' Pia asks as we set off down the steps. She's as immaculate as ever, although more rural than yesterday. The designer handbag has been switched for a spickle khaki rucksack. She wears pale brown linen trousers, a black camisole with a white linen shirt over it, and baby pink lipstick like we used to wear in the seventies. With a hint of gloss.

'Yeah, I'm pretty good. Pretty good.'

The boats are sardined three deep at Commuter Dock, knocking against each other in what sounds like a grumble or cough. I drop her at the loading landing with our bags and baskets and then swizzle into a gap where there's only one boat between the tinny and the pontoon. A single leap into a single tinny and then one more jump to the pontoon. It's a fine day. No breeze. Easy as . . .

I throw Pia the rope. She catches it first go, ties us onto the railing. I leap into a cute little fibreglass dinghy smaller than most bathtubs. I have just enough time to grab the pontoon before it sinks under me. I hang from my elbows, in water from the chest down. Under me, the boat is submerged, stern first. Only the tip of the bow is above water. There are not many things sadder than a sunken boat.

'What d'you do that for?' Pia asks unsympathetically.

'With hindsight, that probably wasn't the smartest boat to jump into,' I say. 'Haven't seen it here much, although I did the same thing yesterday and it seemed quite solid.'

Pia is laughing so hard she can't speak.

'Can you give me a hand out of here?' I ask, treading water. 'It's actually not that comfortable.'

'What we need,' she says, still giggling, 'is a big Maori to come along and lift you onto the pontoon.'

And with that, a big Maori appears out of nowhere, reaches under my arms, hoists me like I'm a featherweight instead of a sodden, spreading woman in her middle-age, and plonks me on the pontoon. Without a word, he turns and walks away.

'Who's that?' Pia asks, wide-eyed with disbelief . . . and a glimmer of admiration.

'I'm fine, thank you. And I've got no idea who he is. The only Maori I know around here is Big Jack, and it's not him.'

Then Brad with the six-pack body arrives and helps us resurrect the dinghy.

'Owe you a beer,' I say, gratefully.

'Nah. You owe the bloke whose boat you've sunk a slab,' he responds, walking off.

'Guess we have to go home so I can change into dry clothes,' I say. Then the two of us start to laugh again. 'Didn't even lose a shoe,' I giggle. 'And, look, the change in my pocket is still there.'

'Thought you said you'd worked out boats.'

'I have, I have! It's just that every so often something comes out of the blue and slugs you. Keeps you honest, though. Even the good life has an occasional sting.'

On the verandah, Bob looks me up and down. 'You're wet?' he says, unable to work out what's going on.

'That's what happens when you sink a boat.'

His face goes white but he doesn't panic. Sinking boats are part of the way of life around Pittwater. They drop to the bottom in storms, when the bilge pump packs up, when you've tied too tightly to a pole in a rising tide. Which is what happened the night we went to dinner at Marg's in Little Lovett Bay. It was the first anniversary of Barbara's death. Bob spent hours on the phone to his kids, talking them through a day that will always be raw. By the evening, he was worn out but he tucked his own sorrow in a corner.

'You look forward,' he always says. 'You have to look forward.'

Halfway through dinner, a neighbour called to say a boat had sunk at the end of the wharf. We all ran out onto the deck. Below us, the *Tin Can* lay with her nose pointed to the sky and her stern embedded in the sandy bottom of the bay. Yellow life jackets, red fuel tanks, hoses and boat paraphernalia floated around her.

Bob's grief ambushed him then, and there was nothing he could do about it. He walked slowly and silently along the jetty to where his boat lay like the dead, and sat with his legs over the edge, tears streaming down his face.

'Bit upset over a boat, isn't he?' asked Marg, puzzled because she knows Bob as a practical, unemotional man.

'Got nothing to do with the boat,' I replied.

And we left him for a while, until he washed his face in water as salty as his tears and called Toby to ask when he and his partner Dave could bring the *Laurel Mae* to crane the *Tin Can* from the seabed and float it again. The engine never recovered but the local kids scavenged all the bits and pieces that drifted in on the tide and brought them back to Bob.

'What d'you want to sink our boat for?' Bob asks me, still trying to intuit what's happened.

'Not our boat. Someone else's. Tell you when I've got some dry clothes on.'

'How big was the engine?'

'Five horsepower.'

And he sighs with relief. No major damage bill in the offing.

An hour later, Bob drops Pia and me back at Church Point.

'Feel up to an Esther visit?' I ask when we're in the car. 'Really want to know what you make of it all.'

'Love to see the old girl,' Pia says.

'Remember when we thought she and your dad might make a couple?'

'*You* thought that, not me. My dad never had time for frivolous women. Don't think he looked at another woman after my mother died, you know.'

'Wonder why?'

'Guess no-one ever measured up to her.'

'Did he ever go a bit silly? I mean towards the end?'

'No. Although he forgot to eat, which is why my brother and I insisted he move to a retirement home. But it was more like a club than an old people's *facility* – sherries in the library at six every evening. He quite enjoyed it.'

'He wasn't there that long. Few months or something, wasn't it?'

'Yeah. The thought of what it was costing probably got to him. Think he made up his mind he'd reached his use-by date and bowed out before he ran through his money. Noble, really. And brave. He was a tough old bugger. Drove me mad occasionally but I miss him.'

I pull into the driveway in front of Esther's unit and let Pia out. Heather from Scotland Island, who works in the nursing home opposite my mother's, is having a ciggie in her break.

'Tell Esther I'll see her in a minute. Just want to say hello to Heather.'

Heather waves and grins, stubs out her cigarette and puts the butt in a little tin. 'Your mother against smoking?' she asks me.

'No. Ran a country pub for a long time. Learned to live with it. And Dad reached for a cigarette before he opened his eyes in the morning.'

'Well, someone's complained about us,' Heather says. 'This is my last smoko here.'

'Lot of folks with nothing better to do, maybe. Don't think it's because anyone's worried about your health.'

Heather laughs. 'No, mate, you're right there. By the way, your mum doesn't get off that sofa very often. Sleeps all day with the telly blaring.'

'Yeah. She's a bit of a worry at the moment. Not settling as easily as we'd hoped.'

'I'll keep an eye on her,' Heather says, turning back to the nursing home. 'Let you know if it gets worse.'

I relieve Pia, who's already looking a bit hunted. My mother wants her to choose a painting before she leaves. One of her own efforts from the days when she took art classes and had everything she ever painted, even the exercises, expensively framed.

'I'm into Aboriginal art, right now,' Pia says, kindly, 'so it's very sweet of you, Esther, and ordinarily I'd be thrilled. But it just won't fit with everything else.'

'Well, if you change your mind . . .'

'What do you think?' I ask Pia over a coffee in Mona Vale. With a tuna and rocket sandwich, which we've halved. Her idea, not mine.

'Well, the noise must be terrible,' she says. 'Apparently she's sleeping on the sofa and she can still hear what's going on.'

'So you think it's true?'

'Well, it is to her. And I must say, she sounds pretty convincing.'

I sigh. Time. Maybe all she needs is time.

That night, the phone rings. The owner of the sunken bathtub is from Frog Hollow. He's rented a house with a slipway for a few months to fix his yacht. Plans to sail around the world. Doesn't everyone?

'Thanks for leaving the note,' he says. 'I'll get a quote to fix the engine and get back to you.'

A couple of days later, he brings around the bill. It's incredibly reasonable.

'Could have done a swifty,' Bob says to him.

'No, mate, I work as an insurance assessor. See so much of that it turns your stomach.'

Simon, a young bloke with corn-silk hair, a blindingly beautiful smile and a faraway look in his eyes, house-sits while Bob and I make a quick trip to Melbourne. He's a naval architect and, like the fella whose boat I sank, dreams of making the great global circumnavigation and then designing the ultimate pleasure cruising yacht.

He's always in demand as a house-sitter. He has charmed us all and he is meticulous, responsible, good with animals. He listens to Pittwater stories he must have heard over and over as though it's the first time. Maybe because he lived with his granny when he was a student. 'She's worked out the internet,' he boasted one day. 'Knows what's happening all over the world! Even though she doesn't leave home much anymore.'

He's the only person who handles Caro's dog, Louie, with ease. She's a pound dog. Nervous, a mad barker and a serious watchdog. But she loves Simon. Rolls on her back for a tummy scratch when he walks past, tongue lolling, her eyes following him like she's got an attack of the besots. I knew he'd handle huge, lumbering, slobbery, increasingly feeble old Wally sensibly and kindly in our absence.

'Hope that dog dies while we're away,' Bob says as we set off.

'Why?' I ask, shocked.

'So I don't have to dig the hole.'

Wally waits until we get home, then within an hour quietly sinks to the ground in the back courtyard and refuses to move. Panting.

'Better get Ray,' says Bob. 'Looks like he's in pain.' He goes to the shed. Picks up a shovel, wanders beyond the chook pen.

Ray shakes his head. 'Spleen's ruptured,' he says after feeling Wally all over.

'That's what happened to my old dog, Sweetie,' I say. So Ray knows I understand what comes next.

Bob digs a hole deep enough to defeat goannas. We lower Wally into it, wrapped in his favourite orange chenille bedspread.

'Don't know how I'm going to tell my mother,' I say. 'It'll break her heart.'

Bob shovels earth. There's nothing to say. Life's a cycle. Everything that is born must die. Once I fought that truth, now I accept it. But it still hurts.

My mother has her own way of handling Wally's death. 'He'll never be dead to me,' she says without a quiver in her voice. 'He'll be over there all the time, on holidays. Getting younger every day.'

A while later she tells me she talks to Wally every night. 'Not much, just a bit of news I think he'd be interested in. Funny thing is, I don't feel frightened at night anymore. I can sense he's protecting me.'

'He probably is,' I reply. But my stomach flip-flops. Fear? She's never mentioned *fear*. Then I push aside my thoughtlessness, like I always do.

≈

A couple of neighbours from my mother's village are having coffee in Mona Vale at the table next to mine.

'How's it going?' I ask. They are a few years younger than my mother. One plays golf twice a week, the other looks after her grandchildren and walks everywhere, even to do her shopping. They are sharp, smart, vibrant women who pay attention to their hair and clothes. They have to, my mother tells me, because if you get sloppy for a minute, people think you are *losing your marbles*. The aged, it turns out, are an unforgiving lot.

'We're good,' they reply, smiling. And we launch into village gossip. The new owners, the new manager, the new units being built. They are against it all – almost out of habit, I think. Why do we all fight change?

'How do you reckon my mother is settling in?' I ask.

'Best thing you could do for her is burn that sofa,' they reply, but not unkindly. 'She needs to move around more.'

And while I may say things about my mother that are neither compassionate nor, occasionally, strictly accurate, I leap to my mother's defence: 'Once she was the doer at the heart of everything,' I reply. And I remember, with a shock, that it's true. I seem to have erased the memories of her running theatre groups for migrant children, carting bus loads of us around the countryside to play tennis. I've almost forgotten her famous picnics when she prepared food so exotically beautiful that everyone gathered around the boot of the car to admire it before we all devoured it. And what about the days when she played tennis five days a week? Ran a catering business? Why is memory so selective when it comes to family, and when did it all change? When my father died? When my brother died? When she started taking so many pills that they had to be bundled together in weekly packs, then set out in kaleidoscopic little groups to be taken four times a day? When she turned seventy, and then eighty? Why do I forgive every slowing moment in my own aging process and get impatient with hers? Perhaps it's fear. That's all I can think of. Fear that one day she'll slow to a complete stop and she will be gone. And it will be my turn to move into God's waiting room.

'She wants to watch her medication a bit more closely, too,' says one of the women. 'Found some pills dropped on the floor and she was taking one very volatile tablet after food when it is supposed to be taken two hours before food. Gives some people hallucinations when they don't follow directions.'

My mind swirls. I barely listen to the chat of these good women. Hallucinations. Not orgies, not senility, not dementia. Just little ol' hallucinations.

I call in on my mother on the way home. 'Let's go through your pills,' I say, 'to make sure you're taking them the right way.'

Orgies are never mentioned again.

Now I see my mother every week, I notice small changes. Unsteadiness. Sitting down when she is on her way to the kitchen to make tea. Three attempts to get off the sofa instead of one. Eating half a sandwich when once she would have devoured two. Her hand shaking when she picks up a cup. And doing everything so, so slowly until it is unbearable to watch and I cannot resist reaching over impatiently and taking away her task. Even though I want to kick myself each time I do it.

'If we don't keep moving,' I tell her when we're off to a doctor's appointment, 'we'll never get there.' She looks surprised, doesn't realise she's stopped walking in the middle of a busy road to talk. She hurries, taking even tinier steps, almost going up and down on the same spot. I mentally tell myself to park on the same side of the road as the surgery in future. It's another lowering of the bar, though, and I hate the thought of it. Is that what happens as we age? The bar gets lower and lower until it – and we – hit the ground?

'Sit,' I tell her in the waiting room of the scrappy surgery with the fake Persian carpet. 'Over there.' I point out a chair nearest the doctor's office.

'Woof!' my mother responds.

The elderly woman next to her turns to face my mother. 'Will she ask you to *fetch* next?' she says.

'No, she only ever tells me to *stay*!'

'I've got a daughter like yours,' the woman continues. 'My other daughter, though, is really lovely!'

'Mine's never been any better,' my mother replies. But the words are without sting. We catch each other's eye. And laugh. Our love for each other is, truly, unassailable.

11

TOWARDS THE END OF a winter so warm we wonder if the world's turned upside down, members of Jeanne's Garden History Society group wander around the house and yard like inquisitive beetles in canary-yellow plastic ponchos. The weather bureau has promised rain, but only a few drops fall from the sky. Not enough to wet the ground. She has brought a cake, of course. I made one – naturally.

I apologise for the ragged state of the garden: 'If we expose even a small group of plants by weeding around them, it's as though we're giving the wallabies a written invitation to dinner. The bracken is like a shield, protecting vulnerable shrubs and flowers.'

'Why would you even want a garden here?' replies a tall bloke with an English accent. 'The water is your garden at the front, and the bush at the back. You've got a lawn, that's enough.'

I look across at Bob, who's holding his tea and smiling like he's listening to a personal symphony.

'Where are the two blokes who reckon Hardy Wilson never came near this house?' I ask Jeanne. She's cutting more cake. Bob grabs the teapot to refill it. It's the large Brown Betty from

Barbara's pottery collection. Does twenty cups at a time. I won't touch it in case I break it.

'They accepted the invitation but didn't turn up,' Jeanne replies. 'Must have had a better offer on the day.'

'Bugger. I'm really curious about the architect of the house. I mean, if it wasn't Hardy Wilson, then who was it?'

Two gardeners launch into a discussion about Wilson's architectural style. I realise I know almost nothing about him beyond Barbara's notes.

A couple of days later, I tell Bob I'm going to the Mitchell Library to do some research.

'Why?' he asks.

'Because I'd really like to know more about Hardy Wilson. It's embarrassing to live here and not be able to answer questions. And maybe I'll find some information that links him to the house. Those two heritage blokes were pretty adamant Hardy Wilson didn't design *Tarrangaua*. I'd like to get to the truth, really. It's a little bit of Australian history. Not that important, but if it's not sorted now, it'll be even harder in another fifty years. Maybe it's the journalist in me. I'm setting myself an assignment. I've always loved the thrill of the chase.'

Bob is silent for a moment or two before asking softly, 'Are you bored?'

'Bored? No! Never! Not for a moment. I love our life. Curious, mostly. Restless, maybe, to be doing more. But not bored. It's a terrible concept, bored. A waste.'

But really, at the crux is a lifetime of seeing words flung around carelessly for effect or gain and regardless of fact. And knowing the damage done can be irreparable.

'Barbara tried to find the house plans in the Mitchell Library and came up blank,' he says. 'Architects rarely kept plans in the 1920s, and they only made one or two copies because they were so expensive. The whole search might be a waste of time. Although she did find a plan for a septic tank that stated quite clearly it was designed for Dorothea Mackellar at Lovett Bay by Wilson, Neave and Berry.'

'I thought she only researched Mackellar. Has there always been some doubt about the architect?'

'Not so much doubt as lack of proof.'

'The septic tank is a good start. Maybe she missed something,' I say. 'Always liked libraries. Silent places that make you feel that all you have to do to discover the secrets of the universe is pull down a gilt-edged tome and flick through the pages.'

The city is chaotic, road rage epidemic. People keep honking. Have I turned into one of those drivers who hunch over the wheel and motor along at forty kilometres an hour? I check the speedo. Forty kilometres. Oh bugger, when did that happen?

I am used to boats now. Going along at a sedate ten knots, checking out the world. Jellyfish a week ago, bigger than a football. Hordes of them floating just under the surface in orange blobs, legs hanging down like fat pantaloons, tops like fringed lampshades. An alien invasion from the bottom of the sea, silent and mysterious. Passing tinnies slowed, heads hung over the side for a closer look.

'Saw a lot of these jellyfish when I was a kid,' said Tanya as we held each other's tinnies to stop them drifting apart. 'They haven't been around for years.'

'Wonder what's brought them back?'

'Dunno. You Woody Pointing?'

'Wouldn't miss it. Bob's been overhauling the sail system. I refused to do more than three tacks up the course and three down. Meant it as a joke. Now he's put in a new self-tacking headsail. Serves me right. It's pretty good, though. All I have to do is get the drinks sorted.'

'Nice job.'

'Yeah, but we don't go as fast. Think he misses that. He's got a new sail that he reckons will speed us up in light winds. A Code Zero. Calls it the secret weapon. Not sure what he means.'

Tanya, an accomplished sailor who grew up in Lovett Bay, raised an eyebrow. 'Within the rules?'

'When would Bob break the rules? Bend them maybe, but never break them.'

In the city, I make a million turns into one-way streets that point me in the wrong direction. I can see the formal columns of the Mitchell Library but it constantly hovers just out reach. I'm about to give up in frustration when a parking station looms directly ahead. I need a rest anyway. Traffic sucks you dry.

I dash into the Art Gallery to go to the loo, then slow down. What's the rush? I'm catching *rush* fever from everyone around me. Outside again, I wander slowly along Sydney's streets, seeing it as a tourist would. The Botanic Gardens. There's a mass planting of dianella in front of an old stone cottage, tiny purple flowers dripping from delicate stems like loosely strung pearls. At home it grows scrappily but it *does* grow, which means wallabies don't eat it. I file the knowledge away.

Sydney's watery beauty glistens. How come I've never noticed a bronze of a very ugly boar, *Il Porcellino*, outside Sydney Hospital? (It was donated by an Italian noblewoman, Marchesa Fiaschi Torrigiani, in memory of her father, in 1968. Her intention was for passers-by to donate a coin to the hospital and rub its nose for luck, as they do in Florence.) I tramped these streets when I worked as a journalist and I never bothered to look around. Always the job. Always the story. Always a rush. Always a deadline.

The library is hot, the stale air chewy. Brown leather-topped tables wide enough to hold a slew of books are arranged in military lines. Stained glass windows of medieval men and white horses surround the room, the name of the benefactor writ large underneath. Buying immortality? It's all very organised, civilised. Quiet. Easy to feel like an interloper in an intellectual morass.

At boarding school we had two libraries, one for the juniors and one for the seniors. They were annexes off the sitting rooms where we gathered in our black velvet dinner jackets and *civi-clothes* (non-uniform) for half an hour before dinner and then again after dinner until it was time for bed and lights out. Like everyone else, I devoured Georgette Heyer's Regency romances and dreamed I'd be rescued from the tower (we really *did* have a tower that rose above the senior library) by a handsome lord. Shy and unsure new girls were told the tower was haunted. Even senior students weren't entirely convinced there wasn't a lost spirit bedded in there for eternity. The tower was always locked, which added to the myth. And when the wind wailed on a freezing winter night like unspeakable grief, few of us slept soundly.

At school, when you wanted to borrow a book, you wrote your name and the title of the book on a page with neatly ruled columns. But when I go to the counter to ask for books on the *alleged* architect of *Tarrangaua*, Hardy Wilson, I am asked for my number.

'What number?'

'Are you registered to use the library?'

'No,' I reply, but I want to mutter darkly about paying taxes and democratic rights. A monumental hot flush surges from my toes. Sweat breaks out on my top lip, under my eyes. Stress. Does it every time.

'It's easy to register,' the attendant says, taking pity on me. She points at a bank of computers near the doorway. 'Fill in your details over there and come back with a number. In the meantime, give me a list of what you're looking for.'

I hand her a scrappy piece of paper with a whole lot of cryptic codes involving letters, backward slashes and dots in all sorts of funny combinations – MAV\SM4\10675. Q728.3709944\10 –

plonked together with no meaning. I got them by phoning the library and asking for anything on Hardy Wilson. They seem to make perfect sense to the attendant I speak to.

The computer doesn't want to know me. It rejects every whack on the *Enter* key. It's hard not to feel like a dunce. An impatient line forms behind me. Nothing works. I finally turn and ask for help, mewling pathetically about being a techno moron. The guy behind me can't get my details over the line either. I feel slightly better but not much. This is supposed to be a pleasure jaunt to satisfy my curiosity, but it's more like being slowly strangled by bureaucracy.

There's a different woman behind the counter when I return without my number. She sighs darkly and follows me back to the machine. 'No number, no books,' she says. 'Name?'

I spell it out for her.

'Address? . . . No, no, you can't do post office boxes. You need a street address. What's the street number?'

'There are no streets. And no numbers.'

It's on the tip of my tongue to add that we manage quite well without numbers, but I hold back. She gives me a funny sideways glance. I can see her thinking *nutter*. I do my best to look like a conservative, sensible, middle-aged woman, not a semi-feral in worn-out boat shoes and ratty jeans. The hot flush isn't helping.

'We're at Pittwater, boat access only,' I explain.

'Ah, where on Pittwater? Scotland Island?' Her face is suddenly all smiley, like we're old buddies.

'No, Lovett Bay. Just around the corner from Scotland Island.'

'Got some friends who live on Scotland Island. They love the lifestyle. Wouldn't like it myself. Not in winter.' She taps more keys and hits the *Enter* key a few times. Then she writes out a number.

'There you go.' We beam at each other.

'Thank you. What was the problem?'

'Someone else with the same name as you, from the same suburb but with a different phone number.'

How bizarre.

The first book comes in a vibrant Chinese red box. *Building Purulia*. It's a specially bound edition with tipped-in selenium toned photographs, printed on thick, textured creamy paper with ripped edges. It's so redolent with self-importance, I feel I should be wearing white gloves to touch it. Then I read it is not an original edition. It was printed by the Guild of Craft Bookbinders in 1982 as an example of their work. WHW is embossed heavily on the cover. The price of the book, $135, is written in pencil.

WHW. William Hardy Wilson. He was known as William until he was elected a Fellow of the Royal Association of Architects for designing a modern Moresque-style building. The building, in fact, had been designed by another William Wilson in a style Hardy Wilson loathed. He couldn't stand the confusion any longer and was just as upset, too, at being credited with what he considered lousy taste. He called himself Hardy Wilson from that moment.

Building Purulia is an essay about building his first home at 16 Fox Valley Road, Warrawee, where he lived with his wife, Margaret. She was twenty-eight when they married. Everyone probably thought she was on her way to *shameful spinsterhood*, but perhaps she was having too good a time to settle down. Or maybe she just had the nerve to wait for true love.

Hardy Wilson wanted *Purulia*, which he began in 1916, to be a masterpiece. Then he 'reckoned the cost'. He couldn't settle on a 'theme'. He worried it would be a 'hotchpotch'. 'In the office', he wrote, 'designs presented no difficulties. When I came to design for myself, there were endless doubts and anxieties.' A little uncharitably, I wonder if it's because spending other people's money is effortless. When it's your own, you remember how long it took to accumulate.

From his essay, I learn that Hardy Wilson never drove a car; that he believed *'confessions are never dull provided they are truthful'*. He also described Sydney as *'where the ugliest buildings are received with the same tolerance as the beautiful'*. Here I am, one hundred years later, in full agreement with him. Underneath a compressed, twenty-first century world, driven by racing technology and an information boom, very little has really changed.

Purulia, I also discover, is named after a house in Tasmania. The word, which has no meaning, is said to sound like the cooing of pigeons, which appealed to Wilson. But it's not an original name, and I feel slightly disappointed: a failing of the imagination in a man who is supposed to be endlessly creative seems odd.

Flipping through a biography by Zeny Edwards (*William Hardy Wilson: Artist, Architect, Orientalist, Visionary*, The Watermark Press) I learn that his design goals at *Purulia* were simplicity, elegance and a practicality that allowed for *'servantless living'*. He even insisted on making the kitchen a pleasant room, *'equal in value to the other principal rooms'*. It was revolutionary thinking. Good on him. The kitchen is the most important room in a house. Being able to stand at a sink, or where you do the chopping, and look out a window at a beautiful garden or view makes the food taste better.

In New York, where I lived for a while in a tiny apartment, the kitchen was the size of a small cupboard, without even a window. A depressing little hole where I never cooked a meal worth remembering. To ease the barrenness, I'd line up water glasses on the counter and fill them with parsley. It didn't help much. To get a bigger kitchen at an affordable rent I moved off Manhattan. It was worth it. I still remember making Christmas puddings and being thrilled it was so cold and snowy that I could hang them outside the kitchen window until they were to be eaten. Not like in Australia, where Christmas means laidback summer holidays, weeks of simmering heat, bodies smelling of coconuts and personal insect repellent. Pinpricks of sweat on tanned arms and legs, making us glow.

When *Purulia* was completed, instead of accolades Hardy Wilson was reviled for creating a house so disgracefully plain it would inevitably drag down property prices in the neighbourhood. He was unrepentant. It took the creation of a carefully planned, wildly colourful and highly scented garden to soften his critics. Those who were '*loudest in their invective, come and lean upon the garden wall. Some laugh, others admire, and all resentment has flown*'.

Wilson encouraged plants to spill and roam. He planted lemon-scented thyme to crush underfoot and enclosed the front garden and rear terrace with a circle of citrus trees. In an era of trimmed hedges, neat lawns and English-style flower gardens, his approach was new and exciting.

During their time at *Purulia*, he and Margaret had a son, Lachlan, their only child. So now I know there is at least one descendant. Maybe Lachlan is still alive. It's feasible. He'd be in his early nineties. There must be grandchildren, too. Someone might remember something useful. All I have to do is find him or her.

I stare at a picture of Wilson's house for a long time: the steps leading to the front door, windows with twelve panes, a steeply pitched tiled roof. Echoes of *Tarrangaua*? I close the books, gather my pen and notes. If I leave any later, I'll hit peak-hour traffic. The thought curdles my mind. All I want is escape. Back to Pittwater, peace and first-hand air.

I turn the corner into Macquarie Street. A man I thought had damaged me forever is walking towards me. At first I think it's an illusion, but it is definitely him. Tricked up in his fancy clothes and talking on his mobile. My instinct is to bolt. Run away and hide in a corner until the *danger* has passed. But why? What danger? Then he looks up and sees me.

'How's it going?' he asks breezily, a smile on his face, as though it's been a day or two since we last met.

'Good. Yeah, it's all good. What about you?' I reply.

'Bought a couple of racehorses. Can you believe that? I'm in the racing game now.'

I smile. 'Well, one way or another, you've had a stake in a lot of racehorses for a lot of years. Every time you put a bet on one.'

He grins. I don't tell him most people go broke when they fall in love with racing. He'll work that out for himself.

And then we have nothing to say to each other. We stand for a moment, awkwardly. Stripped of the godly robes of infatuation, I see him for the ordinary man he is. Around us, people race along the pavement, heads down, briefcases clutched so tightly their knuckles are white.

Probably because he can think of nothing else, he asks if I'd like to have lunch sometime. I decline politely. He reels with astonishment. Was I such a pushover so long ago that saying no to him was unthinkable? Of course I was.

'But I'll take you somewhere wonderful! You love good food.'

It has suddenly become a contest, a question of power. 'Don't have much time for restaurants anymore,' I reply. 'Find them claustrophobic. Rather cook a sausage on the barbecue at home and watch the day shut down behind the hills.'

'You can do that anytime.'

'Yeah, but you know what? Most restaurants are the same. And every sunset is a new experience. Anyway, I'd rather cook for myself.'

He looks at me as though I've gone mad. 'Why would you want to do that?'

'Maybe because I'm menopausal,' I say, suddenly impatient to be gone.

And he's off in a flash, like I've got a highly contagious disease. I stride away, lighter than air.

≈

I tell Bob about bumping into the ex-lover. He doesn't look up from his newspaper.

'He looked dashing,' I say, trying to goad a response from him.

'Who?' he says, still not listening. He grabs a pencil, fills in a number on a Sudoku puzzle.

'Oh, no-one.' I go into the kitchen to chop vegetables for dinner. All that pain and anguish . . . so much of it, I thought I would die. What's the strange glitch in us that dumps reason at the time we need it most? And here I am, with only a few years flown, shaking my head at the absurdity of it all.

A couple of days later, an artist friend, Katie, calls. 'I've done a series of linocuts of Pittwater scenes. Would you let me have an exhibition of them at your home?'

Katie is an exuberant country girl from Temora in central eastern New South Wales. She and her husband Alex, a quiet, shy Englishman, are friends of Stewart and Fleury and visit Pittwater often to escape the deadly dullness of civil servant living in Canberra. Although nothing around Katie stays dull for long. She is full of passion, talks at a thousand miles an hour and doesn't know the meaning of 'go slow'. In the beginning, it was exhausting to be around her for long. Then I stopped trying to keep up and let her run alone, which is when I learned the secrets of her. A single-minded focus under the easy charm. An instinctive spirit of adventure. A good-time girl who is unafraid of the cold hard slog it takes to succeed. Kind, too, and loyal.

Alex is a curious mix. He sets up centre-stage for Katie and then withdraws. I often see him in a corner, observing, saying nothing. At a party but somehow never quite in the middle of it. Until he picks up his mandolin. His eyes close, his fingers pluck, and he riffles the strings in quiet improvisation. Turns out he has a deep and abiding passion for the sixties rock band The Grateful Dead – which seems weird because he looks like he belongs in the village church choir.

Alex was at the helm of Stewart's slim little Soling, *Leda*, when it took a sudden knock, spun and T-boned the commodore's precious antique wooden boat in a Woody Point twilight race. The commodore loved that yacht nearly as much as he did his bad-tempered blue heeler, Badger. The bingle made Katie and Alex famous around Pittwater, but only for a moment. There've been quite a few more T-bones in the twilight series since then.

Katie plays guitar. Together, their singalongs on Stewart and Fleury's moonstruck deck at boisterous post-Woody Point parties kept Towlers Bay rocking into the early hours of the morning. We sang lustily, mostly English, Irish and Australian folk songs. Never thought I'd get a thrill from thumping out the monotonous refrain of 'Botany Bay'. Maybe Pittwater has knotted me firmly to this *sunburnt country* when once home could just as well have been anywhere.

Not long before Alex takes a sabbatical and he and Katie move to Western Australia where the light is fierce and the landscape awash with dense, cartoon colour, Fleury calls to say that Katie has been diagnosed with one of the very rotten cancers. How is it possible? Katie has always been unstoppable. She competed in the double-handed yacht race around Britain and Ireland in the smallest boat in the fleet. At Pittwater, she kayaks around the bays in the rosy-pink light of dawn with her curly-haired spaniel, Holly. Sketchbook in front of her, watercolours in a tin, camera close by. Katie is always the last to fade off to bed, the first to see the sunrise.

'Guess she's a new member of the club, then,' I finally say to Fleury. Because once you have cancer, the world spins differently.

Typically, after diagnosis, surgery and treatment, Katie plunges into work. Now she's put together a solo exhibition.

'When do you want to hold it?' I ask her.

'How about over the Easter holidays?'

'I'll talk to Bob but I'm sure it will be fine. Mind if we turn it into a fundraiser for the Elvina Bay Fire Brigade as well?'

'Great idea. I'll donate a print for a raffle.'

Bob calls Roy, who organises the fire brigade, to help out in shifts during the four-day show. The freezer is filled with cakes and slices. A friend with a small vineyard in the Hunter Valley sells us a heap of wine at cost price.

Katie trucks her prints, packed snugly in the back of a small station wagon, 4000 kilometres across the blistering desert of the Nullarbor, through the brittle red heart of New South Wales and into the blue of Sydney. No-one even tries to tell her the trip is madness. Katie is not going to slow down for a vicious little tumour with a will of its own. In what seems like a flick of time, Katie calls from Mona Vale to tell us she's made it across the desert.

'Be there in ten minutes,' she yells down the phone, excitement trilling her voice.

'We'll meet you at Commuter Dock!'

It's a perfect day, which is the irony of the drought. The sun shines constantly and makes you forget there's a downside.

'Good to see you!' Bob and I yell from the tinny. Katie and an English friend, Liz, are unpacking at the dock. 'How was the trip?'

'Fantastic!' Katie calls back. 'Burned up the tarmac. Gonna go home more slowly and paint stuff. It was just fantastic.' Wind blows hair in her eyes. She flicks it back impatiently, laughing. Always in a rush. She looks so well, so strong. If anyone can beat the odds, she can.

At home, the prints are unveiled one by one: a series of almost thirty Pittwater boatsheds. Glamorous, quirky, crumbling. Throbbing with light on water, shadows on walls, windows, trees. There are bigger prints of a deserted Morning Bay in the oily lustre of dusk. Woody Point seen through a web of skinny young spotted gums. And *Tarrangaua. House Among the Trees*, she calls it. Moody. Evocative. *Home.*

'Technically,' she tells us, '*Tarrangaua* is one of the best prints I've ever done.'

'It's wonderful, Katie. They're all really wonderful,' Bob and I say. And she shrugs because she's smart enough to be suspicious of quick praise. But there's a small smile, too, because she *knows* she's caught the spirit of Pittwater.

'Had a coffee in Mona Vale before coming over,' she adds. 'Saw a pair of pink Ugg boots in a shop. Funky as anything. If I cover my costs I'll buy a pair to celebrate.'

We leap into setting up the exhibition. Our paintings come down from the walls. Barbara's pottery and family photographs are carefully put away. The house stripped bare looks forlorn and, for some reason, shambolic.

'Now,' says Katie, picking up a long, thin print of Woody Point. 'How about here?'

Bob looks at her in disbelief. 'There's no hook there.'

'But there's no other place for it!'

Hanging the pictures turns into a nightmare. Understandably, Bob doesn't want new holes in the walls. And where is there a space big enough to hang the massive boatshed series? He and Katie bicker. They are both tenacious about their points of view. Then Bob disappears into his shed. Katie, Liz and Fleury, who's dropped in to help, hover over mugs of tea on the verandah. The fire's gone out of us, even Katie. No-one's quite sure what to do next.

'Think this will work,' Bob says a while later, holding a few bits of wood. 'Means we can layer the boatshed prints so they're all in one place.'

We look at him standing in the kitchen doorway with long thin strips of timber in his hands. None of us has the faintest idea what he's talking about but he goes away humming off-key and we all decide we might as well have some more tea. And a bit of cake. 'To keep our strength up,' I say. The cake slips down easily. The fire brigade profits drop.

Bob builds a light frame and anchors it on the benches in the hallway, tilting it until the overhead lights hit the prints at a perfect angle. It's a breakthrough and we're all revved again. Especially Katie, who wonders if it might be a good idea to move all the furniture. Then she sees Bob's face. 'Maybe not,' she adds hastily.

By lunchtime on Good Friday, every work is polished and hung. Straight. Pia arrives to help with the fundraiser part of the weekend. She's elegant, gorgeous, spotless. Author Di Morrissey and her partner, Boris, lob in. Di will officially open the exhibition.

A long time ago, Di was a wild Pittwater child who lived in a little white fibro shack with an enclosed verandah not far past where Lovett Bay spreads into Pittwater. She was a curious kid with secret hiding places in the bush and a vivid imagination. Once, she hunted for fairies with Dorothea Mackellar after the poet found her searching for them under bracken. 'May I help?' asked Mackellar. 'If you like,' shrugged young Di.

On a cold winter afternoon when the water was choppy and the wind temperamental, Di's stepfather and baby half-brother drowned as they returned home from The Point. No-one really knows what happened, but it's generally believed her 18-month-old stepbrother fell overboard and her stepfather drowned trying to save him. 'A life given for his son,' says the tombstone where they are buried together. Di and her mother moved away from the fibro shack and Pittwater. How could they ever cross the water again without tears and rage at the senselessness of it?

Now Di is back, for the first time in years. 'In a way,' she says when she arrives for the preview in a swirl of blonde coiffure and dainty high heels, 'this is a pilgrimage.'

The first guests come up the pathway for the preview. Jeanne is amongst them. She waves from the lawn, her face jammed tight with smiles. Her clothes flow around her lightly, anchored by her black orthotics.

'The moment of truth,' says Katie, taking a deep breath. She wears white cotton trousers and a navy and white striped top, like a sailor. Alex, who has flown in for the opening, smiles at her. Before long, little red stickers appear on frames. Slowly but surely.

We pass around lush cheese, tomato and zucchini tarts made from one of Jeanne's recipes. A couple of garlicky chicken and pork terrines wrapped snugly in bacon slices. Little duck sausages. Michael, who took over the house I rented on Scotland Island before moving to Lovett Bay, and his friend Kal, a meat exporter, barbecue thick slabs of rump steak to pinkness, then slice it thinly in a way the Americans describe as 'London broil'. Some of us eat it with our fingers, others make little sandwiches with a slash of French mustard and a handful of rocket.

'You Pittwater people know how to live,' says Jeanne, when she pokes her head into the kitchen. 'Is life always like this?'

'Like what?' I ask.

'*Fun!*'

'Yep!'

She wanders back to the sitting room where she's found a friend she hasn't seen for years. Alex picks up his mandolin, Katie grabs her guitar. In the middle of a Joan Baez tear-jerker, Michael casually picks up an armchair and carries it outside, high-stepping across the room like an eccentric character in a comedy skit. It's puzzling, but I soon forget about it.

A while later, he sidles over and whispers in my ear. 'Jeanne's had a fall. She's outside lying on the lawn. No-one wanted to tell you.'

I bolt out the door and find Bob kneeling near her, holding her hand. Her eyes are closed and her face is white. Damn. Bloody damn. A fall any time you're over fifty years old is a bugger. You never quite recapture your old mobility. I lift her head and rest it in my lap.

'Ah, there you are,' she says. 'Wondered when you'd appear.'

'No-one told me. Nearly had a fit when I heard. What hurts?'

'My hip.'

'The original one or the new one?'

She smiles for a moment. 'Can't remember which is which anymore.' She closes her eyes again. I stroke her face, her arms, her head.

'The water police are on the way, with the blokes from the ambulance. Just have to wait,' Bob says.

The moon is high and bright. A giant yellow ball in a black sky, making midnight more like dusk. Six blokes with eager young faces come up the steps with a stretcher and a medical kit – none of them puffing. Three are water police in blue overalls, three are medicos dressed in navy pants and white shirts. They amble towards us, then surround Jeanne in a thick, handsome wall.

'Jeanne?' I whisper. 'Help is here.'

She opens her eyes. Blinks. 'Have I died and gone to heaven? Six gorgeous young men?' She tries to smile but can't pull it off.

The bloke with the medical kit kneels beside her, asks what hurts. He moves her hip a fraction and she lets out a scream loud enough to break your heart.

'Don't!' she says, gritting her teeth. 'Do. Not. Do. That. Again.'

The medico stands up. 'Better get her on the stretcher and into hospital.' He looks around. The water police have disappeared.

'Stewart's taken them on a tour,' Bob explains sheepishly. 'They've never been here before.'

'Right, mate. Well, we better get 'em back. It's gonna take all of us to get her down to the boat.'

'Use the ute if I could,' Bob says, 'but it doesn't have lights. Sorry. We carried her up in an armchair from where she fell. Do you want to try it?'

'We're used to carrying stretchers down steps around here. Every house is the same. Steps up. Steps down.'

He gives Jeanne a shot of painkiller. Bob's daughter, Kelly, who's a nurse and visiting from Melbourne for Easter, goes across the water with her and stays at the hospital until she's settled.

Inside the house, the singing fades. The party's over. Torches are grabbed and the tinnies firing up sound like a rush of small explosions. Boats slink out slowly, their wakes spreading like silver-blue fantails in the moonlight.

'Think she'll be there at least a week,' Kelly says when she returns, her face white and tired. It's almost three am. 'She's strong, though. Wasn't going to let anyone touch her without knowing what they were going to do.' She starts to help load the last of the dirty glasses into the dishwasher.

'Go to bed,' I say, pushing her away. 'You've done enough.'

Pia's taken Di and Boris down the hill to Stef and Bella's, where they're all staying while Stef and Bella are away.

'What a bugger,' I sigh. 'Don't know how she'll manage when she goes home. She's got steps everywhere.'

Walking down the hallway feels like wandering through a stranger's house. Bob turns out the lights and Katie's gorgeous boatsheds fade to black. Bob and I slide into bed. He grabs my hand.

'She'll be fine,' he says. 'She's one of the toughest women I've ever met.'

'Yeah. Maybe.'

I wait until nine the next morning to call the hospital.

'Jeanne who?' asks the receptionist.

'Villani. V-i-l-l-a-n-i,' I spell out.

'She's not listed. Oh, here it is. She was discharged early this morning.'

I punch in Jeanne's number. 'What are you doing?' I ask crossly. 'You need looking after!'

'Hate hospitals and I certainly wasn't going to spend Easter in one,' she says. 'Nothing's broken and I can move around with a crutch. I'm an expert with crutches. Learned to use them when I had my hip replaced.'

'Jeanne, your bedroom is up a flight of stairs . . .'

'I'm *especially* proficient with a crutch on stairs.' And there's nothing more to say. I want to be like her, I think to myself. As I grow older I want to find ways to grow stronger instead of weaker.

On Saturday morning as the first guests arrive to see Katie's exhibition, Roy drives the Lovett Bay fire truck out of the shed and onto the lawn. He pulls on the handbrake and every shiny-eyed kid runs over to the glittering red and chrome vehicle. They stand and stare . . . with dreams in their eyes.

The first lot of volunteer fireys appear at the top of the steps, resplendent in bright yellow. There's Dan, who has a beautiful tenor voice, the two Alans, who are fiercely protective of our environment, Nick and Ann, who wear away the weeds in the bush. Roger, who has an encyclopaedic knowledge of crustaceans, and Kylie, whose dad Stacky died and whom we all miss. And Lisa, of course, who keeps us laughing but never misses a detail. They whiz around like bees. Every kid thinks they're heroes.

They take turns pouring endless cups of tea from large, speckled blue enamel teapots, safer than using Barbara's rare old Brown Betty. They slice cakes, replenish plates and look after old ladies who are a bit wobbly on their pins or in need of gentle resuscitation after the walk up eighty-eight steps.

'This is a busy house,' says a woman with white hair and a walking stick, 'like houses used to be.'

'Like I'm sure you are,' I reply, and she smiles.

'You're dead a long time. Shame to waste a minute,' she adds. Then she wanders down the hallway, looking at Katie's boatsheds intently. 'Ah,' she says, turning back to see if I am still watching her. 'This is my son's boatshed. Thought it might be here.'

'Guess you'll want to buy a print, then?'

She nods. I run off to find Katie.

Lisa and I work the lunch shift for the fireys and people who thought they'd come for half an hour and have decided, instead, to spend the day. Bob and the fireys, all armed with fact sheets about the house and the poet, answer questions. Alex washes mugs until the skin on his fingers begins to peel. A bosomy woman in a floral dress pushes him aside. None of us has a clue who she is.

'Got a bit of time and this bloke looks like he needs a break,' she says, plunging her hands into a sink of hot, soapy water.

'Are you up to it?' I ask.

'Not like you need a degree or anything,' she says.

Mackellar's old writing room becomes known as 'The Exchequer'. Caro, with Louie asleep at her feet, keeps a tally of art sales, tea sales, cake sales and any donations thrown in a blue plastic bucket at the top of the steps to the verandah with 'Fire Brigade' written on it. The kitty kicks along. The bay glitters like silver baubles. Blokes, women, kids, dogs, old people, youngies, singles and families, they keep trekking up the steps. Slowly, moderately, quickly or flat-out. Day after day. Spilling onto the lawn in red, pink, blue, green, like exotic flowers, eating cake and drinking tea. Staring at Lovett Bay, the boats, Matty's ferry, the *Fruit Box* – a rough, homemade houseboat that never leaves its mooring – the ancient escarpments and, for a moment, our two resident sea eagles returning to a nest high above the green water.

'There's a whole lot of pink tulips arriving,' my mother calls from where we've stationed her in a cane chair on the lawn. It's a perfect spot. Nearly everyone asks her if she's ok and she gets to talk all day to an ever-changing audience.

I look down from the verandah. About a dozen women in pink T-shirts are coming up the steps in single file. They are locals who paddle dragon boats as part of Dragon Boats Australia, raising awareness for breast cancer and supporting women – like themselves – who have been diagnosed with it.

'Great to see you,' I yell.

They wave, come up for tea and cake.

'We paddle around Pittwater every second Sunday. Thought we'd check out Salvation Creek and stop in for a bit of culture,' says one of them.

'You all look so fit!'

'We are! Why don't you join us?'

I laugh. 'Maybe.'

By the end of Easter, red dots cover Katie's prints like confetti. The Woody Point edition sells out. The pink boots are a certainty. The fire brigade will get a couple of new pumps and still have money left in the kitty. Katie's got a hit on her hands. Cancer doesn't bear thinking about.

When it is all over and the last mug has been packed away in a box and returned to Bob's loft for storage, we collapse into bed, so tired our voices are hoarse.

'Houses have spirits, you know,' I mumble.

'You're not talking about ghosts again, are you?'

'No. I mean the way some houses can inspire you. *Tarrangaua* draws people. It has such . . . such presence. And history. It can be a tool to do good for the community, if we want it to be.'

Bob sits bolt upright in bed, looks at me in shock. 'You haven't said we'll do another exhibition, have you?'

'No, but there are so many wonderful artists living around here. If we need another fundraiser for the fire brigade, it would be good to keep it local, don't you think?'

Bob slides under the covers. 'Why don't we recover from this one before thinking about anything else?'

I lie there for a while, wide awake. An ancient saying spools through my mind: *Noblesse oblige*. Loosely, it means if you are fortunate, you have a responsibility to give back.

A month later, Jeanne is recovered enough from her fall to plod her garden paths in her black orthotics. 'Can you come and help with my Open Garden weekend?' she asks.

'What do you want me to do?'

'Wash up, mostly.'

'Should be ok. Will you be making those lemon and ginger muffins?'

'Why?'

'I wouldn't mind watching how you do it. I've made them a couple of times and they're dry.'

'Come over on Monday in time for morning tea. We'll make them together.'

Jeanne and I sit at the trestle table on the verandah near the front door. It's a warm, sheltered and sunny spot overlooking layers of garden. The morning tea tray is set with a china milk jug, pretty blue sugar bowl, flowery mugs. Cakes and muffins are arranged on a handpainted plate and dusted with icing sugar. Enough for two each. Or three.

'There's been a worldwide death of busy lizzies,' Jeanne comments, looking forlornly at the flopped flowerbeds in front of us. 'Not sure about South America or the Himalayas, but they've all died in England and Australia. No-one knows why.'

'How bizarre. Do busy lizzies know something we don't?'

'All plants know more than we do.'

Near the front door, Jonnie the canary sings joyfully, his silky little throat pulsing frantically. A fearless young brush turkey fossicks under three bird-feeders hanging from the branch of a tree with wrinkled pale brown limbs reaching heavenwards. A couple of kookaburras zoom in like stinger missiles, fixating on our plates.

'Greedy birds!' Jeanne admonishes them. 'I've fed you already this morning.' They are unabashed, their shiny eyes never wavering.

'Can never get over all this wildlife. You've got eight cats!'

'I have a secret weapon.'

She reaches onto the bench beside her and brings up a plastic water gun. Mischief, a brown, wavy-haired Rex is stalking something hidden from our sight. Jeanne aims the gun and squirts. The cat yelps and leaps into the air, his coat sodden. Jeanne gets a filthy backwards look. Wilfred, a grey tabby, slides onto her lap and puts a paw up to her face affectionately. Jeanne scratches him behind the ears.

'Poor old Wilfred, he's got dementia.'

'Seems happy enough.'

'Yeah, well, I suppose every moment's a new moment. Must make life pretty exciting.'

'What made you buy the place? It was a little fibro shack, wasn't it? And you were an advertising bigwig. Drove a Porsche, lived in an apartment. Bit of a change, all this.'

Jeanne laughs. 'Places find *you* sometimes.'

I know, I think to myself. *I know.* That's how Barbara felt the day she and Bob stumbled on *Tarrangaua* when they were walking in the national park.

'I read the ad in the paper,' Jeanne continues. 'The property sounded too good to be true, but I decided to have a look on a dull drizzly October day. I opened the gate and it was . . . wonderful! Much better than the ad described.'

She had, she says, a vision from the first glimpse. 'The cottage was quite sweet with a pleasant little garden around it. But there was a glorious, towering rainforest alongside a creek. And a waterfall. Imagine having a waterfall in your own garden! The whole place felt quite magical. I had to have it!

'I later discovered lots of people had already inspected the property, lured by eight acres in the heart of a northern beaches suburb! I suspect the gleam of profit from subdividing had a bit to do with it, but the site was daunting. Sheer cliff faces, gullies, steep rocky hillsides and impenetrable native bush almost completely strangled by lantana. And anyway, the council wouldn't allow the land to be cut up. They walked away.'

It was 1982, two years after her husband, Matt, died. The cottage, she thought, was adequate for a weekender. She wouldn't waste time fixing it. Her passion, anyway, was to build a magnificent garden. With the help of friends, invited for weekends of Jeanne's food and company, she began by clearing the lantana and stumbled over stone walls, flights of steps, camellias, abelias, hibiscus and hydrangeas. The skeleton of an old garden. Someone, at some time, had carved out pockets of gentility from the thorny bush.

'The surviving exotic plants had thrived despite total neglect. Worth knowing what plants are unbeatable when you're trying to start a garden,' Jeanne says. 'The crepe myrtle was here too. Probably planted in the fifties at the same time as the shack was built.'

Then, in 1988, the rains came. Not sudden cloudbursts over in a flash, but torrential: thick, flat walls of water on hot and humid days. Sydney was bearded with mould, rivers flooded, strange mushrooms sprouted in dark houses. The sagging city reeked of decay.

In Jeanne's garden, the waterfall roared, fast and furious, like rapids over massive boulders. 'But the house was well above the creek and the water followed an age-old course, so I wasn't worried about flooding.'

What she didn't know, though, as she squelched towards the cottage late one Friday afternoon in April, was that a water pipe had burst and had been leaking steadily for weeks.

'I heard a crash in the middle of the night. I staggered out of bed and saw that a stone statue of a cat had fallen off the mantelpiece above the fireplace. Ah, I thought, that's what the noise was. I went back to bed.'

The next morning, still groggy with sleep, she put on the kettle and picked up the statue to replace it on the shelf. The weight of the statue made the whole wall slowly tilt forward.

'I was so stunned I just stood there! It felt like it was all happening in slow motion. I remember calling my business partner and screaming down the phone: "The wall's falling down. What should I do?" "Get out of there as fast as you can," he told me. So I did.'

The leak and the rain proved too much for the cottage. It was unsalvageable and Jeanne had it demolished. A vague idea took shape, one she'd shoved to the back of her mind for a long time: 'I decided to build my dream home and a garden that might – one day – be enjoyed by other people,' she says. In 1989, *Waterfall Cottage*, with a pitched green roof and gables, was completed. She began opening it to visitors as part of the Open Garden Scheme in 1994.

Jeanne reaches for a slice of carrot and pineapple cake. What the hell! I reach for another muffin.

In Jeanne's kitchen, a wide window above the sink is framed by pure white angel trumpets (*brugmansia*) and shell ginger with waxy yellow, white and pink flowers. Blood-red bougainvillea splashes against the sky. Little firetail finches, lured by goodness knows what, bang into the glass then fly off unsteadily, probably to nurse a headache for a day or two.

'This is so beautiful, it could be a movie set,' I say, looking at glossy copper pots and pans, bunches of dried flowers hanging from a French herb-drying frame, and bowls of fruit and paintings everywhere. 'It's the country kitchen you dream of but never quite achieve. And also utterly functional.'

'Let's get started,' Jeanne says, rolling up her sleeves. 'We're going to make two hundred and eighty-eight muffins in three separate batches.

MAKING LEMON AND GINGER MUFFINS WITH JEANNE
Makes 20.

125 g butter at room temperature
1 cup granulated sugar
2 large eggs
2 tablespoons peeled and coarsely chopped fresh ginger root
2 tablespoons finely grated lemon peel
1 teaspoon baking soda
1 cup plain yoghurt or buttermilk
2 cups plain flour
¼ cup freshly squeezed lemon juice
2 tablespoons granulated sugar, extra

Pre-heat the oven to 375 degrees. Beat together the butter and one cup of sugar until pale and fluffy. Beat in the eggs one at a time, then add the ginger and lemon peel. Stir the baking soda into the yoghurt. It will start to bubble and rise up. Fold the flour into the egg mixture, one-third at a time, alternating with the yoghurt mixture. When blended (do not overmix or the muffins will be dry and tough), scoop into muffin tins. Bake for 18–20 minutes or until lightly golden and springy when touched.

While the muffins are baking, mix together the lemon juice and extra sugar until the sugar dissolves. When the muffins are baked, remove them from the oven and let them cool for 3–5 minutes in the tin. Remove them from the tin and dip the top and bottom of each muffin into the lemon syrup. Note: If you have a food processor, put the lemon peel, ginger and sugar in the bowl and process. Add the butter and process until creamy. Add the eggs one at a time. Scrape the mixture into a large bowl. If it looks curdled, don't worry. Continue as above.

Carefully measured and weighed ingredients for three batches of muffins are separately grouped near the food processor. Twenty-seven lemons float in a sink full of water.

'Wash every piece of fruit before you grate it,' Jeanne says. 'You never know who's handled it or what it's been sprayed with.'

There are three giant stainless steel mixing bowls with two cups of plain flour in each. At the far end of the kitchen, on the bench closest to a barn door, eight muffin trays are lined with paper cases, like a frilly-collared army waiting to advance.

'Why the paper cases? The pans are non-stick?'

'It's less trouble if you're making huge quantities but they're not necessary for smaller batches.'

Jeanne hands me a can of non-stick spray. 'For the paper cases.'

'But you don't need it, that's the point of paper cases.'

'I remove the muffins from the cases as soon as they come out of the oven. so I can dip the whole muffin in the lemon syrup. The muffins come out perfectly if the paper cases are greased.' Then she gives me a grater and nine lemons she's towelled dry. 'Now, let's really get started!' she says, happily.

Music wafts. The house smells sweetly of oriental lilies from a vase in the front hall. A cookbook lies open on the dining table with a photograph of a cheese and fig tart. There's a bowl of shiny lemons – extras, if we need them. Old dressers lining the walls sag with colourful plates of all shapes and sizes, each arranged like a still life. Out of every window, the exquisitely tended garden seduces.

'One day, I want to come here to dinner in the middle of winter. I want the fire roaring, the smell of roasting beef and potatoes seeping through the house, wine glasses glittering on the table. I'll bring dessert.'

'No you won't. There's only one cook in this house.'

'One cook and an apprentice,' I reply. I look at Jeanne's pile of lemons. She's already grated six and I'm still on number three. 'I'll have to speed up a bit or I might get fired.'

'Not a chance!'

I watch Jeanne work like I'll be examined. Every good cook has tricks that no cookbook ever reveals, and Jeanne is a master.

'One step at a time, that's how you do it, and it all works out. Rushing never helps. Remember to keep the recipe in front of you, no matter how many times you've made it. It prevents mistakes and you get the same result every time. And measure all the ingredients,' she adds firmly. 'I know a chef who even weighs her eggs. Baking won't tolerate rough guesses. It's more science than skill.'

The butter goes into the food processor and gets whizzed. The eggs, broken into a china jug, are tipped in slowly while the machine whirrs. When the batter is thick and pale yellow, Jeanne reaches for a stainless steel mixing bowl, stirs the flour quickly with her hands and adds the batter and the yoghurt in one go. She grabs a long-handled stainless steel slotted spoon and gently folds the mixture. Does air go through the holes in the spoon – helping to keep the mixture light?

'Don't be silly,' she says. 'It's just the biggest spoon I've got!'

When the mixture is still lumpy and barely combined, she declares it ready.

'I've been overmixing,' I say.

'Fatal,' she replies, picking up an ice-cream scoop and filling each paper case with a perfectly equal amount so the muffins will cook evenly. She scrapes the sides of the bowl until it's clean, squeezing two more muffins out of the mixture. Another lesson. Don't waste a skerrick.

'Now, whack them in the oven and turn the trays anticlockwise every four minutes. That's your next job. I'll get a new batch going.'

I am far too cavalier in the kitchen. I measure roughly, substitute one ingredient for another if I don't have the one in the recipe, and I never open the oven once the tray's gone in.

'Why not?' Jeanne asks, perplexed again. 'Without a perfect oven, which is very rare, most food cooks slightly unevenly unless you turn it.'

'Doesn't a rush of cold air make cakes sink?'

'Only angel cake. If a cake sinks it's because you're cooking at a temperature that's too low. Or you've pulled it out of the oven before it's fully cooked.'

'Oh.' Another misconception gets torn up and thrown away.

Two and a half hours later, the muffins are defrocked, dipped, lined up on melamine trays and wrapped in plastic film.

'Don't you wait for them to cool?' I ask, watching Jeanne wrap the final tray.

'I think they stay more moist if you get them into the freezer before they've cooled down completely.'

And another myth gets blasted into the stratosphere.

'Want to stay and have a glass of wine and some cheese?' Jeanne asks.

'Thanks, but no. Got a car full of shopping and I've arranged to meet Bob at The Point.' I hug her so easily to say goodbye. What always drags me back from showing my mother affection?

When the groceries are loaded onto the boat, Bob and I zip across the water. The afternoon sun is a blinding ball hovering above the gully in the hills beyond Lovett Bay. Bob opens a parcel he's picked up from the post office. I push the throttle forward, urging the tinny to go faster, tired from shopping, muffin-making and in a hurry to reach the house. Fighting the growing crowds in Mona Vale for a parking spot wears me out. When did it suddenly get so busy? I am locked, I realise, into the way it was when I first moved here.

For some reason, and neither of us will ever know why, Bob looks up. 'Stop!' he yells.

I see it at the same time. The *Amelia K* is hurtling from Halls Wharf towards Elvina Bay, ploughing through the water in a straight line. I swerve, missing the ferry by less than a foot. Bob's fists are balled against his eyes. It was too terrible to look. I nearly killed us both.

'I'm sorry, so sorry. I just didn't see it. I looked and looked. You know how careful I am! I just didn't see it.'

It takes Bob a few minutes to speak. The engine idles, the boat rocking roughly in the wake. Groceries roll all over the deck. I am too frightened to move either backwards or forwards, numbed by a fear so intense my legs and arms prickle with pins and needles.

'The sun,' I say, scrabbling for a reason for roaring so close to disaster. 'Couldn't see the ferry through the sun. That's it! I'm getting new glasses! And we need new windows. These are crazed by the salt. And –'

'It's ok. We're ok,' Bob says, diverting fear that's quickly turned into anger.

'You drive. Please.'

We swap seats. For some reason I want to whack something hard. Smash it. It was so goddamned close. I wasn't careful enough, assumed life would keep me safe for a long time yet. As though I'd earned the right.

'Bit of a reality check,' I say, calming down as we reach our pontoon. Bob nods. His face is still white, which makes his eyes look blacker than coal.

'Reminds you to be humble,' he says.

I fumble around for words to say how sorry I am. A split second would have changed everything. That's all it can take – a split second – and there's no going back.

'I'm so sorry, Bob, so sorry.'

He puts his hand on my knee, big and warm, and there's no blame in the touch, only comfort.

For the next few months, I slide from shore to shore as slowly as Bainy, the local marine engine mechanic. He has a pocked, yellow fibreglass boat with broken windows that he also uses as storage space for odd engine pieces and a small 9.9 horsepower motor. Crosses the water at the speed of a royal barge, Greek fisherman's hat pulled low on his forehead, a spiral of smoke rising from under the peak. He waves royally, a single hand twisting above his head, when you overtake him. As everyone does.

'Give you a lift?' he offers Mary Beth early one morning when she's on her way to work.

'No thanks, I'm in a hurry. I'll wait for the ferry,' she replies.

'Don't say I didn't offer,' Bainy responds, shaking his head sadly. 'Gave you a chance to ride in style and you turned it down.'

My courage in the boat gradually returns, but I am almost pathologically vigilant for a while. I buy new glasses with non-reflective lenses and remind myself over and over not to take paradise lightly. It sneaks up behind you and nips you on the back-side if you're too blithe.

12

Brigitte (a different Brigitte from the one in Lovett Bay) is the diplomatic custodian of local information which she puts together in a regular bulletin called *Bay News*. It is sent via email to people in the bays and Scotland Island and keeps us in touch – with each other, with local issues, and with the wider world if it is relevant to our small community. It is a Herculean task and she does it with fervour and grace. She and her husband Andrew live in Frog Hollow with their twin boys.

Each year the five houses nestled in this dreamy little half-moon bay with its lush rainforest and, when the rains fall, a busy creek organise a pump day. 'It's to make sure we're set for the bush-fire season,' Bob told me not long after I moved into the *Tin Shed*. I had no idea, then, that bushfires were to become a fact of my new life. Nor did I have even a slight understanding of what pumps were all about. 'Come and see what happens,' Bob said. 'You'll need to buy a pump of your own.' Barbara was still alive, then, but too ill to take part.

He handed me a schedule beginning with his name and followed by other names, listed in half-hour increments. At two thirty on the dot, his allotted time, he pulled the start cord and his pump worked first go. Spumes of water flooded the sky. He'd prepared and tested it the day before. In Frog Hollow, though, none of the pumps started quite so effortlessly. One of them, the cleanest and neatest, didn't start at all. 'That's why we have pump day,' everyone tells each other soothingly, 'to check out the equipment.' And they cast accusing looks at Bob, as though he's shown them up. Which he has, of course.

It's traditional for everyone to bring a plate and join together for an early dinner after all the pumps have been put back in storage. The first year I went to pump day, Brigitte's twins were not even a year old. They were tiny babies, one snowy-haired, the other with hair darker than a moonless night. Both had streaming colds and we took turns holding them until they fell asleep on our laps, eyelashes fanned over their rounded cheeks, their skinny little legs still at last. They grew up quickly, those boys, with a lust for adventure spurred on by living with the bay at their feet, sheer cliff faces at their back and the bush above.

Bob and I are fixing an old garden seat when we hear the high-pitched, whining thwack of a helicopter above us. We look up, curious but not alarmed. Until it hovers over Frog Hollow for far too long and so low and close to the houses, surely it will clip a tree and spin wildly into the water. At first we fear it might be having engine trouble, but the fierce wind from the propeller turns the still, emerald waters into a swirling cauldron, flattens the cabbage palms. The engine doesn't miss a beat. Then a bloke attached to a line drops from the helicopter door, swaying back-wards and forwards over the pontoon until he lands safely.

'It's got to be one of the twins – or both,' Bob says. I nod, my stomach filled with dread. Hoping whatever has happened is not unthinkable.

'I'll go and call Jack and his wife. They're close friends. Tell them they might be needed,' I say. Truth is, I cannot watch. I cannot bear to think that a single reckless moment may have led to an eternity of grief.

Later in the afternoon, we hear what happened. One of the twins fell nearly fifty feet from a ledge of the cliff behind the house. On his way down, he hit a tree fern that broke his fall and probably saved his life. When the doctor checked him over, he was certain his back wasn't injured but he was worried about internal injuries and a badly broken leg. The chopper ferried the boy to hospital where X-rays revealed a single, broken right femur and cuts and bruises. His body was encased in plaster to the neck and he came home, flat-out on a trolley, a few weeks later.

'Might slow him down a bit, the accident,' we all said. But it didn't. As soon as he was out of plaster and could ride his bike again, he raced to the top of our track, hesitated for less than a second, then pedalled hell for leather, bouncing over rough sandstone, to the water.

I caught him the next day and threatened to take his bike if he wasn't more careful. Bob heard me. 'When I was a kid, we stayed away from mothers like you,' he said.

'I worry,' I replied.

'Kids are kids. You can't change them.'

Since Brigitte began her newsletter, the fire-shed dinners – held on the first Friday of the month, although they're on Saturday's now – in Elvina Bay have become even more of a community highlight and fire brigade funds are fatter than they've ever been. The *chef du jour* is announced (which puts pressure on the cook, but not too much), along with any highlight of the evening. Usually, it's a bake-off competition. You bring a dessert and someone judges it. Then we all eat the entries.

There's a crowd at the shed by the time we arrive on an early spring evening. Bob lets me off at the ferry wharf then swerves to park three deep along the jetty. He jumps from boat to boat, arms held out for balance. Sometimes he pretends he's about to fall, but he's showing off. He's not nearly as nonchalant at the end of the night, though, after a few glasses of wine. Still, if he falls, it's a soft landing into glistening black water – unless it's a really low tide. It's always wise to check.

When Bob has tied up the boat, we wander along the jetty. Wheelbarrows are lined up along one side, one per house, for residents to cart their shopping home. It's the day after a full moon, the air is thin and crisp. Kids run helter-skelter in the silver light, barefoot despite the stony ground. We adults are more languid and stand in groups, touching base. Which is part of what makes us such a strong community.

'What's on the menu?' we ask Stewart and Fleury.

'Slow-roasted lamb shoulder. Chicken in spices. A salad of some kind,' Stewart replies, handing us both a glass of wine.

'Better than the Ritz!'

'The view is certainly ahead of the Ritz,' he says, looking around.

Through the casuarinas, Elvina Bay is black marble smooth. Yachts rest on their moorings, the fire brigade tinny amongst them. It's a good solid boat, bought with donated funds, although none of us ever wants to see it used.

Someone calls out to the kids. 'Dinner's on. Come and get it. Now!'

Not one child slows down, but they somehow get fed anyway.

'Bit light on desserts tonight,' I say when we sit down. 'Should have made an effort. Getting lazy.'

'I used to make bread and butter puddings all the time. Never did much good in the judging,' says Jenny. 'Then one of the Alans gave me second prize. Told me I was such a trier everyone felt sorry for me.'

'Bit hard to stuff up bread and butter pudding, isn't it?'

'Not for me,' she says, laughing. 'I'm probably the only person around Pittwater – male or female – that isn't a star chef.'

'Ever think of leaving here?' I ask, because she has raised her son alone since he was born and water access living can wear you out.

'Once or twice. On a grim day when I'm too tired to think straight. But then I look around. Everyone here is family. If my son's not at home, I know he's around somewhere and in good hands, with plenty to do. He's nearly ten years old, and perhaps it will change as he gets older. But I hope not.'

She sighs and rests her knife and fork on her plate, hesitating before she speaks again. 'I don't know if this makes sense, but living amongst community instead of within the narrow confines of family has made my son aware of a bigger world from the time he was born. He accepts that people are different. And all that matters is kindness and compassion.'

'Good start in life,' I reply.

'The best.'

I have more or less forgotten the architect debate until Jeanne sends me an email that is typically succinct: 'There's a talk by Zeny Edwards about Hardy Wilson at *Eryldene* this Saturday. You should be there.'

'Do you want to come?' I ask Bob.

'Interesting house. Hardy Wilson designed it. Went there with Barbara once, not long after we moved into *Tarrangaua*. Yeah, I'll come.'

'I'll ask Esther, too. Try and get her out and about.' When I call her, though, she's busy.

'There's a classical music concert in the main room,' she says. 'I'm looking forward to it.'

When I tell Bob, he nods with relief. 'Might be a good idea to keep Esther and Jeanne on different social circuits,' he says. 'Esther likes you to herself.'

Eryldene was built in the Sydney suburb of Gordon in 1913 for linguist and camellia expert Professor EG Waterhouse. The two men recognised a kindred spirit in each other from the moment they met and the relationship between Wilson and the professor, both newly married to Scottish wives, developed into a strong and enduring friendship – an unusual result for Wilson, who typically complained about and ultimately fell out with many of his clients. According to Zeny Edwards, *Eryldene* became one of the most photographed and publicised properties of the 1920s and 1930s. Wilson and his partners, Stacey Neave and John Berry, designed seven new features for the house over a 23-year-period, including the Tea House, Wilson's oriental-inspired *pièce de résistance*.

On the allotted day, we park the car and walk along an ordinary suburban street to a woman sitting at a table selling tickets. As Bob pays, I stand and stare at the house and cannot help feeling disappointed. The verandah is almost decorative, as though no-one was ever intended to sit on it in the cool of a summer evening to hear a kookaburra's last hurrah. The double columns framing the front door are slim, delicate almost, whereas at *Tarrangaua* they are solid and massive.

'Think those heritage blokes might be right,' I suggest, but Bob doesn't reply.

We wander through dining rooms, sitting rooms, bedrooms where the scale, again, is small. Bob studies window ledges, flagstones, the verandah. The key, he says, is almost always in the detail. But although there are similarities everywhere, nothing is intrinsic. The back door leads to a flagstone courtyard but it's circled by Grecian columns and lacks the simplicity of *Tarrangaua*'s. Beyond, the garden sprawls. Gum trees soar nakedly to a crown of hangdog foliage against a pure blue sky. Camellias in pots and in the ground bloom in swathes of red, white, pink. Citrus trees bend with bright globes of fruit: oranges, cumquats. The colours all fight each other. Two dogs bark, backwards and forwards, like they're having a conversation.

'Jeanne!' I call out, waving across the lawn. She's part of a group near the Tea House. Black orthotic shoes, black trousers, a pale green round-necked shirt, a soft green sweater around her shoulders – unmistakably Jeanne. We wander over.

'This is Zeny,' Jeanne says, introducing us to a quietly beautiful woman, all style and perfect skin, with eyes that don't miss a nuance.

'We have your book,' I say, shaking her hand. She nods.

'We're here on a mission,' I add. Her eyebrows go up but she doesn't say anything. 'We live at *Tarrangaua*, in Lovett Bay, the home Hardy Wilson is supposed to have built for Dorothea Mackellar. We're trying to establish whether it's his design or not.'

'It isn't,' Zeny says flatly and firmly.

'Why not?'

She is nonplussed by the question, hesitates for a moment.

'Have you ever seen it?' I ask.

'No, but if it were his design, I would know. There's nothing in the archives. It isn't his house.'

'Maybe, maybe not. I'd like to know for sure. Some people,' I add, 'think the Queensland architect Robin Dods may have had a hand in it, but he died before she bought the land.'

'It took a long time to do property deals in the twenties. Maybe he did a rough plan before he died. You could ask Robert Riddel. He's doing a thesis on Dods. You'll find him in Brisbane,' Zeny says.

'Thanks. I'll chase him up.'

'What do you think?' Zeny asks, turning towards a tall woman standing next to her. She has tinted reddish-brown hair, wears well-cut trousers, a finely knitted sweater with a string of pearls, plain brown shoes. She looks like a sensible, no-nonsense woman.

'This is Margaret McCredie,' Zeny adds. 'Margaret is one of Hardy Wilson's granddaughters.'

I glance at Jeanne. She looks smug, a half-smile lifting the corners of her mouth. 'See what happens when you get out and about?' she whispers. It's a dig. She's been after me to join the Garden History Society for months. So far, I've resisted. Societies of any kind have never been a passion.

'I'd love to come and have a chat, if you have the time,' I say to Marg. We exchange telephone numbers, set a date. 'Do you think Hardy Wilson designed *Tarrangaua*?' I add.

'No.'

'Why not?' I ask again. And she cannot give me an answer.

A few weeks later, Margaret McCredie leads me along her hallway and opens the door to a spare bedroom. She points to a camphorwood chest with brass hinges pushed against the wall.

'Everything that is left is in the chest,' she says, turning the lock with a key. 'There's not much, I'm afraid. He sold or bequeathed most of his work at various times throughout his life. I inherited a sideboard. With a bullet hole. Dad was playing with Grandpa's gun and it went off! I have a sofa, too, that we kids would lie on during the day if we were unwell. A few other things but not much.

'When he remarried after my grandmother died in 1939, I think Dad felt that a few bits and pieces which should have come to him never did. Hope you discover what you're looking for,' she adds, pulling the door closed behind her.

I lift the lid of the carved brown chest. I am hunting and my old journalistic instincts click in, my stomach fluttering with the excitement. But I have no idea what to expect.

There are magazines, scrolls, notebooks with silk moire covers and leather spines, blank sheets of tea-stained paper, photos of furniture, old press clippings of his published essays. Bryant & May's Redhead matches lie in a cigar box, alongside tweezers, a box of Benson drawing pins made in Belgium, and measuring calipers. There's a beautifully stitched leather pouch with sky blue silk lining: 'American Express Travel Department'. It is empty.

Books – Chinese legends, Chinese painters, Japanese painters – an *Australian House and Garden* magazine dated 1986 which features a story on *Purulia*. Notebooks filled with neat writing, the pages hand-numbered. There is nothing about a house on a high, rough hill, though.

A telegram expresses deepest sympathy at Wilson's death. ' . . . A splendid man', says a condolence letter, 'kind and gentle. A big man in every sense of the word.' His obituary is small and discreet. 'Tribute to Architect', it is headed, and it is barely a few paragraphs. By the time he died of pneumonia, Wilson had lost his status and was even regarded by some as irredeemably eccentric.

'What was he like, your grandfather?' I ask Margaret when the lid is closed on the camphorwood box.

'My memories are vague. I was eleven years old when he died. I remember one thing quite vividly, though. When I stayed with him, I was expected to say goodnight, standing in front of where he sat in his armchair, with my hands clasped together and raised to chest height. "Good night, Grandpa," I had to say. Then I bowed my head as though I'd been raised in the East. And he'd nod silently while I rushed away to bed.'

When Wilson's son Lachlan married and began practising as a physician in Launceston, in north west Tasmania, Wilson offered to design the young couple a new home at 15 Lord Street. 'My mother, Jean, took one look at the Chinese upturned eaves and decided conservative Launceston wasn't ready for them. Nor for the blinding Chinese red pillars at the front door. Although she liked the idea of the green shutters, sadly, we couldn't afford them. They cost a fortune, apparently, in those post-war days.

'She also wanted to be able to walk from the living room into the garden and Grandpa's plan didn't allow for that. I was too young to understand family politics but I believe there was a cooling-off period between my parents and Grandpa. "My plan's not good enough for you . . ." or words to that effect. Grandpa felt they should have been falling over backwards to have him design a house, that they should love it as it was. That's the kind of man he was.'

'I'd like to show you our house,' I say as I pack up my note-book and tape recorder to leave. 'Would you come over the water to us one day?'

'Love to! I've always been curious about *Tarrangaua*.'

'Find anything interesting?' Bob asks when I get home.

'Kind of weird, going through all his stuff. Got a clearer picture of the bloke, though, especially from reading some of his note-books. He was into quality, that's for sure. Everything he owned was the best money could buy. But no, I'm no closer to solving the mystery. Might chase up that fella in Queensland, the one Zeny suggested. Visit Pia at the same time.'

'Wait till the end of the sailing season. Be good to go after the Woody Point Annual General Meeting. More time then.'

Woody Point Yacht Club is a club with no clubhouse and very few rules. Except that any race protest must be accompanied by a slab of beer when you lodge it with the current commodore, and all funds remaining at the end of the season must be spent at the Annual General Meeting knees-up, which is traditionally held at the Lovett Bay boatshed where we dance on sloping concrete and dodge the metal boat-cradle tracks.

George Bennett told me the tracks came from the old Pitt Street tram lines when the tram service was abolished in 1957 to make way for a new public transport system based on buses. 'They were perfect to slide the boat cradle along in my new boatshed in Lovett Bay.'

'You built the original boatshed?' I asked him, surprised, because I didn't think it was more than thirty years old.

'Took me three years to get the plans through council.'

'Nothing changes, does it?'

'Not much.'

Every year, one or two people come a cropper at the AGM party on those tram lines. It's a badge of honour, really, to take home a few scars.

If you don't want to dance dodging tram lines, you can fish from the jetty. Or sit by a washing machine drum with a fire roaring inside. Or hang out on the lawn and look up at the stars. Or climb into your tinny and rock with the tide, a glass of wine in your hand – tied to the jetty so you don't end up bobbing towards the Pacific Ocean.

The new season twilight sailing series begins with daylight saving. Every Wednesday, we all emerge from our houses at five o'clock as though we're in some kind of trance: Jack, Stef, Bob, Mick, John. There is a dreamlike quality to the scene, I sometimes think, as we climb into tinnies and motor slowly through the moorings to our boats. Like we're on a silent, almost sacred mission.

Jack sails his much-loved family boat, *Birrah Lee*. He gathers his boys in the cockpit, wide-brimmed straw hats tied under their chins like African field workers, and sails with louche serenity, engaged, as he mostly is, in the physical world.

Stef's boat is a fast Farr 37 called *Kookaburra 11*. It has two sofas and a fridge. Glasses, plates, cutlery and bathrobes, too. 'If it gets too blowy,' Bella warns him, 'I will go below, put on my terry towelling robe, climb in between my four hundred thread count sheets and read a book.'

'But, Bella, you look like a queen when you ride in the cockpit with us.'

'Flatterer!' she says. 'But it won't work.'

I have seen her, though, wrapped in wet-weather gear, wind and rain blowing her red hair flat. Seduced. I've seen her in the robe, too.

We hoist our mainsails while we're still on the mooring, almost in unison. They unfurl like butterflies emerging from a chrysalis. When the headsail is set free and fills with air until it is as gently rounded as a woman's breast, the engine is switched off and we glide soundlessly, except for the murmur, like whispering lovers, of water parting under the keel. On summer evenings not long before the sun leaves the bays, water explodes with heavenly light and white sails fill with gold until they look like falling angels.

Each year the club grows bigger. When I first started sailing, we thought it a busy night if thirty medium-size boats gathered politely at the start line, skippers and crew with drinks in hand, main sheets loosely held, sails reefed safely if the winds were strong. Now, at least sixty yachts jockey for a prime start each Wednesday, so huge, some of them, they are like tankers alongside the smaller boats. It is frightening and for a while I want to with-draw from the fray.

'It does you good,' Bob insists every week.

'I'm an amateur. If we get into strife I won't know what to do. I'll be a liability.'

'You won't learn if you stay home.'

Nick and Ann sail regularly. Nick is ex-British navy, expert and unflappable, always polite and proper. Ann is quietly capable and sees problems before they happen. They sailed from England to Australia with their two small boys and are our core crew. Others come and go – fair-weather sailors, we call them with affection.

About the third race into the season, it's a foul, blustery evening. The wind is cold and erratic, blowing first from one direc-tion and then another. The fleet is a crowd at sixty-three yachts. The start is a frantic melee of tacking boats, shouting skippers and, occasionally, bad temper.

'This used to be a race for gentlemen,' yells one of the oldest members. He's sailing a cosy Jubilee and trying to fend off a pugna-cious 'big shitter' bullying to push him out of a well-judged start.

'They come to escape the rat race in the bigger clubs and bring all their bad habits with them,' Bob says, shaking his head.

I let off the mainsail to slow the boat. We have two minutes to start time. We won the series once and now carry a handicap that ensures we'll never win again – another club rule.

'Need to tie a bucket on your keel,' I yell as John glides past in *KA2*. Therese pops her head out of the forward hatch, waves.

'You look good from the back!' Stef calls when we pass him.

'You look good from the back,' we yell when he passes us.

On the home stretch but before the third and final marker, the wind drops to about ten knots.

'Where's that big shitter?' Bob asks, bending to look under the sail. 'Ah fuck!'

He suddenly tacks the boat. A yellow hull cuts in front of us, ignoring sailing racing rules in what it probably believes is a show of balls but in reality is ignorant, dangerous thuggery. It's so quick, Nick, Ann and I don't have time to cross to the other side. Our bums drag in the water as the boat heels. Nick grabs Ann's leg, I grab her arm. She's flat against the lifelines. Nick and I hold on to our ropes for support as water floods over the side. There's another boat on a collision course in front of us. Bob tacks again. Quick as a flash, we're back on the dry side. Nick and I pull Ann to safety.

'Jesus!'

'Do they know they were in the wrong?' I shout angrily. 'We were on starboard!'

'You ok? Everything ok?' we ask Ann.

'Yes. Yes, of course.'

'Nearly lost you overboard.'

'Not at all. No danger at all. Anyway, I'd rather die in a yacht race than in bed,' she says, grinning.

Later at home, I mutter angrily about the new machismo taking over our little club that was created thirty years ago. Anything that floats can race. 'Doesn't matter if you win or lose, it's how you play the game, isn't it?' I ask, remembering one of my mother's lines from the days when I played tennis in junior tournaments all over Victoria.

Bob is noncommittal. 'It's a race, Susan. Races are about winning.'

'Not at any cost, surely?'

'No, of course not.'

We drop the conversation.

A week later, when the wind's lighter than fairy floss and Bob's secret weapon, the Code Zero, helps us win the race by two minutes, I bounce around the boat in jubilation. 'We won! We won!' I shout, slapping backs. Then I look at the shocked faces around me. 'Not that it's important,' I add hastily. 'It's the experience that counts.' Not a soul believes me.

Over the years, we've cooked many different dishes for the end of season Annual General Meeting, from basic bangers with tomato, onion and basil salad to a fish stew redolent with fennel and garlic. The chicken curry laced with chopped peanuts and basil was by far the easiest for a big crowd. It's made from thigh fillets diced into big lumps and cooked on the barbecue. The meat's then whacked into a catering-size stainless steel mixing bowl and a large pot of pre-made curry sauce is tipped over the lot. I put a bit too much chili in one year, but sailors are a tough lot. The baked beans are a popular dish, too, although Stewart says septics all over Pittwater struggle for a few days afterwards.

The best meal ever, though, was when Tim barbecued tender lamb cutlets and made a lemon, thyme, green olive and butter sauce to dip them in, a sauce so deliciously pungent and rich we tipped it over the salad, dunked our bread in it and sipped it like soup from empty plates. Tim's used to barbecuing under pressure. At home in Towlers Bay, as soon as the chops go on, five svelte, drooling reptilian heads with glittering eyes peer longingly from the cliff overhanging his hotplate. Goannas. He stores a few old gumboots close by to chuck at them, but they keep coming back. Smart goannas. Tim's a great cook.

Bainy, the gifted local boat engine mechanic, is chief custodian of the Temprite for the beer kegs for the party, which he instals with passion and precision. And a few expletives if it's been borrowed and returned with dirty hoses or a missing washer. He's meticulous about the whole set-up: the table, the right size blocks of ice, the hoses, gas and even the type of beer (lager or pilsener). But he is especially fastidious about testing. 'When a beer's poured,' he says, 'the glass must be angled. The tap flicked quickly. On. Off. And no more than half an inch of froth, mate. That's it. Any more and you've poured it wrong. And, mate, it's gotta be cold.'

'Does anyone care, Bainy, if the beer's not perfect?' I ask him.

'Mate, everyone's a critic. Trust me.'

On the big night, he slips out of his blue singlet into a white dinner shirt, clips a bowtie around his neck, pulls on perfectly creased black strides and stands firmly behind the bar. Unrecognisable, except for his fisherman's cap.

A few weeks after nearly being T-boned, there's a message on the answering machine from an old colleague. A retired editor and editor-in-chief of *The Australian Women's Weekly* is dying. At one time, when she prowled the corridors at Australian Consolidated Press, she was indestructible. A tiny redhead with flashing green eyes who could flatten you with a look, she worked for the Packer family for fifty years to the day because she was a woman, she said, who liked neatness.

I ring her immediately. 'You up to visitors?' I ask.

'Of course.'

A few days later, I join a couple of friends who still work at *The Weekly* to beat through Sydney traffic to St Vincents Hospital.

When we get to the swinging glass doors, memories of long nights with death hovering at the foot of the hospital bed, of tubes and sacks of fluids, of looking in the mirror and seeing a strange, distorted body with one breast instead of two, roar through my mind.

'You'll be right,' says Kay, seeing me hesitate. She grabs my arm, leads the way.

It takes a moment to recognise my old boss. No green eye shadow, no painted lips. The days of using eighteen different cosmetics at one time are over. No vibrant floral prints either, only a girly pink nightie with a tiny lace frill around the neck. But her toenails flash boldly, and jewellery glitters on her fingers and wrists. Still true to the old image. Although the core is waning.

'Tell me about cancer,' she says. To the point, as always.

'You leave hospital. Go home. Then you begin again with a new set of rules.'

She is silent for a moment. 'Not sure about any of that,' she finally replies. And I realise she has accepted that she will not get well.

Three weeks later, the funeral notice appears in the paper and the phone rings again. 'Can you pick up Sharon and bring her to the funeral?' asks a former colleague who's moved into the more predictable world of administration. 'She lives near you in a retirement village at Bayview.'

'No problems. I even know where it is. It's just up the road from where my mother lives.'

'I'll come with you,' Bob says, because he knows funerals make me feel like I'm standing against a brick wall while someone kicks me in the guts for an hour or two. Even after all this time.

Sharon is already waiting for us in the car park, dressed to kill in a beautifully tailored black suit and a black and white houndstooth scarf. She folds her walking frame and Bob puts it in the boot, but she keeps her matching walking sticks close by as she struggles into the seat. Her long, slim legs won't obey her orders. She uses her arms to lift them into the car, one by one.

I want to ask her age but I know she'll hate the question. I do a few mental sums. She must be in her late eighties or early nineties. Her skin, though, is so flawless she could be sixty, and her mind is razor sharp.

'I'm the person that journalists phone when they're doing a story on the history of *The Weekly*,' she says with a grin, 'because I go back further than almost anyone. Don't know what everyone will do when I go.'

'What was it like, when you were there?'

'It was a different world. More genteel, if you like. If Sir Frank [Sir Frank Packer, founder of *The Australian Women's Weekly*] were still alive he'd be appalled at the way I'm dressed for a funeral. No hat, you see. We always seemed to be rushing to funerals in Sir Frank's day. He felt it was important to show respect if a staff member died, even if you didn't know the person. Had to dash out to David Jones to buy a new hat nearly every time. I had a cupboard full of hats by the time I retired.'

Later, when I know her better and it becomes a habit to cook a little more than we need and then take Sharon a small plate or two, I ask why she never married.

'My own fault, really,' she says. 'I fell in love but the war came along. My friend gave me a ring but he insisted I wear it around my neck. If he returned from service wounded in some awful way, he didn't want me to feel tied to him.' She dabs her eyes with a corner of her linen handkerchief. Not crying, more as if to give herself time to get her story in order.

'Well, he returned unharmed, but he was not the boy I knew anymore. He was a man and very changed. I'd changed, too. I had a job as a journalist, I was free and independent and enjoying life. I wasn't ready to settle down.' He married another woman on the rebound, a staunch Roman Catholic who believed her vows were inalienable. They had a child, and when the marriage foundered, though they agreed to live apart, divorce was never discussed.

'I ran into him one day, years later. I was coming out of a hotel in Double Bay with a carton of beer. "Can I carry that for you," he asked. "No," I replied. "You're as independent as ever," he retorted.

'He told me he and his wife lived apart, so we saw each other from time to time. One day he took my hand and said that if his wife would give him a divorce, would I marry him? "Yes," I told him. "Yes." '

By this time his wife was far less emphatic about the rites of her church. She still said no to a divorce, though, because she couldn't bear to hurt her devout parents. Sharon says: 'He told me the news, which didn't really matter to me. It was the sixties, life had changed. "I'll live with you anyway," I told him. But he shook his head. "I can't do that to you, Sharon," he said. "It wouldn't be right." And I never saw him again.

'When he died, his wife phoned me to see if I wanted to come to the funeral. I'd just had my hip replaced and couldn't walk but I thanked her for asking me. "Your name was on his lips as he died," she told me. Which must have cost her, I think. Such a waste, all of it. But my own fault. You see, I had the opportunity to marry him when he came home, and I refused it.'

I pick up my empty dishes from the kitchen to take them home to refill.

'If you are making those little lemon cakes . . .' she whispers shyly as I open the front door to leave.

I turn and smile. 'As it happens, I am.'

Impulsively, I return and lean to kiss her cheek. Why can I never do that with my mother? What is the dark abyss that stretches between us sometimes? I have no idea. No memory. If there even is one.

13

FLEURY TELLS US THAT Katie is having an exhibition in a gallery in Canberra. Desert art, inspired by the return trip to Perth after her show at *Tarrangaua*.

'Tell Katie we'll be there for the opening,' Bob says.

'How you doing?' I ask when we all meet up on a stinkingly hot summer evening.

'Fantastic,' she replies.

'Good.'

She has done prints of red sands and blue-green spinifex, and brought the desert alive. But alone on a wall there's a massive, powerful print of a vast, grey ocean. Empty, except for a single, small rowboat. A wordless revelation.

On New Year's Eve, a night so explosively hot even the frantic castanets of the crickets slow to a tepid beat, the round table in the western corner of the long verandah glows in the flickering light of a single candle. It is set with my grandmother's white lace tablecloth, my brother's crystal glasses, my mother's silver cutlery. And the expensive silver ice bucket she hid from my father for about two years before she found the courage to tell him she'd bought it.

Near the candle, in an old blue vase, roses from a friend's garden in the high, cool ranges west of Sydney flop in riotous colours: red, yellow, orange, hot pink. Only Bob's table napkin ring is new, a Christmas gift. Because he once mentioned that he liked the idea of them. You can use a napkin three or four times before it has to be washed.

'Seems appropriate, don't you think, to surround yourself with the past when you're about to begin a new year?' I ask Bob.

'Prefer to look forward,' Bob replies. 'Always have.'

Earlier, we sat neck high in the cool green shallows of Lovett Bay to escape the prickling noon heat. Skittish baby bream with flirtatious tails swam around us. Gentle waves spilled over a starfish, mute and motionless on the sandy bottom near where the seawall holds back the erosion of time, tide and weather. But nothing ever really stops time.

'We'll be hot and sticky after we climb the steps back to the house,' Bob murmured, waving his arms slowly below the water to keep afloat.

'Worth it,' I replied.

He heaved a deep breath and slipped his head under, blew bubbles. Came up laughing because he reckoned I'd fall for his trick.

'Saw you blowing.'

He grinned and let rip with noisy wind. 'Gotcha that time!'

'Bastard!' I swam away from him, towards Jack's second boat, a gleaming wooden skiff called *Dorothy*, after his mother. He is passionate about the boat and cares for it reverently. He glides through the water single-handedly when he's going off fishing alone, his long body curved into the same quilled shape as the headsail. If he's not going far he rows, dipping his oars into the water with long, even strokes. Stretching forward, leaning back, stretching forward, leaning back – so perfectly rhythmical that to watch him is like meditating.

Saw him in the skiff with one of his children a few days ago. White-haired with skin seared by the wind and sun and folded into deep lines. His son beside him was satin smooth, his face already losing the jellied edges of boyhood. Jack threaded a sail shaped like a wing into a track on the mast, explaining each step. The boy watched, nodded, intent. He was about to go solo in his father's precious boat for the first time. A rite of a kind.

After our swim, Bob and I climbed eighty-eight steps to the back door in the lurid glow of the setting sun. Bob opted for a shower while I set the table. For two. These final hours of the old year are about counting blessings, not wishing on the future. What could we wish for anyway, beyond health?

'Still scorching,' Bob says, coming into the kitchen. His hair is wet. Water trickles down the deep grooves in his face. 'Where's the sea breeze when you need it?'

'Never known it this hot.'

'Yes you have. You've just forgotten.' He is right, of course.

'The table looks beautiful,' Bob adds hesitantly, lifting the bucket to fill it with ice and a bottle of champagne. 'Sure you don't mind just the two of us?'

'Can't think of anything better.'

He slips an arm around my waist, leans his head against mine. I kiss him lightly, this quiet man with fine instincts, this man who is the real reason my mother found the faith to pass on her cherished silver. She trusts him to always be around as she has never trusted me. With good reason. 'Here! You can clean it now,' she huffed when she handed it over. What she meant, though, was that I'd finally come of age. Settled. She can safely give me her knives, forks, spoons and the ice bucket knowing I won't abandon them in some far-flung corner as I chase the next assignment. 'My gypsy daughter,' she called me once. But I suspect my restlessness was inspired by her. On my twenty-first birthday, she handed me wings she'd drawn on a card. 'Fly,' she said. And the word twanged with her own awful longing. She'd never been further than inter-state, then.

Looking at the table, I suddenly understand why she refused to buy all new furniture when she moved from her home to the retirement village.

'I'm old,' she snapped when I tried to drag her around stores to see lean couches and sleek sideboards more suited to her new, small space than the pink chintz granny couch and recliner armchairs, and Dad's old writing desk with the wonky drop board. 'I want old things around me.' And she defiantly plonked her faded burgundy Carlton Ware vase with the gold trim that she was given as a wedding present on the too-big dining table. 'When you're eighty-three,' she added, 'you can do as you damn well please.'

I'd sighed with the automatic intolerance that children have for their parents and given in to her. Yet here I am, no different really. Grey-haired, like her. Surrounded by the past, like her. When did I stop desiring *new*? Sometimes I catch a fleeting image of a tall woman with a matronly bosom in a plate glass window. I do not recognise her until much later when I realise it is me, as I am now. Not as I still think of myself – a red-headed thirty-year-old with the strength of an ox.

The champagne cork pops – is there any sound so universally celebratory? Bob pours two glasses, hands me one.

'To us,' he says.

'To health,' I respond. To me, *us* is a given.

'Garlic and lemon prawns, with a hint of chili. Pasta. Salad. That suit you?'

'Yep.'

Without fail, Bob tells me, I have *never* kept to a food plan. By lunchtime, the menu has changed at least three times. By dinner, it's anybody's guess. So he nods in agreement to every suggestion at every stage of the day. I mentioned snails once, hoping to trick him into a debate, but his eyes lit up enthusiastically. 'With lots of garlic butter?'

'You don't *like* snails, do you?' I asked in disbelief.

'Love 'em.'

'Well bad luck, there aren't any.'

'What about the garlic butter? Can we have that? It's the best bit.' And I love the way he plays the game.

Water boils for the pasta. Steam rises to the ceiling then drops like sweat. Or rain. Summer in Sydney: clammy skin, slippery legs, clothes clinging wetly. The humidity is suffocating. No rain, though. None that counts anyway. Just a light drizzle when the dogs swam from Scotland Island to Church Point in the Christmas Eve race. But the clouds drifted away, as though it was too much effort to perform.

When dinner's ready, we turn off the lights in an attempt to lure buzzing Christmas beetles, suicidal moths and flying insects out of the house and back into the bush. It's too late for the termites. Thousands of their fragile dismembered wings make the floorboards shimmer like shiny fabric.

'Music?' asks Bob.

'Nah. Clash with the rhythm of the crickets.'

'Thought about next year?'

And it is peculiar to think it is only a few hours away. Like my mother, I have always loathed the fanfare of New Year's Eve, the pressure to party. It is, after all, only another day. But rituals stick, even after they have lost their meaning.

'Nope. Not much. Have you?'

Bob coils linguine on a fork, the wine and butter sauce dripping from the pasta. The seaweedy smell of seared prawns lolls in the air with the nutty scent of garlic. 'Everything seems to be heading in the right direction,' he says finally.

Bob mops the dregs of the sauce with a piece of bread. When he finishes, I pick up our empty plates and take them into the kitchen.

'There's dessert,' I call out, when I hear him getting up to help clear the table. 'Stay where you are.'

It was too hot to go shopping for supplies, so dessert, like our main course, is made out of ingredients from freezer and pantry staples. Another sign I'm slowing down – or perhaps simply shifting priorities. Once, nothing short of an earthquake would have stopped me from slogging around Mona Vale in search of fresh produce. Today it's mixed (frozen) berries cooked in a friend's homemade cranberry sauce (pantry) then poured over small cubes of brioche (freezer). On top, I've piled a heart attack amount of heavy cream lashed with honey melted with a whisky liqueur called Glayva.

I stack the dishwasher, swizzle the kitchen, return to the verandah with dessert. Bob looks at the bowl. A slightly anguished sigh escapes him.

'Cream's good for you,' I insist. 'Makes you feel decadent . . . and daring.'

He sighs again and lifts his spoon. The crickets hush so suddenly it takes a few moments to hear the quiet. At the water's edge, the blur of high humidity hovers like misty rain. Yellow lights come on in houses on the other side of the bay, reflections stretching from shore to shore like golden legs. Spotted gums, one hundred feet tall and rampant with green, brown and gold in the sun, turn flat black, as one-dimensional as cardboard cutouts. Behind them, undulating hills fade to blankness against a deepening sky.

We sit, mostly silent, until it's midnight. Candlelight catches the crystal, shooting sparks of celebration. Bob reaches into the ice bucket and refills our glasses. We clink.

'Happy New Year,' we murmur.

New Year's Day is hotter still, a suffocating forty-six degrees. Lovett Bay looks limp: flat water, flat colours, nothing stirring. Not even a seagull.

'Fleury should cancel her lunch,' I call to Bob from the bathroom where I'm standing under a cold shower. 'It's too hot to eat.'

'Fleury won't cancel. It's a tradition. She might feel it's giving in – or up.'

I sigh, turn off the water. Wish I could skip underwear. Once, I would have. Why do I feel I'm too old to go without knickers? It's not as though anyone will know. The uninvited and unavoidable boundaries of late middle-age?

'Chippy, let's go! Chippy?' No response, not even a yap. I find her lying on her back on the sofa, legs sticking straight up, her freckled pink belly exposed to the world. No middle-aged modesty here. Her brown eyes slide around to look at me, but she doesn't move.

'Want to come and visit your friend Bailey around in Towlers Bay?' She loves Bailey, the hip-wiggling, good-willed but extremely dumb golden retriever most of us call Brittany behind Fleury's back. But Chippy still doesn't move.

'Let's go!' I say again. She sighs loudly, stretches. Lets me strap on her harness, topples to the floor, too sapped by the heat to jump.

The tinny feels hot enough to fry an egg. We push through glutinous water, air thick as custard. Sweat streams down my back like a personal waterfall. A dreaded hot flush rips up from my toes. *Pins and needles. Anxiety. The sky is about to fall. The world is ending.* The urge to strip off and slide naked into the water is overwhelming. Will they never cease, these cruel reminders of the relentless march of time? Two years or ten years, the doctor told me. I mentally gave my body two years but it's ignored me. Five years down. Five to go.

Woody Point is flattened by the heat. The smell of baking earth drifts towards us, biscuit dry. We slow the boat and glide alongside another boat at the dock.

'Happy New Year!' we shout, but not loudly. It's too damn hot. We loosely tie up, clamber over the other boat.

'Bugger!' I yell as Chip Chop takes off, slipping out of her harness. I've got a leg in both boats and they're drifting apart.

'Christ,' Bob explodes. 'Here, give me the peaches.'

Bringing dessert is another tradition. Fleury cooks the main course on New Year's Day and I do a pudding. Sometimes I get it right, sometimes guests are very polite. I made some apricot cupcakes once. They were harder than bullets but no-one said a word and everyone ate them – a true measure of friendship on Pittwater.

This time, the peaches are poached almost to the point of collapse in rosé and sugar. Made a mango and Galliano sauce and a raspberry coulis to go on top. Red and yellow. A sprig of mint in the middle. Looks like a Christmas bauble. Overdone, as usual.

Bailey wades into the water but Chip Chop hangs back. She's not a good swimmer. Nearly drowned once when she leapt off the pink water taxi at Commuter Dock. Frightened she might be left behind, she jumped too early, missed the dock by about three feet and quietly sank, her eyes wide open with shock and fear under the water. I was about to jump in when Bob pushed me back. He leapt over three tinnies and scooped her up, wet but unharmed.

'Didn't want to have to rescue you, too,' Bob muttered, handing me a soggy dog. We were driving to Melbourne that day, to visit Bob's children. The car stank of wet wool all the way.

At lunch, Fleury brings out a huge baked ham, glistening in an orange and mustard sauce. Blackened at the edges, it looks luscious, but it's hard to want food. It's so burning hot on the deck that even the red wine in our glasses starts to fizz.

'Never seen this before,' says Tim, a guest, looking at the pink froth. 'It must be scorching!'

Fleury, typically, pretends it's just another Pittwater lunch. She's elegant in black with a little gold necklace and earrings. Though her red hair is damp around her forehead, it's smooth and sleek. Of all of us, she is the only one who still struggles against the lure of clothes that conform to our figures instead of fashion.

Towlers Bay is filled with yachts, like a private pleasure navy, sleek white hulls, furled sails and gleaming woodwork. Each year, the boats seem to be bigger – almost ships, some of them, with three or four storeys and good-looking blokes in clean white uniforms to touch the switch to raise and lower the anchor. Or just to hang out on the bow like young gods.

From Fleury's house we can see people rolling off decks into the water. It's too fervid even to jump. Every so often, the sound of laughter floats across to us. Idyllic, I think. This is all so idyllic, heat or no heat. And with that thought comes a niggling sensation of unease. It erupts out of nothing except a languid thought that while *traditions* are the comfortable fabric encasing our lives, there is something chilling when they become the sole focus.

After lunch, we return home to singed agapanthus leaves and a bush that's so flattened by the heat it looks weirdly empty. The landscape is almost white, like it's been bleached. Eerie. Perhaps that is why, I think, I'm filled with unease. This is an unnatural, end of the world kind of heat.

'What's on tomorrow?' I ask Bob as I ask without fail every night.

I watch his face as he replies. It is disengaged. He yawns, takes his time replying. Yes, he has plenty to do each day. So do I. Yes, neither of us is ever bored. But where are the challenges? For so long, I dreamed of the moment when the struggle would be over and now that it is, am I missing it?

~

A few weeks later I look at Bob over a plate of paella. An explosion of pinks – prawns, chorizo, rice cooked in broth and tomatoes. The scent of smoked paprika hovers over the pan like a campfire.

Bob looks at the food intently. It's more exotic than usual for a middle of the week night. He realises something's brewing but can't think what.

'If you open the conversation with "*Now, darling*", I'll know I'm in trouble,' he says finally, but his eyes are laughing.

'Remember that rug we bought for the bedroom floor? The one that looks like a blast of colour, with the initials of the weaver on it?' I bought it after a midnight dash to the bathroom across icy floorboards. When you live on the water, you often forget the sting of winter.

'Ye-e-s.'

'You ever feel curious about her, what she's like, how she lives?'

He is silent, pushing around the rice until he exposes a prawn. He spears it and puts it in his mouth, chewing slowly.

'Should I be?' he asks eventually.

'No, not necessarily. But I was curious. Tracked her down through the rug seller. She lives in a small village in Turkey. Thought it might be interesting to visit her, learn more about rug weaving, have a holiday at the same time.'

As I say it, I realise it is only part of the truth. I am restless, filled with vague yearnings. Sometimes, on days when there's nothing to disturb the still green waters except the shadow of a sea eagle soaring overhead, I am filled with needless anxiety. My mother would say I am feeling like I'm in a rut. Maybe. But now that I no longer trek to an office each day, I have the luxury of my own time. I want to learn, explore, be stimulated beyond my own world . . . even if it's only to reassure myself that I am still a long way off placing the fluffy slippers neatly by the side of the bed. Where will the challenges come from, I wonder, if we don't look for them ourselves? Am I drifting dreamily in nirvana and letting my world shrink and even slip by unmarked?

I say none of this, though, as Bob takes another mouthful, because I realise I will sound spoilt and ungrateful. There was a time, after all, when simply breathing was gift enough.

'How much money's in the holiday fund?' he asks.

There's a tin bowl on top of the fridge. Any small change lying about is flung into it. At one stage, I am so enthusiastic about collecting coins, Bob says a newspaper costs him $5 because when he hands over a banknote, I scoop up the change. Eventually, of course, he gets me to buy the papers.

'I'll count it after dinner,' I reply, smiling. He and I both know trekking from one side of the world to the other in search of a weaver is nothing but whimsy. Just as we also know that the real reason for the trip is to break routine, rattle our comfort zones. And even, perhaps, because we know that one day, travel will be beyond us.

'Thank you,' I add. Because I understand he's doing it for me when he'd probably prefer a new sail.

'We're off to Turkey. On a holiday,' I tell my mother when I arrive to pick her up to go shopping. 'Be away for two months.'

She is suddenly forlorn on the pink granny sofa. Her face closes down as though she's just learned of a terrible death.

'Lisa's offered to run you around to do your errands while we're away. Or do them for you, if you'd rather. You'll be ok.'

'We need to have a serious talk,' she replies.

My heart sinks. I can feel the Sarah Bernhardt side of my mother's personality is about to take over. Or am I being unkind? I haven't left her for more than a couple of days since she moved closer to me. Disappearing on her for so long must make her feel vulnerable.

'Ok, what about? Shall we chat in the car?'

'No, this is serious. Sit down.' She leans forward, resting her elbows on her knees.

'I'm getting old,' she begins.

'No you're not. You are old. I'm getting old.'

'Just be quiet and listen.'

I sit on one of the recliner chairs, cross my legs.

'I want to know what will happen if I die while you're away,' she says, spinning the rings on her fingers and looking out the window.

'We'll make sure you're put in the fridge until we get back for the funeral. Is that all? Can we go?' It's a clumsy attempt to make her laugh. It doesn't work, but this is all about manipulation and I won't let her get away with it. Not anymore.

'No. It's not all. Stop trying to rush me. I haven't finished. What kind of a funeral will you have?'

'What kind would you like?'

'Church of England. None of the non-religious stuff. I've always believed in God.'

'Done! Now can we go?'

'I haven't got anywhere to be buried. I bought a plot next to your father but the time limit's expired. I only had a twenty-year option.' I add up the figures. She's about twelve years overdue.

'Well, we'll find you a nice sunny plot somewhere.'

But I'm surprised she bought a plot next to my father. My mother was over him before they even married. Told me she grabbed Dad on the rebound, married him to hurt someone who let her down. In those days, though, divorce made you socially unacceptable. Better the devil you know, she often told me, than the devil you don't. As if *everyone* was a devil, just to varying degrees.

'I don't want to be buried anymore, anyway. I want to be cremated,' she says firmly.

'That's fine. No problems. Consider it done.' I stand up, smooth my jeans, ready to go.

'Sit down, I haven't finished.'

Her face is severe, with the no-nonsense look in her eyes I remember so well from my childhood. I sigh, fall back into the recliner, cross my legs. Again.

'Where will you scatter the ashes?'

'I don't know.' I'm flummoxed. This is a new question in an old routine. 'Lovett Bay?'

'You can't throw me in Lovett Bay,' she snaps. 'There are too many people scattered there already.'

And I cannot think of a single thing to say until much later when I wish I'd made a crack about how she wouldn't have to travel far to haunt me if we tipped her in the bay.

14

WHEN I FIRST TRAVELLED to Turkey thirty-five years ago, it was raw and tribal. I joined throngs of skinny hippies with hennaed hair and heavily kohled eyes trekking overland from London to Katmandu. We thought we were on a search for our souls – or at the very least, the meaning of life. I know now that we were just delaying climbing on the treadmill, putting off the dastardly business of growing up.

On that first visit, I was young and broke enough to be beguiled by any place where I could afford to eat more than once a day. Turkey was one of them. I left London, where I'd been working as a (very bad) temporary typist at a time when the swinging sixties had spilled well into the seventies. Turkey was like stepping into a different century. Small villages were often primitive, and sometimes men spat at us if we exposed our arms or legs. This was not a land rocking with flower power and free love.

But Istanbul, a small city of narrow streets and swarms of bone-thin men bent almost double from the loads they carried on their backs, was mostly tolerant. And cheap. For a dollar or so, we could loll for hours on gaily woven cushions around knee-high tables, eating small plates of deliciously spiced vegetables. Drawing in cool, apple-scented smoke from water pipes. Sipping sooty black coffee. It was exotic, intoxicating.

That is what I want Bob to see. Perhaps I am hoping he will get a glimpse of the way I was. Which is impossible, of course. The clock only ever goes one way.

The skyline of Istanbul is pierced by minarets and tides of domes swelling like waves. There are rug shops everywhere. Windows throb with colour, bold and unapologetic. I suspect *neutral* is not a familiar theme here.

Excitement takes the edge off jetlag. We're in a new world and it stirs the instinct to wonder, the desire to be inquisitive. Is curiosity the real key to eternal youth?

'I feel like lounging around on red and gold velvet divans and smoking water pipes. Do you?'

Bob looks at me. 'You'd want to have a cuppa tea first, wouldn't you?'

I lean across and kiss him hard. 'Darling, this is the *land* of cups of tea. You will be in heaven.' I'll mention that it comes in delicate little tulip shaped glasses, not large mugs, later.

In our cramped hotel room, mustiness wafts out of closets and the window looks onto a light well, but the shower is hot and hard and the bed firm. The owner of our hotel, a bearish, chain-smoking Bulgarian with a buzz-cut, hangs around the foyer all day with the hotel's breathy resident singer who I suspect is also his mistress. She sits for hours in the one place, stroking her Siamese cat, Sheba. Her English is perfect. She learned it from songs, she explains, reaching always for another cigarette. It's a skill, I decide, to be able to hang about doing absolutely nothing.

'Join us!' shouts the hotel-keeper when Bob and I return, map in hand, from our first walk through the old city. A giant, shiny black cake with baby pink icing waits on the coffee table. It is the singer's birthday, he explains, through curling clouds of smoke. We must accept, he insists, or how will we ever understand the meaning of Turkish hospitality? The chef and waiter stand alongside the cake. Where are her friends, or do mistresses give up everything when they choose the murky world of the illegitimate?

On our first night, we splurge what seems like most of the 'holiday fund' on a Turkish feast at a restaurant recommended by the hotel-keeper. He gives us directions verbally and hands us a piece of paper with the address. 'It's genuine Mediterranean food,' he insists. 'Very fresh. Very good. Not like kebabs you will get if you go to restaurants for tourists.'

We follow his directions down dark laneways. Boys play soccer in the fading light. Gossiping women wearing long grey coats and black headscarves hover in doorways. A mangy cat pounces, traps a squealing rat. Bob and I stare, then look away. We walk on, searching for the address on our piece of paper, but there are no numbers and only one streetlight which casts a small, weak yellow pool. Eventually, we hold the paper out to show one of the boys. He looks at it, scratching his head. We mime eating. 'Ah!' He nods, pointing behind us. We are standing at the back of the building. We need to walk around to the front.

The restaurant shimmers. Gold tassels on cushions, tablecloths, window sashes – even carafes of water. Little boys in bow ties, girls in lacy dresses. The delicious smell of garlic.

'How good is this?'

Bob nods. Plate after plate of small tastes of Turkish cuisine come steadily from the kitchen. He is game for any dish and plunges in while I hang back. My old country kid nervousness around strange food kicks in.

'You're not very adventurous for a foodie,' he says.

'I've always been a lamb chop, mashed potatoes and peas girl at heart.'

'Never can understand why you'll cook food for people that you don't like to eat yourself.'

'I grew up in a country pub where it was steak, chops, steak and kidney pie, or a roast. Made me suspicious about anything different. I've come a long way, considering.'

'Try this,' he says, putting a tiny piece of cured salmon on his fork. I hesitate, then bite. It is smooth and tender, almost sweet. He cuts a long, curling octopus tentacle, charcoal-grilled to blackness, offers it.

I hold up my hands. 'No. Looks too close to the real thing. I'll hit the vegetables.'

Butter beans in dill cream, eggplant, zucchini, tomatoes, cucumbers and spoonfuls of satin smooth yoghurt. Mint, tarragon and dill lift the mundane to exotic heights. Herbs on top of herbs, mixed in ways I wouldn't dream of.

'Gotta get a Turkish cookbook. This is really wonderful food.'

Later, out of the warmth and crowd of the restaurant, the streets are empty, the shadowy light unnerving. Only the cats remain – ginger, black, tabby. So many ginger cats. They are furtive, like thieves, and slink off into black spaces as we approach. Everything looks different. Is this the way? Or perhaps that? There's a tingle of fear. What was it the guide book said about muggers? Bob holds my hand tightly, smiles at me and swings my arm like we're teenagers, killing my dread. This kind of loving, when you are wise enough to understand each other's frailties, when you learn to match one person's weakness to another's strength, is the very best.

'Tomorrow,' he says, still swinging my arm, 'Gallipoli!'

He skips a couple of steps, his face smooth and young in the stifled light. It is almost 25 April, Anzac Day, when Australians remember the dead at the Battle of Gallipoli in 1915. It was his only request when we began our holiday planning. Small enough, considering his interest in my weaver is minimal.

It's barely light and still very cold. Our bus to Gallipoli can't make it around the narrow Istanbul streets. The guide leads us three blocks to where it is parked. We carry our bags. Packed too much, but the seasons will change from late spring to summer while we are here, which means warm clothes as well as light ones. The bags get heavier with every block.

'The traffic will be bad,' the guide explains. 'We need to get out of the city before it reaches peak.'

On the bus we drift for five hours along the blue and gold shores of the Sea of Marmara. Houses, fields, trucks passing on the way to Greece. We doze, warm in the bus. Lunch is kebab and pide (grilled meat on a skewer and flat bread) and a glass of ayran – a thick, slightly sour yoghurt drink – in a seaside café at Eceabat. Here, the wind is so cold and fierce we sit inside, huddled in jackets and scarves.

'Thought the weather would be warmer,' we tell our guide, but not as a complaint.

'In Turkey, we say now is the time to dress like cabbages,' she tells us with a smile. 'Layer by layer. So you can peel each one off as the day grows warmer.' Her name is Yasmin and her hair is cropped into triangles so it looks like a black pixie hat. She smokes from the moment we step off the bus until we climb back on board. And she has a wicked hangover.

'Thought drinking was a no-no in your culture,' I remark, hoping I don't sound like a censorious old woman.

'It is,' she replies and laughs loudly. She is studying English at university, guiding and doing translations to pay her way. Drinking is a way of life, she tells us, for students. A way of rebelling against their parents, authority, politics, religion.

'My generation was no different,' I tell her, watching her eyes widen in disbelief. 'We burned our bras, marched for women's liberation. Every generation rebels. I think it's programmed into us biologically.' But she finds it hard to believe, looking at my whitening hair and sensible walking shoes.

At the Gallipoli Peninsula, the tweed hills are bleak and disturbing, the wind still ferocious. We tread the narrow, pebbly beach at Anzac Cove. So much death. So many cemeteries. The futility of it all. Who died in this trench, now crumbling and empty? Who played cricket on this beach while shrapnel and bullets whined overhead? Who stood where I am standing? What did he talk about? What were his hopes and dreams? Did he survive or is he lying under a simple white headstone with a wrenching epitaph. 'Rest, my son, rest', says one, as though a mother cannot bear the thought of death and chooses instead to believe her son is merely sleeping. For eternity. Whose sons, whose husbands, whose brothers? I knew none of them, but the ache of loss comes pounding back.

Only a few days earlier, though it already seems a lifetime ago, as we left Church Point for the airport, Marg from Little Lovett Bay rushed up and grabbed my arm: 'See if you can find a razor case I donated to the museum at Gallipoli, will you? I sent it to a lovely man a few years ago, who drove me there from Istanbul, in his taxi. He said he'd pass it on.'

I nodded. Not a chance in a million is what I thought, though. Then, suddenly, there it is in the small Kapatepe Museum, amongst the relics and the frail reminders of daily life in the trenches – rusted nail scissors, a battered Players cigarette tin, broken pieces of pipes: 'This razor case was made by Corporal Albert Bassnett in April 1915, doneted [sic] by the Molley family on behalf of Sergeant Tom Molley 1st AIF (Australia) who served with him on the Peninsula throughout the Gallipoli Campaign April–December 1915'. Only the name is spelled wrong. It should read 'Molloy'.

Tom was my neighbour's husband. How casually I'd fielded her request, not even bothering to ask why she would donate something to a faraway museum. Bob photographs the exhibit. 'She will be pleased,' I say. But I'm ashamed at my offhandedness with her.

After a few hours' rest in a hotel in a distant town we return to Gallipoli for the dawn service. Trudging for an hour and a half under a full moon along a dirt track, past silent, humble shacks with small flocks of sheep tucked into front yards. Every shadow feels like an echo of the past.

At Anzac Cove, the chill ground is lumpy with bodies, sitting, lying, sleeping, dreaming. Spotlights scour the night sky like air-raid lights from World War II. It looks more like the site for a rock concert than a memorial service. Giant television screens show old videos of the Bee Gees, Olivia Newton-John . . . There's scaffolding, cameras on cranes, long lines of Portaloos. But the atmosphere is strangely quiet, the crowd subdued and polite.

'Hard to find a spot to sit.'

Nearly everyone is so young. Why are they here? They have no experience of war, or even – hopefully – of loss. We throw down our plastic groundsheets bought in a nearby village, squeeze in between groups of prostrate bodies. Soon, we lie like everyone else. A young woman with flaming red hair sleeps with her head on my thigh.

Nearly five hours to dawn. When the redhead gets up and goes for a walk to get her blood circulating, a young Turkish woman and her husband mutely offer to share their blanket. We smile at each other and make room for them on our groundsheet. Within minutes we are all warmer.

As the light turns to a lemony blush, we struggle to our feet, stiff-limbed and numb, faces red raw with the cold. But it is not the finely honed words of the politicians that move, nor the prayers, although where there is death, ritual is always a comfort. Some inner core shifts when I see the Australian destroyer, HMAS

Anzac, in the distance, a simple red kangaroo painted on its funnel. It triggers a yearning for a landscape of gum trees, for the peppery smell of scorched earth on a westerly wind, for a clean blue sky. An ache for everything deeply, intrinsically Australian. For Pittwater. For home. In the orange glow of sunrise, a lone bugler in a slouch hat with a scarlet band plays 'The Last Post', and I think of Lovett Bay and our simple service at Church Point.

'Feel like crying.'

'You *are* crying,' Bob replies. And his eyes, too, are filled with tears.

We cross the Dardanelles by ferry later in the day. My body is screaming with tiredness. Once I could go without sleep for forty-eight hours, adrenalin pumping, and still function. Now I feel the strobing threads of a migraine. I tell my body to behave but it refuses to listen. Does this mean that I have to shift the goalposts? Keep reducing the distances to the touchline? Is every year going to mean being less and less capable?

I glance at Bob, who looks like he's had a ten-hour sleep on a feather mattress, and wonder at the biology of men and women. I close my eyes. All I want to do is lie down. For a moment, I am filled with the same old regrets. Regrets that so many years slipped by without me taking note of the great moments. Regrets that I failed to understand the effortlessness of youth until it began to slip away from me. Regrets that I didn't cram in more. Regrets that I wasn't more useful when it would have cost so little. A ping of regret for the old times, because when you are past fifty, they truly are the *old* times.

Then I slam back the ball of self-pity. I force myself to remember, again, the day I sat on a cracked leather chair in a fluoro-lit office and had a weary but decent doctor tell me that

I had cancer. After that kind of wake-up call, life in any form is a gift – young, old, ancient. My mother insists these are the most contented years of her life, perhaps because her countdown is speeding along and only a fool would squander what is left in a mire of bitter regret.

'Here,' says Bob. He holds a glass of hot tea and two painkillers. Thank you, I think, for not making me feel like a liability. But I know I have changed enormously from the woman of even five years ago.

When I was young and tired I could always find some inner reserve. Now when I am tired and I search for the spare tank, it isn't there. I get furious, furious that my body makes decisions without consulting *me*. Furious that I cannot control the where or when of a migraine, a hot flush, fatigue. Furious that menopause has changed my entire bodily frame of reference.

'So what do you want to do?' Bob asks. 'Give up everything? Give up living? Just exist?'

'It's you I worry about. You just keep going and going. I'm always holding you back.'

He grins then, and his big capable hand reaches for mine. 'Don't worry about it. We're a team. I paddle hard too. I just hide it better.'

He leads me to a bench, makes me lie down with my head in his lap. How did I get so shockingly lucky?

We wind through an almost biblical countryside. Dry stone fences, fields spotted with red poppies, hills carpeted with chamomile, campanula and wild geranium. Women sell olives and wild pistachios along the roadside, men guide horse-drawn ploughs. Shepherds, cigarettes dripping from bottom lips, ride sturdy brown donkeys or trudge the tracks, crook in hand, with flocks of well-mannered fat-tailed sheep. Once or twice there is the tender sight of a young man gently nursing newborn lambs still slick with afterbirth.

About an hour inland from the icy Aegean Sea and not far from the ragged urban sprawl of a town called Ayvacik, we turn towards the red-tiled roofs of an untidy, ramshackle village perched on a rocky hillside, a town so high and quiet, the song of night-ingales ripples clearly. Only the sound of our feet treading the rocky ground sounds discord.

As we walk towards the village square, where we will learn about vegetable dying and rug weaving, dirty white geese eye us suspiciously. Sharp-eyed chooks stab the dusty ground and cats, dozens of them, laze in thin sunlight, watchful and unmoving. The narrow streets are pungent with the smell of cow dung. Piles of compost, taller than a man, wait in lanes to be spread over freshly planted vegetable gardens.

In shaded corners women, their hair covered and wearing floral trousers, sit in doorways on the street, rolling creamy wool between tanned, callused fingers, or crocheting delicate white lace. They smile shyly as we pass, but do not speak. At the tea house, cloth-capped men with five o'clock shadows slouch under a fruiting mulberry tree, drinking weak black tea from tulip-shaped glasses, playing backgammon.

My weaver, when we meet her, is not the firebrand of my imagination. She is a short, plump, cheery-faced 45-year-old mother of two, with a couple of cows, forty sheep and a much treasured new calf. She also has the commercial instincts of a shark. Within five minutes of being invited into her home, she produces a few crocheted borders she wants to sell.

'How much?' I ask, expecting to pay about five dollars.

'Fifty lira [about $50],' she replies promptly, knowing she has me. And I laugh as I pay because I like her toughness, her instinctive ability to seize an opportunity. Doesn't matter if you can read or write, to survive is what it's all about.

'What are your dreams?' I ask when we are ready to leave. Because I am curious. Is acceptance of age-old tradition the key to happiness?

She thinks for a while, taking the question very seriously. Then she slides her arm around my waist as though we have always been friends. A new dress for her daughter, she says eventually, because there is a wedding soon. She is hoping her Emine will catch the eye of a suitable young man.

And that, it turns out, is the reason for the huge price for the crocheted borders. The money will buy fountains of fabulous fabric for Emine, a stocky, rosy-cheeked young girl with the light of desire in her eyes. Shades of my own mother, I think, who dressed me in frills and, once, a petticoat so rigidly hooped that when I sat down my skirt reared up in front of my face. It was at a kids' party and I can still hear the laugher. It's probably why I have always preferred wearing trousers.

Later, Bob and I walk into a forest of elegant pines. Rugs and more rugs, masses of them, are tossed casually on the ground. Cushions are scattered amongst beaten silver tables on wooden bases loaded with plates and glasses. We kick off our shoes and run like kids across the velvet softness of red, blue, gold and purple.

'Kings used to live like this,' says Bob, his face full of excitement. It is pure fantasy. Only the camels are missing.

'There's a tree over there,' Bob adds, pointing away from our carpeted picnic ground. 'I'm told it's called an erik tree. If you tie a ribbon on it, you can make a wish.'

'I can't think of anything to wish for.'

'That's good,' he says, his face serious.

We sleep that night on a homemade mattress filled with cotton in the garden of the village headman. A doona stuffed with wool, thick and toasty over us, we drift off. When it is late, a low whine creeps up the valley. Then the wind blows. Little green plums, hard as bullets, pelt our heads and caterpillars, squishy and sticky, fall on our faces. Dust gets into our ears and we snuggle deeper as the wind builds to a gale. Rugs set out for us to look at fly everywhere. Sleep is impossible.

'Do you think kings had to deal with weather?' I whisper.

'Everyone has to deal with weather.'

We wait for dawn and this is magic.

We continue our journey for another six weeks, riding local buses, getting stranded by roadsides, holding our breath around hairpin bends with sheer drops to the sea below. Then our credit card is stolen from us in a scam of breathtaking finesse. After dinner one night, we are mellow, not concentrating.

'There's an ATM. Should we get some cash?'

We are in a tourist area, which means there's a chance the ATM directions will come up in English. Bob puts his card in the machine. A young man hovers behind us. He's scruffy, in dirty clothes and when he smiles, his teeth are black with decay. I smile back but inch closer to Bob, uneasy. The directions on the ATM come up in Turkish.

'Let's wait till the morning,' I say.

Suddenly, the man behind us snatches the card from Bob as he's putting it in his wallet.

'Hey!' Bob shouts, grabbing him. The man smiles again and slips the card into the machine and brings up the directions in English. Ah, we think, Turkish kindness.

'Thank you,' we say, smiling. He shrugs as if it is nothing and walks away.

Bob punches the keys. Nothing happens.

'Bugger it,' he says, slipping the card into his wallet, 'let's do this tomorrow.'

But he's puzzled. Something makes him pull out his card again.

For a moment, he looks confused. The card is a Japanese credit card. Then we realise what's happened. Our hotel is just a few doors away so we run in and call up our account on the internet. The hotel staff try to phone MasterCard to cancel our account. While the phone number remains engaged, we watch the purchases made by our thief tally up on the screen.

'Let's go home,' I mutter to Bob as we lie in bed later that night. I feel violated, betrayed.

'Don't be so silly,' he says. 'It's only money. No-one got hurt.'

He's right but it takes me days to let it go. I have seen a million scams in decades of travelling. I should have twigged.

'So should I!' Bob says when I chastise myself once again. 'It's not just you, you know,' he adds. 'I wasn't concentrating.'

We travel on, stumbling over the remains of long-dead civilisations: sarcophagi in main streets, Roman columns used as bases for café tables, tombs cut into hillsides that cast the uneasy shadow of our own mortality.

I get mean with money and insist we stay in cheaper and cheaper accommodation until Bob complains: 'The noise is terrible, the bathroom is dirty, there's no hot water. Why do you want to punish yourself like this?'

Because I was stupid, I want to scream. Because I am frightened I am getting old and silly and that the next time I fail to be vigilant something bad might happen. What I really mean, though, is that my confidence is shattered.

In Ankara, the capital city of Turkey, Bob chooses a bed-and-breakfast in the crammed and crumbling old part of the city, away from concrete footpaths and office buildings. Our cab driver gets lost amongst narrow, nameless streets. I feel the anger of fear and a tingle of shame when I suggest heading downtown where the hotel staff will certainly speak English. I am not so intrepid anymore. I have stepped over the line separating traveller from tourist. I want each day to be easy. Challenges are wearing me down.

'Let's give it five more minutes,' Bob says.

The driver calls to a bunch of black-eyed kids playing soccer in the street. They point to a high wall about fifty yards away in a lane too skinny for even one car to pass through. The driver gets out. He disappears inside a door. A few minutes later, he returns with the hotel-keeper.

'Come,' says our host in perfect English. 'You need tea. And maybe a little pastry.'

Yes, I think with relief. That's exactly what we need. He shouts to the kids, who run over and grab our bags. He leads the way into a richly coloured haven where the floors are covered with dozens of quite small but utterly exquisite old carpets and every bedroom is a sumptuous suite.

'It's glorious, Bob. Quite glorious.'

'Are we done, then, with doing it rough?'

'Yes. Oh yes.'

'How was it, mate?' asks Toby when we return to Pittwater. There's a mug of coffee in his hand. It's the beginning of winter but he's still in shorts, with a blue flannel shirt. Heavy socks, too, under his dusty work boots. His partner Dave is already sitting at one of the picnic tables at The Point, coffee steaming in front of him, newspaper opened to the sports pages. The voluptuous *Laurel Mae* is tied up at the end of the ferry wharf.

Dave smiles his angelic smile. He's a hellraiser, though, if he's in the mood. Toby, too. But they never lose their manners, no matter how late it gets.

'Welcome home,' Dave says. 'Have a good time?'

'It was fantastic!' we reply. 'But it's good to be home.'

Pittwater is golden in the early morning light. Church Point looks polished, details are sharp. Being away makes it new. Tinnies rock on the waves and dogs sniff around. The old *Curlew* drops off a boatload of bleary-eyed commuters, her navy body hanging ever lower in the water. The ferry driver yells at Toby to move the *Laurel Mae* from the ferry wharf to the cargo wharf.

'Right, mate, just picking up a coffee,' Toby calls back, cheerfully, waving his styrofoam cup.

Phil, who drives the water taxi, zips into the store to warm his hands on the coffee machine. He's finishing the night shift and is frigid after sleeping on the sofa on the houseboat that's head office. It's moored at the mouth of McCarrs Creek, like a pink mother ship for the small fleet of pink water taxis.

'How was it? How was it?' we are asked over and over, as though we have returned to family.

'We're gonna make a Turkish dinner. We'll call you,' we promise, loading our stuff onto the water taxi, anxious now to complete the final lap.

'Any rain?' Bob asks Phil as the water taxi swings away from the ferry wharf.

'No. Not a drop. Think it's forgotten how.'

Behind us, the boat's white wake, a symbol of separation from one world to another, plumes out. Home.

During the next couple of weeks, it is the tough moments we recall and laugh about.

15

'MIGHT GO AND VISIT Pia in Brunswick Heads. Talk to that person Zeny Edwards suggested – Robert Riddel,' I tell Bob when we are well back into our routines at home and the old question about *Tarrangaua*'s architect begins to niggle again. After meandering through ancient Turkey where anything less than one thousand years old is considered new, it seems absurd that a detail from less than one hundred years ago could be so elusive.

'Might come with you. Not much on at the moment,' he replies.

At Brunswick Heads, Pia has a new project underway. She has sold her house and bought a block of land in the heart of town to expand her wonderfully eclectic shop, Secondhand Rose Emporium.

'You're a property developer,' I say enthusiastically when we meet.

'Hardly. Just a couple of shops and an apartment,' she explains, as though it's nothing. But it is everything. She is renting an upstairs flat next to the local service station until the building is finished. Not a typical choice for a woman with a glamorous past.

'It's all I need,' she says, unlocking the front door. 'Prefer everything simple these days.'

Inside, of course, she has made it look beautiful despite the mustard carpet, which is a real achievement.

The next day Bob and I drive to Brisbane to meet the architect, Robert Riddel. He is a long, thin man in black jeans and a striped cotton shirt, wearing round black glasses and with a ponytail trailing down his back. He lives and works in a converted office building on the edge of the Brisbane CBD. He's kind to Chip Chop and lets her roam even though he must know she's going to shed bright white hairs all over the polished concrete floors, rugs and seventies retro furniture in his funky warehouse-style apartment.

'Could Dods have designed *Tarrangaua* for Dorothea Mackellar?' I ask as he puts his thesis on Dods on the table in front of me and opens it at a page marked with a yellow sticker.

'Well, they were in love, we know that much,' he says.

'What?' I am shaken out of my slouch.

'Yes. Haven't you read her diaries?'

'Years ago, when Bob and his first wife loaned them to me. I didn't find anything about a romance.'

'She wrote about Dods in code. It's all there. Have another look.'

He has an appointment downstairs in his office and leaves us. Bob gets up to take Chip Chop for a walk. I open the pages of his thesis and there it is, carefully culled from *I Love a Sunburnt Country: The Diaries of Dorothea Mackellar*, edited by Jyoti Brunsdon, published in 1990 by Angus & Robertson. The references to Dods are in bold type, translated from coded entries in the diaries, and refer to a time when Mackellar visited Queensland and stayed for a while with Dods and his wife Mary.

Thursday August 4 [1910] . . . Mrs D. [Dods' wife] went to bed early and he kept me up awfully late yarning. He's such a dear. It does make things really hard . . .

Tuesday, August 9 . . . He does like me, but he was very good driving home and I tried to help him and we succeeded! It will be alright now I think . . .

September 10 . . . Mrs D. has nerves, but I of all people and to her of all people ought to be patient.

Thursday, October 6 . . . R.S.D. [Dods] and I was very weak and I gave in without saying anything – but he knows I like him now and I'm glad in a very queer way.

There are more references but when Mackellar returns to Sydney, the references to Dods end. The following year, 1911, though, they begin again when Mackellar returns to Brisbane for the social season.

Wednesday, August 2 . . . R. [Dods] met me in Finneys and would insist on buying me stockings.

Tuesday, August 8 . . . Assembly Ball. Mrs Dods didn't go. Very good. Only stayed 8 dances, but loved each of them. It will be some time before I forget the drive home, but it's too long to write here! Only he was touching me and – I said I was rather a bad little girl, and it hurt him. We were both upset and it got much more serious . . .

The diary entries about Dods fade away over time. Was it really an affair? Or a light flirtation? Dods was married and Mackellar would never flout convention. Or would she? Some kinds of love know no reason and it means *Spinster* and all its dreaded connotations did not apply to her. Did she know, no matter how briefly or inappropriately, passion?

I flick through the pages of Riddel's thesis looking for similarities in the design of *Tarrangaua* and Dods' work. 'Front steps leading to an elevated verandah. Steep roof lines. Paned windows. Columns. Simplicity.' It was a reinterpretation of our colonial tradition. Many architects were following the style with slight, individual differences.

Hardy Wilson and Robin Dods, I also learn, were friends. Dods, who was thirteen years older than Wilson, encouraged the younger man in his quest to find a style of architecture that belonged uniquely to Australia. When Dods relocated his architectural practice to Sydney in 1913, the two men became even closer, moving in a small, cliquish circle founded on old money and powerful families – such as the Mackellar family. They went to the same art openings, functions and parties. It is inconceivable that Wilson somehow failed to meet Mackellar, inconceivable that she didn't at least discuss with him her desire to build a summer house on her *high, rough hill*.

'Do you really think Mackellar and Dods had an affair?' I ask Riddel as we leave.

'I doubt it was physical. But perhaps romantic?' He shrugs.

'The frustration of time gone by,' I say. 'Hard to find the facts. You're nearly always forced to make guesses. Hopefully well-informed, but guesses nevertheless.'

'That's why I did a thesis on Dods. He was an amazing architect and his buildings are being pulled down or altered beyond recognition. It seemed criminal to let his work fade to nothing.'

He opens the door to his office, where a client is waiting.

'Do *you* think Wilson designed *Tarrangaua*?' I ask again.

He closes the door, leans against it. 'That's what I've always been told and believed. And it looks right, although I've only seen pictures. I've never been inside.'

'Could Dods have had a hand in it – given the friendship or whatever between him and Mackellar? And even Wilson?'

'Maybe. When was the house built?'

'1925.'

'That makes it simple. Dods died in 1920.'

'Yeah, I know, but I've been told plans were often drawn up long before land titles exchanged hands.'

'Sounds like a long shot but you never know.'

'Yeah, right. Anyway, thanks for your time. Appreciate it enormously.'

'My wife and I spent a few months living at *Eryldene*,' he says, opening the door to his office again. 'I'd just returned from working in London and the Trust in charge of the property needed a caretaker.'

'What was it like?'

'Exquisite.'

'Your wife enjoy the experience?'

'Yes. I think so. She died of cancer, though. When she was thirty-two years old.'

'I'm so sorry.'

'Yeah, well. I know that you know what it's like. In time, you build a new life. In time.'

'Let's call in to say hello to the nun?' I suggest to Bob on the return drive to Pittwater. 'She might be able to fill in some gaps.'

We phone her and she says she's not busy so we pick her up from her home and drive into booming downtown Lorn, near Newcastle, for a sandwich and a cup of tea. The Buddhist nun, Adrienne, looks fit and well. She is less hesitant with almost no sight than my mother, who doesn't even need glasses.

'I cannot believe I am well into my eighties,' she says. 'Who would have thought I would still be alive?'

She was diagnosed with cancer in her early forties and told to get her affairs in order. Five years later, after sailing around the world with a temperamental skipper, she thought death was taking so long she might as well rejoin the world of work and resumed her nursing career. In her sixties, her eyesight began to fail and she was told there was no cure.

'All I really miss are books,' she says, sipping her tea and nibbling her sandwich in small bites, careful not to spill anything.

'Do you think Dorothea would have had an affair with Robin Dods?' I ask.

'Absolutely not!' she replies, outraged at the suggestion.

'But there are a lot of vaguely romantic references to him in code in her diaries.'

'She may have had a crush but she wouldn't have had an affair. She was terribly conscious of her social position and, to her, dignity was everything. No, no affair. No way.'

'What about the house? Do you think it was designed by Hardy Wilson?'

'Dorothea designed it herself. She was incredibly proud of it.'

I don't pursue the topic. Mackellar may have made changes and added personal touches, but she couldn't have sited the building or designed it. Every architect who ever walked into the house has sighed at its balance and grace, its presence and perfection. An overprotected little rich girl without training could not have created it. But Mackellar was astute about the power of money and she may have insisted on so many changes that Wilson, a man who was passionate about detail and impatient with difficult clients, might have walked away in disgust.

A couple of months later, I remember I have a phone number for Jyoti Brunsdon, the woman who researched Mackellar's diaries. It was given to me when Bob and I called in to the Gunnedah Tourist Information Centre and mentioned that we lived at *Tarrangaua*. Gunnedah, where Dorothea's father, Sir Charles Mackellar, once owned four large properties, has claimed the poet as its own and runs an annual poetry competition to encourage young writers.

'We're researching the history of the house,' I told the helpful young woman behind the desk, and she came up with a contact number. I sift through my old notebooks. There it is, in neat writing instead of my usual scrawl. After only a slight hesitation, I pick up the phone.

'Is that Yoti? Or Joti?' I ask, unable to pronounce her name.

'Joti,' she says. 'Yes. Speaking.'

I explain my search, and I hear her sigh.

'Dorothea Mackellar. It's quite a long time since I've thought of her,' she says.

We chat for a while about small things. I discover she loves books and each January she ritually sets aside time to air and dust every single one she owns. 'Books hold the key to so much,' she says. She teaches the flute for a living and although she's had a couple of health scares, she is well now, and life is good.

'I can't understand why there's not a single mention in her diaries about building *Tarrangaua*,' I say, broaching the subject at last. 'I know this is rude, but are you sure there aren't more diaries somewhere?'

'As sure as I can be. I went through every diary at the Mitchell Library. Every single page of every book. The reason there's no mention of the house, I suspect, is because by the time she built it, she'd stopped keeping a detailed record of her life. Her diaries noted appointments with doctors and dentists, days at the milliner or dressmaker. Not much else. Except that she felt poorly a lot of the time. Dorothea suffered from "nerves" and her father, a doctor, dosed her with opiates, which was accepted treatment. Later on, she became more than a social drinker.'

'You cracked the code and unravelled a romance with Robin Dods. Do you think they were lovers?'

'Good God, no. Dods was a man who flirted madly and he probably chased Dorothea but her closest friends told me she ran a mile from any bloke who went after her. Her allusions to romances were fairy stories. All in her imagination.'

'But Dods bought her silk stockings, dined with her in her bedroom . . .'

'There is no primary evidence they had an affair. He probably waltzed into her bedroom to cheer her up when she was ill. He was a notorious flirt and womaniser. Completely charming, witty and well-read. And Dorothea, for all her wealth, led a very repressed life. She was the only girl in the family and she was groomed to stay home to look after her parents in their old age. She was really quite an innocent about romance.'

One of my mother's sayings flashes through my mind: 'A son is a son until he takes a wife, a daughter is a daughter for the rest of her life.' In Mackellar's day, it was common practice to expect the youngest daughter to dedicate her life to caring for elderly parents. My mother's generation was the same. Her sister Belle, Uncle Frank's wife, looked after their parents. Deep down, no matter what she may say to the contrary, is that what my mother expects of me?

'I think the closest relationship Dorothea had was with the poet Ruth Bedford. In one of her diaries, there was an entry about the two of them acting out a scene in bed together. The next two pages had been ripped out. I've always wondered what was written on those pages. Nothing improper for the era, I'm sure, but she might have revealed her yearnings. Her deepest desires.'

'Maybe she knew someone would read the diaries one day. I wonder if she ever felt a twinge of discomfort when the accolades rolled in for "My Country"?'

'You mean the similarities between it and the Maybanke Anderson poem?'

'Yes. I've never seen any acknowledgement from her for Maybanke Anderson's inspiration.'

'The words were her own. She just wasn't original. It's hard to know how she could have been when she lived such a sheltered life.'

I think back to an exhibition of Van Gogh at the Louvre in Paris a few years ago when I was traipsing around the world as a travel writer for *The Australian Women's Weekly*. It was mounted to show how he'd been inspired by the works of an earlier artist, Jean François Millet (1814–1875). The subject matter and composition of peasants working in the fields of Normandy were almost the same and yet the works could never be confused. Each artist saw the scenes with individual eyes. At the time, I couldn't work out whether the exhibition was criticising or explaining Van Gogh's work. But aren't we all inspired by others? First by our parents then, if we are lucky, by our teachers. And if we are truly fortunate, by our partners.

I am curious about the diaries, wonder what it would feel like to thumb through their pages. I imagine boxes full of notebooks bound in leather and cracked with age, gathering dust at the Mitchell Library. Shelves of them, like the ancient books I once saw in a church library in Lima, Peru. God, how I coveted that room with its long, thin windows and floor to ceiling shelves bent under the weight of hand-tooled leather-bound volumes. As I walked around, wide timber floorboards groaned and squeaked. Tomes with gilded titles, and measuring up to three feet, were frayed with age. What lurked inside them, waiting to be discovered? On a lectern a massive book, exquisitely handwritten and illustrated, was opened and a scholar was reading. I asked what he was learning.

'These words allow me to know the life of men who lived four hundred years ago,' he told me in lightly accented English.

'It is amazing,' I replied, 'for tourists like me to be able to see and touch these books.'

'Yes, but it will change. Peru is beginning to understand that they are treasures. In a few years, you will be able to look in from the doorway only, not enter.'

His words are swirling through my mind when I set off for the Mitchell Library. I have an email in my bag from three women who hold copyright to Mackellar's estate, giving me permission to access the diaries but not to photocopy any material without further consent. In a cordoned-off section of the library reserved for people working with rare and original materials, I reach for two denim-coloured boxes the librarian places on the counter.

'Thank you,' I whisper, overawed by the surroundings. He nods.

I find an empty table and lift the first lid – hesitantly, oddly nervous. It feels intrusive, voyeuristic. How many years need to pass before digging into the past switches from *prying* to *researching history*?

'What is your motive?' the Buddhist nun once advised me to ask whenever I felt unsure of my actions.

Before I reach for the first manilla envelope, I stop and think. Knowledge, I tell myself, that is my motive. Knowledge so that half-remembered truths don't slide into oblivion forever. But I am not being completely honest. I yearn to understand what the woman who once wandered through the rooms of *Tarrangaua*, who fed king parrots on the verandah, was really like. Not just where and when she was born, educated, lived and died. Voyeuristic or not, I want a sense of her lifeblood. Like the scholar in Lima, I want to step back in time and into another person's life.

Inside the manilla envelopes, there are several packages wrapped in white tissue paper and bound, like a gift, with cotton tape. I unwrap one with great care – and almost burst out laughing. It's a horoscope Mackellar had done for the years 1928–29, three or four years after she built *Tarrangaua*. A horoscope! Then I pause. Why would a well-educated woman who theoretically had everything money could buy go to the trouble and expense of having a personal horoscope done? Because she was lost and unhappy, I think to myself. Her father had recently died, her mother was increasingly frail. The family framework that had defined her world was crumbling. Who loved her? What lay ahead? Where did she belong? Money, if that's all there is, can be a cold companion.

In the next package there is a leather-bound book with a brass clasp, dated 1900. But it is not a diary. It is filled with quotes from Voltaire, HG Wells, de Montaigne, Rosetti, Vernon Lee, Rebecca West and St Catherine of Sienna. Quotes carefully copied because the words struck some inner chord with a sheltered, privileged fifteen-year-old girl who dreamed of being a writer herself one day. I think back to the calendar Dorothea Mackellar made for Dr Fraser in 1927. It, too, was full of wise words from famous thinkers. What was she searching for? I wonder. A creed? Understanding of the human spirit? A way of making sense of the world? Or simply meaning?

I unwrap two diaries for 1910 and 1911. 'Collins Handy Diary', written in gold type on an oxblood cover, small enough to fit in the palm of a hand or a small handbag. Inside, the ink is blotchy, the writing cramped. The entries are mundane: 'Morning sunny . . . Town shopping (a very little) . . . Dentist. Long and beastly . . .' And on 30 December 1911: 'Clairvoyant'. So her habit of seeking esoteric direction began when she was in her twenties.

There's a loose piece of paper, speckled with dried mildew. Black ink has faded to brown:

A RECIPE FOR SPICED COTTAGE CHEESE CUSTARD

2 cups milk
3 eggs
3 tablespoons sugar
1¼ cups sieved cottage cheese

¼ teaspoon salt
1 teaspoon grated lemon rind
½ teaspoon cinnamon
1 teaspoon vanilla
cooked or canned apricot halves – drained
[¼ cup sugar extra, not listed in original recipe]

Heat milk in top of double boiler. Beat two eggs and one egg yolk, add quarter cup of sugar, cottage cheese, salt, lemon rind, cinnamon and vanilla. Stir to blend. Slowly add hot milk stirring constantly. Place two to three apricot halves in bottom of six, buttered custard cups. Pour custard over them. Place in a shallow pan of hot water and bake in a slow oven for 40 minutes or until custard is almost set and lightly brown. Beat remaining egg white till stiff and add remaining sugar, a dessertspoon at a time. Beat until stiff. Top each custard with meringue. Brown in oven or under griller. Serve warm or cold.

Late in the afternoon, in another box under the name of Marion Mackellar, Dorothea's mother, I find an invitation to a dance and a handful of receipts for clothing and riding gear for her son, Keith, who was killed in the Boer War. It is the thought of a mother hoarding scraps of paper for no reason other than that they were a frail link with her dead son that undoes me. I close the boxes and return them to the counter.

16

SHARON IS ILL.

'They tell me I have breast cancer,' she says, surprise and disbelief on her face. 'I feel quite angry. I thought as I'd made it this far I'd escaped that whole dreadful cancer business and something far more civilised would probably get me.'

It's late afternoon. There's a vase of lavender on a side table. I squish some silver leaves in my hands and the scent floats through the room. The perfume is supposed to quieten anxiety, but not today.

'What have you been told?' I ask, sitting in one of the armchairs opposite her.

'I have to take some tablets. A form of chemotherapy.'

'Not much fun. No, no fun at all. But not impossible.'

'I thought you'd understand about it, because you've been through it. Or I wouldn't have mentioned it.'

'And here I am, Sharon, eight years later. You'll be fine. Treatments today are amazing.'

She smiles. 'I felt quite frightened for a moment, but I'm past that now.'

'Might have to make you a few delicious little dishes to keep your strength up. Fancy a light chicken stew made with mushrooms, pancetta and leeks?'

'Sounds lovely,' she says. 'Will be you making any of those little lemon cakes . . .?'

I laugh. 'As many as you like.'

Instead, I make butter, coconut and almond cupcakes, to give her variety. I drop them in the next day. For the first time since I have known her, she is still in her nightie at lunchtime.

'How're you feeling?'

'Not bad. Not bad.'

'Need help with anything?'

'Oh no, thank you. I'm a bit slow today because I found a red-bellied black snake in my living room this morning. Gave me a terrible fright. It's gone now. One of the gardeners got rid of it. But I'm still recovering. Haven't got around to my shower or dressing yet.'

'Your number's not up, then, Sharon. The snake didn't get you. You've got a long way to go yet.'

And she smiles. Then laughs. 'I think the snake was more frightened than I was!'

'You are so, so tough, Sharon. You'll wear this thing down.'

A week later she politely tells me that the almond cakes were lovely but there's nothing as light and luscious as the little lemon cakes.

The year flies so fast, and I am no closer to discovering who designed the house. Life intervenes. How can I rush when the sun peels back the gloom of a winter day? How can I ignore the pleasure of standing quite still as that great golden orb sinks over the hills that cradle Salvation Creek? A thin crust of light etches the landscape then drifts into a yellow sky. And just before black enfolds the evening, the bay is flecked with silver. Satin smooth, alive and mysterious, it anchors and restores.

One night I cook a feast of lamb ragout on a bed of silken eggplant puree. For dessert, I slow-cook cubes of pumpkin with water, lemon juice and sugar until it is sweetly tender. It's piled in a glass bowl and sprinkled with chopped walnuts. I'll serve it with double cream.

'Out of the big Turkish cookbook or the little one?' Bob asks, looking at his plate, which is like an abstract painting, splattered with green and red slices of capsicum and tomato on a smooth caramel-coloured background.

There was a moment, in an Istanbul bookshop, when my lust for a cookbook filled with large glossy pictures of Turkish food irked him. Mostly, it's his habit to turn away when I am seduced by what he sees as inessentials and he lets me decide for myself whether to splurge or not. But this day – almost at the end of our holiday – he gets angry and storms into the street. I have bought one Turkish cookbook already. He cannot see the point of two, and it is expensive because it's in English and we are in Turkey. I was going to put it back on the shelf, even though it's the only book I've found that describes how to cook a whole baby goat, but instead I buy it – and two other paperbacks – because I don't give in to pressure anymore.

'The little one,' I reply, string-lipped with the memory.

'You ever going to cook that goat?'

'One day. Maybe.'

'I could rig a spit. If you wanted.'

'I'll think about it.' And I smile so he knows I understand. He grins back. We both know I will never cook a whole baby goat.

'Would have been interesting, though, to check out that archaeological site.'

Halfway through our Turkish holiday, we climbed onto a bus for an eight-hour trip south to the turquoise coast. Bizarrely, there was a lanky, freckle-faced Australian wearing well-pressed desert fatigues in the seat in front of us, so raj he would have been at home in an Agatha Christie mystery. Turned out he was an archaeologist specialising in ancient coins.

'Off to a dig in Syria,' he told us. 'Filling in for another bloke who's sick.'

Ever since I was a sunburned country kid with spindle legs and copper hair, I've wanted to go on an archaeological dig. I have no idea why. Maybe I've just always loved treasure hunts.

'We could go with him,' I suggested to Bob quietly but enthusiastically, when the archaeologist drifted into sleep. 'Wouldn't it be fascinating? A dig! The stuff of dreams. When he wakes up shall I ask him if there's room for a couple of willing helpers for a week?'

'We'll see what happens.' Which meant *no way*.

'Why not?'

'Let's stick to the plan,' he said.

I didn't argue. We're a team. Give and take. He reached across and lifted my arm, tucking it under his. Then he held my hand in a firm warm grip and closed his eyes. Beside us, the bleak high country rolled past.

Bob doesn't look up from his dinner. 'Thirty to forty degrees in the desert every day. Can get a bit stressful when it's that hot and there's no escape.' No escape for me, he means. He would have handled it easily. He probably even wanted to go.

'Yeah, but sometimes you've got to have a go, even if the whole thing turns turkey.'

Already, warmer weather fingers its way down the hills to the bay. The old uncle who came to live with us for two years and stayed until he died told me over and over to live in the present, not the future, because you get to the future soon enough. I was a little kid then who didn't want to wear steel tips on the heels and toes of my shoes because they clattered when I walked around the classroom. I pretended to believe him, hoping he'd let me skip the tips, but he put them on anyway. Shoes lasted twice as long after he'd doctored them, which was the last thing I wanted them to do.

He was a frugal man, my Uncle Ted. My mother said he was the kind of bloke who still had the first penny he'd ever earned. But when money was short, he always came good with a few hundred pounds or so, until my parents staggered over the lean times and frolicked back into plenty.

Like the old bloke in the corner milk bar, he was right about time. Now that I am well and truly in my fifties, it rockets. Which seems odd because my own pace has slowed considerably. I cannot help noticing that my ankles take a moment or two to lose their stiffness in the morning, and occasionally I find myself dreaming about a project then pulling back: 'You're too old for that,' I hear an inner voice admonish. And I am struck by a wave of nausea that can only be fear. Not of death, or so I like to think, because I faced it years ago and it is absurd to fear what cannot be escaped. No, it's fear of a diminishing future and, mostly, of quitting this physical world. Even I can't pretend that I am only halfway through my life. I am almost on the brink of the final third. Then I think of my mother. I cannot withdraw from challenges because it heralds the beginning of *lying down*. Instead, I think of Jeanne and Sharon, of Ann and PD James, who is still writing books at eighty-eight! *So many challenges ahead, so little time.* I wriggle out of the suit of despair. Live for the day. *I am strong.*

Bob and I walk down the steps to the waterfront. It's take-mother-shopping day.

'Why can I be kind to Sharon without any effort and my mood

turns black before I even walk out the door to see my mother?'
I ask Bob.

'Family. Goes way back.'

Is that all it is? It cannot be memories of childish hurts, surely.
To hold on to them at my age would be . . . well, childish. And yet
when I scrabble through the past, I am niggled by unease. My
mother competed with me. She fired arrows with frightening
precision that wiped me out for days at a time. She coveted my life,
she told me one strange day when she was unwell and thought she
might die. How could you covet your own child's life? Was her
own life so mired I was her only way out? Yes. But I've always
known that and what does it matter?

'One day, I will ask her a single question. And perhaps I will
understand it all,' I tell Bob.

He looks at me hard. 'Some questions,' he says slowly, 'are better
left unasked.'

I smile as I walk down the pathway to the boat, flicking aside
cobwebs as frail as necklaces. Bob is the only person I know who
is wise enough not to ask what the question would be. Some
questions, I also know, can open vaults that should never be
disturbed.

A small spider scuttles down my shirt front. I squish it, an
instinctive reaction. I loathe spiders. Is all loathing based on fear?
There's a muddy brown mark on my shirt. Dirty already, and I'm
not even in the tinny yet.

Michael walks down the jetty at the boatshed, all skin, bone
and flowing blond hair. A cigarette hangs out of his mouth. We
wave. He jumps lightly into his tinny, sits and grabs the tiller. Then
there's an almighty yelp. A split second later, in what looks like a
single motion, he lands back on the dock.

A diamond python raises its head above the gunnel, looks
around casually then slithers silently onto the pontoon to bake in
the morning sun.

'Jesus!' says Michael when we come to have a look. 'Never moved so fast in all my life. Scared the shit out of me.'

When I settle my mother in the car for our shopping trip, it is on the tip of my tongue to query odd moments in my childhood. Then I look across at her. The smudged lipstick on her teeth, a spill on her jacket that she hasn't noticed. Sacrilegious slip-ups for a very vain woman. She is too vulnerable, too easy a target. I let the moment pass. And I always will.

The snake quickly becomes a boatshed mascot. It lingers, coiled, on the pontoon, rocked by the water. Sleepy and full, its stomach distended. A rat maybe. The boys step around it to do their work. It stays for three days, through an entire beautifully sunny weekend. 'Saw a lot of boats slide alongside the pontoon to tie up,' says Michael later. 'Then quick as a flash, off they went. Most peaceful weekend I've had since we bought the boatshed.'

When someone does the wrong thing in our little community, it doesn't take long before we all know about it. The word flies around faster than baitfish and for a while a grey gloom seeps into our lives.

One day Bob and I are told someone is suing a man whose only sin was to volunteer to run a community event. During the weekend of the event, a terrible windstorm rampaged through Pittwater, lifting roofs, felling trees and smashing tinnies until they lay flat on the bottom of the seabed. Items loaned for the event were damaged beyond repair, but only a single person decided to sue. The word goes around the bays. Dismay hangs heavy in our hearts, like someone has hammered so hard that our belief in ourselves has cracked wide open.

'It isn't right,' everyone says, shocked. 'Good communities look after each other.'

We send emails of support to the hapless volunteer, who is distraught. Will he lose his home? Where will it all end?

One day when there's a huge crowd at The Point early on a Friday evening, the person at the heart of the trouble gets off the ferry. People stand back to let him walk along the pontoon and jetty. As he passes, they whisper:

'Arsehole. Arsehole. Arsehole,' in a breathless chant that ripples through the crowd as he moves along.

A few weeks later, we hear the lawsuit has been dropped.

Obea is dead. The big, boofy labrador with Rhett Butler charm and a noble profile will no longer pad through the bays sniffing out a party or a barbecue, breathing so heavily and humanly he made our hearts thump until we realised it was only Obea, not a primeval boojum following us in the dark on the back track. His tail will no longer thump enthusiastically at the sight of us as though we had never done, and never could do, any wrong. He will no longer lean heavily against our legs, looking up into our eyes in silent thanks for a chop or sausage. Obea is dead. A chapter in Lovett Bay history has gently but firmly closed.

Obea was here when it all began, this new life of mine. A golden head as big as a football swimming across the bay to say hello no matter how choppy the water, how fierce the wind. He sometimes stole a sandwich or two out of one of the boatshed boys' packs, but no-one minded. He charmed us all. Oh, how he charmed us. Such a powerful dog and, for so long, invincible. Or that's how it seemed. But there's no cheating death. His liver, Ray the Vet said, was worn out. It is not a bad thing, though, to die with your head cradled in a loving lap, to die knowing you finally found where you belonged.

'How old do you think he was?' asks Tanya, who runs her own

real estate agency now. We are at The Point, passing through to our boats.

I think back. 'Maybe twelve?'

'He turned up on my deck the day my mother died,' she says. 'Sat there for three days, being beautiful and charming. The way my mother once was. I know this is going to sound weird, but I felt Obea knew she'd died and he was helping me through my grief. He stayed until the funeral was over. Then he went home to Gill and Ric, as though he'd done his duty.'

'Yeah. That sounds like Obea.'

17

AROUND PITTWATER, PEOPLE DREAM of boats and sailing, of endless voyages across comforting seas to remote shimmering coves in a lush paradise where the natives are very, very friendly. The search, of course, is for freedom, finding a life beyond the suffocating reach of bureaucracy, not a pretty white beach with a bending palm tree.

Occasionally, sailors with faraway places in their eyes need crew. Big Dave tackles Bob when we're passing through The Point one night 'Want to come to Hobart?' he asks. 'Jackie and I are taking *Intrepid* to the Wooden Boat Festival in Hobart, in February. Then circumnavigating Tasmania.'

Intrepid 11 is a pointy-nosed 52-foot crayfishing boat from Western Australia that Dave and his wife bought a couple of years ago. Built from jarrah, a Western Australian hardwood, it's part of Big Dave's plan for when he walks away from his highly stressed cop's life. Jackie, who makes the best wontons on Pittwater, was emphatically against the boat. 'I don't like it, Dave, I don't like it. It's too big. I don't feel comfortable on such a big boat,' she insisted.

Big Dave won her over with promises of fridges, sofas and

double bunks. A large gas stove and even an oven. Two bathrooms, one ensuite. 'A fantastic boat,' he whispered seductively, 'smooth as silk. Think of us gliding along the Hawkesbury, stopping for oysters. Or prawns. The back deck is meant for champagne, Jackie. Oysters and bubbles. Can't get better than that!'

Her complaints about scrubbing decks, hulls and windows on every day off from her work as a midwife dissolved in a flash of graceful moments on the gunmetal waters of the giant river. Big Dave never mentioned the open seas, though. He saved that for a couple of years later.

When I return from the mailbox with a fistful of letters, Bob's eyes have a new, mirror-sharp gleam in them. 'What do you reckon?' Big Dave asks Bob, beer in hand, rocking back on his heels. 'Need a couple of blokes on board who know what they're doing. The boat's comfy for six. That'd be ideal.' Bob looks at me.

'We'll think about it,' he tells Big Dave. 'Go home and have a talk. Let you know.'

'Plenty of time. Festival starts on 9 February. Give ourselves eight days to get there. Stop in some nice little inlets for fresh lobster and champagne along the way. Lovely!'

'What festival? Get where?' I ask Bob as we walk along the new ferry wharf, a long slim metal jetty leading to a concrete pontoon. There's a see-through shelter with a wall down the middle so you can dodge gales by moving to one side or the other. But a six-inch gap at the bottom means no matter where you sit, if the wind's blowing cold, your backside still freezes through to the bones. The chipped, white wooden rails, oyster encrusted pylons, yellow-coated steps and leaning shed of the old ferry wharf still lie alongside, abandoned and slowly rotting. It's like watching another era disintegrate.

'Dave wants to take *Intrepid* to the Wooden Boat Festival in Hobart, then go around Tassie. He's looking for crew,' Bob explains.

My heart sinks. Ten days of vomiting. Got carsick as a kid, get airsick before take-off. Winding McCarrs Creek Road always makes me queasy unless I drive so slowly the cars behind me get ratty. Sometimes I really wonder if I'm cut out for travelling. Or boat access life. But you can't give in, can you? *Lying down* on the sofa is not an option.

'Could go. Always wanted to check out the Wooden Boat Festival,' I say.

'You'll be sick as a dog all the way. Not worth it.'

'Like to see Bass Strait, too. Must be magic. And it's a great way to lose a few pounds, especially after Christmas. Be slim as a sardine by the time we get there.'

'Sardines aren't thin. They're just little.'

'No chance of little.'

Stewart and Fleury are horrified. 'I forbid you to go!' says Fleury, shaking a finger at me. As a young woman she raced yachts with Ted Turner, became famous for her on-board desserts. Never told a soul they were frozen Sara Lee. But she's been over the glamour of boats for twenty years, knows they're hard, dangerous work. 'He went to the stern for a pee in the middle of the night. Never saw him again.' Happened to two friends. Not much glamour in death.

'There's some pretty good seasick pills around now, and Jackie's a nurse. She'll know the best kind to get. It'll be great. Bit of a challenge.'

'I forbid you! I absolutely forbid you to go. You'll be throwing up before you even get to Lion Island.'

I'm about to deny it, but I pause. Have I ever made it past the corkscrew currents of Broken Bay, where the Brisbane Waters meet the Hawkesbury River and Pittwater, beyond where a sou'easterly hurtling straight from the Pacific Ocean spins a boat like a toothpick on rollercoaster swells? Nope!

'I'm gonna go, Fleury. I want to be with Bob.'

'You'll be over that by the time you get to Long Reef. I'll pick you up at Middle Harbour. That's about four hours from Church Point.'

'I'll be fine.'

'Like hell.'

Fleury is helping her daughter to prepare for her first full-time job since finishing university. 'Got to find a flat, a fridge, a bed and a sofa. And all in Adelaide!' she groans.

'I hate to sound like my mother, but how did she grow up so fast?'

Wasn't it only yesterday that she lay politely in a bassinet under a table while we all dined on navarin of lamb in a long-gone little Paddington restaurant called The Brussels? And now she is about to start her adult life.

'If you fall in love,' I tell her sternly when she asks for a couple of easy recipes to take to her new home, 'I want to know imme-diately. You may tell me anything and trust that I will not pass it on to your mother. Unless I feel I should.'

'I want a few cooking tips, Susan, not a recipe for living.' She smiles wickedly. 'Anyway, seems to me I spent my teens making sure *you* got home safely. It wasn't the other way around!'

Bugger.

I think long and hard about what to write. And after deleting twenty ways to avoid romantic disaster, because as my wise old dad used to say 'Experience is the only way to learn,' I come up with:

RULES FOR COOKING

1 *Always use the best ingredients you can find (or afford), which usually means getting them from a good deli or good food stores. Buy less and buy quality.*

2 *Always use proper stock — make it yourself, especially chicken, or buy from a good deli.*

3 *Vanilla is important. Use beans. If the recipe calls for extract, use Herbie's or Madagascar (shockingly expensive but it lasts a long time).*

4 *Use very fresh eggs. The whites should hold together like gelatine and the yolks sit up like a glossy, golden dome.*

5 *Get to know your butcher. He will always help you if you establish a relationship with him.*

6 *When stewing chicken, use thigh meat. It can be cooked for longer without drying out.*

7 *Swiss brown mushrooms are preferable to regular mushrooms. They're worth the extra money.*

8 *The Tasmanian Honey Company makes wondrous products – I use leatherwood honey, which has more oomph. Experiment with different flavours. Honey should have far more overtones than just a flat sweetness.*

9 *Rice is tricky. Use the right kind for your dish. Calasparra is good for paella and there's an Italian risotto rice, Ferron, that is great. (I will murder you if you use poor quality rice – there's not enough starch in it to give you a creamy result.) But: you can use jasmine rice for Chinese dishes, although I use Basmati for everything apart from paella and risotto. You can buy this from supermarkets. Basmati is a beautiful long grain that must be cooked by absorption method only. (Measure the rice and the water according to the instructions on the packet and turn down the heat to almost nothing the moment the water boils, then turn off the heat just before all the water is absorbed and leave it with the lid on for another five to ten minutes.)*

10 *Use what's in season. It's always best. Get to know your greengrocer, who will also look after you if you establish a relationship.*

11 *Fresh herbs are superior to nearly all dried herbs. If I can't get fresh, I change the menu. If you need tarragon, it must be French or, at a push, winter. Don't go near Russian, it has no flavour. Flat leaf (Italian) parsley is best. Dill needs to be very fresh or it gets dull and slightly bitter. Rosemary is queen – but it's got to be fresh and if there are flowers on it, try to avoid it as it means it's past its peak and will be*

slightly bitter and very strong. That applies to all herbs. Basil must be very fresh and smell heavenly.

12 *If you're making fresh pasta, use double 0 (00) flour only. Other flour glugs up. Let the pasta dry for at least half an hour before you cook it. Overnight is still good.*

13 *Pastry is best made at home (unless it's puff or filo, then you're definitely allowed to buy it from the supermarket). If you have a food processor, it's easy. Just use frozen butter instead of cold butter. Also, I often use lemon juice instead of water. Always rest pastry in the fridge before rolling it, then rest it in the fridge again after rolling it. If you don't it will shrink. Also, if you use too much water (or lemon juice — whatever fluids) it will shrink. If you're using filo, rest it on a damp tea towel to stop it drying out and breaking up.*

14 *Use uncultured unsalted butter for everything. If you use margarine, I will take out a contract on your life. If you use salted butter, I will haunt you.*

15 *Make your own mayonnaise. It's easy and quick, especially if you use a food processor, and it tastes so different from bought products they could be from different planets. If it curdles, take another egg yolk and whip the curdled mixture into it.*

16 *Always use good chocolate — Valhrona or equivalent. Cocoa — Dutch is good. The Valhrona one is almost too rich.*

17 *Cream — thick (not 'thickened') is fine. Don't bother with double thick or very expensive creams. If you want to dress it up, add icing sugar and vanilla. The icing sugar makes it stiffer.*

18 *Always spin your salad greens until they are dry. If you don't the dressing won't stick. Never let your salads swim in dressing and dress at the last minute to stop sogging.*

19 *Use Murray salt (pinkish) on salads. It's fabulous. Maldon is also wondrous but always try to buy Australian if you can.*

20 *Easiest ever dessert: Fresh strawberries — the best you can buy — accompanied by sour cream with dark brown sugar stirred through. HEAVEN!*

Final advice: Almost anything tastes good if you're hungry enough.

When I give it to her, I'm puzzled. 'You know, darling, there are a squillion great cookbooks around that will tell you all this and more. Why don't I get you a couple as a going-away present?'

She smiles, that clever young woman who will always be a child in my eyes, and shakes her head. 'Cookbooks have no soul and aren't filled with our own history,' she replies.

Then I remember Barbara's recipes. Handwritten or clipped from magazines and filed together in a loose leaf folder, with notes along-side: 'This is quick and easy for a big group', 'Use half the amount of butter', 'Don't overmix'. Bob gave the book to his youngest daughter. Hopefully, she will keep it and pass it on to her daughter – with recipes of her own added with handwritten hints. It is the resonance of the past that is compelling and comforting. Any food, if it's cooked with care and love for the people you are feeding, turns out ok.

On a walk along the back track, I run into a neighbour and tell her about writing 'Cooking Rules' for Fleury's daughter.

'Glad she appreciated it. I was at a twenty-first birthday party recently, where an ancient aunt lovingly handed over her mother's recipe book to the birthday girl. It was clearly the most precious thing in her life and to part with it was a measure of her love and hope for her grand-niece's life ahead. As soon as she turned away, the girl and her mother whispered, "Cheapskate!" behind her back. Felt like snatching the book away from them. They didn't understand what it was all about.'

'Yeah, it's the past that reminds us who we really are, no matter how many times we reinvent ourselves along the way.'

Late October and jacarandas froth along Pittwater Road in purple splendour. Bougainvillea spills in red and pink rivers over fences and corrugated iron rooftops, flounced like chiffon. Jasmine clings to walls, its tiny white flowers like the night sky.

The colours are so lush it's difficult to believe the drought goes on. And on.

Big Dave's working to get the boat ready, sanding timber, polishing steel. Painting, cleaning and lining up Bainy to service the engine to purring contentment. He's also getting anxious about crew for *Intrepid*. Bob is keen to explore the wild coastline of Tasmania but doesn't want to do the numbing slog from Pittwater down the coast to Victoria and across irritable Bass Strait to Hobart. He's done it too often, mostly as either skipper on his own boat or crew in the iconic Sydney–Hobart Yacht Race when, every Boxing Day, a fleet of svelte yachts glides out of Sydney like a flock of giant seagulls or parrots, depending on whether they've hoisted pure white sails or rainbow-coloured spinnakers.

Bob was in the blow in 1998 when thunderous waves rose higher than a city skyscraper and six men lost their lives. He was one of seven crew on *Bright Morning Star*, a 55-foot yacht fitted for cruising not speed, owned by Hugh Treharne, Bomber's brother. Hugh was tactician the year Australia won the America's Cup, in 1983. I was still living in the low-slung timber house at the water's edge on Scotland Island the year of the horror Sydney–Hobart and I knew Hugh and Bomber but Bob was in the future.

When the storm hit between Christmas and New Year, Pittwater, normally raucous with parties, went silent. It was a dreadful time, the whole community huddled around the radio and television waiting for news. Big Dave was on a boat, as were Zapper from Scotland Island, Bob and many others. Pittwater was lucky. Everyone survived. There was no backslapping hurrah for the men when they returned, though. They came home silently and for a long time no-one asked what it was like that night. But slowly, the stories came out.

'I was on the helm,' Zapper said. 'The noise was horrendous, like the world was being hammered to pieces. Then suddenly there was absolute silence. My glasses floated in front of me. I reached for them, my arms slow and heavy, like I was in a dream. I realised we were under water. The boat had rolled. Then the roaring began again. We'd righted.'

I didn't hear Bob's story until a couple of years later. 'The storm reached a peak as I came off watch,' he recalled. 'I was exhausted. The boat was chaos. Stuff rolling, falling, crashing, banging.' He had one dry change of thermals in his waterproof bag. He hesitated. Should he change or not? Just as he stripped, a wall of deep green water exploded though the hatch, filling the cabin like a backyard pool. A round pink shape hurtled towards him and landed heavily on his chest. For the first time in his life, Bob thought he might die. He couldn't breathe. He was drowning.

'Another bloke was thrown out of his bunk and landed on me. Bomber's son. I shoved him off. The boat righted. The water sloshed to the floor. I was winded but I could breathe again. I managed to pull on my wet-weather gear, strapped myself to a safety harness and went on deck. The mainsail was reefed three times but I watched a wave shred it like a cotton handkerchief. We were doing six and a half knots under bare pole. If you looked behind, all you could see was a sixty foot green valley.'

At four o'clock in the morning, they made it to the shelter of Eden, an old whaling and fishing town on the coast just before the halfway mark. They tied up to a barge on a mooring and waited for light.

'All I wanted was a hot breakfast and dry clothes,' Bob said. 'But we couldn't get a taxi. The bloody media had grabbed the lot. We all walked to a café in town, ate everything we could see. Then we went to the laundromat and washed and dried our gear. Felt almost normal.'

Not for long, though. Later that afternoon, Eden was a graveyard of battered boats and bruised and battered men with sunken eyes black with shock.

'Never should have stripped in a storm,' he said, over and over, shaking his head. 'You keep your clothes on, wet or not. A bad decision like that can cost you your life.'

It's a crystal-clear evening after a roaster of a day. Far too hot for October. Makes me wonder if the apocalypse is coming. Or doomsday. When I was a kid, the school playground was always rife with prophecies of doom. 'The world will end next week,' little Gunther would insist, eyes wide with fear, skinny legs poking out of leather shorts with embroidered braces. And the rumour would take hold until we scared ourselves silly, running home to ask our parents if they'd heard. *The world is coming to an end!* And my parents would laugh, the best cure for fear, and my brother and I would have to do our homework after all.

But when the weather is weirdly wrong for the time of year, or a storm lashes so violently that the back track is strewn with fallen trees or when the sky is orange from the smoke of bushfires, the doomsday words of long ago claw back. For a split second I wonder, is this it? Then I shrug. What will be will be. Don't sweat what you can't control.

'Got your crew yet?' Bob asks Big Dave when we meet, as usual, passing through The Point. Around us, people stand chatting in groups. Curly-haired Scotty with his shy smile and handsome Thad with his devoted brown border collie, Griffen. Bainy, his fisherman's cap titled forward against the setting sun. Toby, khaki shorts overcoated with red dust, and thoughtful Dave with his big, slow smile, dreadlocks shorn. Matty, red-faced and grey-haired, less able to charm and dangerously oblivious to the penalties of reckless living. They all look knackered and hold their beers like the brew has been sanctified and will lead to everlasting life.

Heather, Scotty's partner, still in her navy blue and white

nursing uniform, sits at one of the wooden tables with a rum and coke in a can. She's a natural comedian – the humour black when she talks about working in the dementia ward of the nursing home that is part of the retirement complex where my mother lives. 'Mate,' she'll say, 'the posh old girl with the plum in her mouth. Every time you go into her room, it's *hello, how are you, how lovely of you to visit, how's the weather, seen any shows lately.* You're in and out about ten times a day and it's always the same: *Hello, how are you, how lovely of you to visit . . .* She cracked it today, though. One of the *wanderers* nicked off with a photo from her bedside table. Nothing posh about her today . . . Mate, words *I've* never heard!'

And the sad stories. 'Couldn't get Mrs Kafoops showered. Shrank in the corner whimpering like a baby. Must've been raped as a kid. There's a few like her. Lived with it all their lives and probably never told a soul. In those days, women shut up. Buried it in their heads until dementia cross-wires their brains and opens the box. Now it haunts them. Breaks your heart.'

Groups dissolve and reform with a slight turn of a shoulder. The talk rambles on. Who fell out of a tinny? Who ran aground? Even small crises are recreated in comic skits. 'Mate, I was busting for a pee. Busting! So I scooted through the moorings. Bloody water police got me. Didn't want to know about my bladder. If men had babies they'd be more understanding. Well, I *couldn't* wait while he wrote out my ticket. Peed over the side. Never seen a boat move so fast. Still haven't got the ticket.' But occasionally, voices shrink to a murmur about a struggling marriage, a health crisis, kids careening down the wrong path under the illusion it's nothing more than good fun.

Big Dave sways backwards and forwards on his heels. I look at him sometimes and wonder whether he locks pressure inside because he's a man and a cop and he's not supposed to have frailties. But we all do.

'Got a team together for the trip,' he tells Bob. 'Only thing is, they're all women.'

'Nothing wrong with that,' I blurt.

'Not a thing, except they don't know anything about boats.'

'Who are they?'

'Kerry, from The Island. She's retiring from work, said she wanted a challenge. Well, we can manage that. There's one little problem, though,' he says, screwing up his face with concern. 'She's scared of boats. Little ones, like tinnies. Hates them. Not sure she'll feel much better on a big boat, which will make it a bit hard ferrying her on and off when we throw down the anchor.'

'Bit of a handicap, yeah,' says Bob. 'Who's the other person?'

'Annette. From The Island. She's done some sailing but she's been a bit crook. A lung transplant a year ago. She's good now, but wouldn't like to push her too hard.'

Bob's eyes start to spin wildly. He sips more quickly. The great circumnavigation is starting to look wobbly. A woman with flyaway red hair and Cleopatra eye makeup rocks up.

'This is Annette,' Big Dave says happily.

'Signed on for the big adventure then?' I ask.

'Yep. Always wanted to go to Tassie on a boat. Looking forward to it. I'll fly home from Hobart, though. Don't want to go around the island and one way to Tassie is enough.'

Bob gets a hunted look on his face again. His forehead is tight, his mouth stretches into a thin line.

'What I reckon,' Big Dave says, 'is that we should all get together for dinner at home. Work out what each of us can do on the boat.'

'I can do food,' I offer.

'No way!' Big Dave says.

'What do you mean?' I splutter. Everyone lets me cook. Then I remember. He and Jackie came to dinner a few months ago. I gave Bob a container of marinated lamb chops to barbecue. Garlic, rosemary, preserved lemon. A hint of fresh oregano. When he lifted the lid it smelled like Greece. I thought he'd cook enough for four of us but he cooked every one of the thirty-two. Even I thought it was excessive.

'I can do the food,' Annette offers. 'I'll cook up a few meals and freeze them in packs. Easy.'

Big Dave, who loves a bargain and always buys everything *really cheap*, says he'll do the shopping for staples such as pasta, biscuits, bottles of water, cereal, tea and coffee.

'We'll organise tea!' Bob and I say simultaneously. For us, tea is lifeblood.

'No, no, I'll get teabags. I can get 'em cheap,' Big Dave insists.

'Dave,' I say, slipping my arm through his, 'if there's only teabags you'll never get Bob on board. Let me organise the tea, ok?'

'Jackie will get proper tea. It'll be fine.'

'Jackie will get jasmine tea. We like stuff that sticks to your ribs.' But I can feel it's an issue that could escalate. 'You get what *you* want,' I suggest, 'and we'll buy what *we* want. And we'll bring a proper teapot. Stainless steel so it won't break.'

We found a design we liked a couple of years ago. It edged out the china teapot overnight. Makes a stunning cuppa every time. He thought so much of this honest little pot that Bob bought one for all his kids – even his son who lives in Pittsburgh and doesn't drink tea.

'It's for us!' Bob confessed when I tackled him. 'For when we visit. We'll buy leaf tea at home and take it with us. That ratty floor dust they call tea in America isn't fit for humans.'

I laughed but I wondered when the thought of a crummy cuppa became intolerable. Is it age, or the pursuit of excellence?

Big Dave looks at Bob. His putty face beguiles and there's the beginning of a wheedle in his tone. 'Need at least another bloke on board for the Sydney to Hobart leg and I'd be happier with two more,' he says.

Bob is silent, takes more quick sips of his beer. The ugly tin ferry blasts its horn. Five minutes to departure. The blokes who are regular last-minute dashers land smooth and light. The *Grey Ghost* reverses from the pontoon, churning the waters. Bob shuffles. He knows he's snookered. He's going to be crew all the way. He has one last go, running a few names past Big Dave, who shakes his head.

'Wrong time of the year for their holidays,' Big Dave explains. 'Not long enough after Christmas.'

Bob drains his beer, blows into the empty bottle like it's a whistle. 'Ok, I guess I can find the time. I'll do the whole trip.'

Big Dave's face wrinkles with gratitude. He wraps a beefy arm around Bob's shoulders. They look like Jack and the Giant. Bob gazes at the ground, his mouth lifting into a smile.

Rain. Steady, soaking rain. We laugh and joke and the weariness of the endless dry fades away. The waterfall gushes as a grey film coats Pittwater for three gloriously muted days. Then blue sky returns and brings a heat so fetid it's as though someone's lit a campfire under the earth. Once again, the festive season will be like sitting on a tinderbox with a flaming match in your hand.

My Uncle Frank says they will have to plough all but six rows of peach trees into the ground at the orchard at Wangaratta. If there's another year without rain, even those rows will have to go. A lifetime of work bulldozed into mulch. No more ghostly armies of trees reaching towards the Victorian Alps in the light of a full moon.

'What then, Frank?'

'We'll wait for rain and plant new trees,' he says. 'Or maybe sell. Doctors are buying up land for wood duck money.' But his voice doesn't lift at the prospect of slippers and sleeping cosily late on icy winter mornings. It's the challenge of each season that makes him thrive and he knows it.

Once, on an assignment for *The Australian Women's Weekly*, I crossed the border from Peru into Bolivia and stood amongst the massive granite stones of an ancient temple from the Tiahuanaco civilisation of 400 BC. The culture collapsed after a seventy-year drought. Seventy years! And we are only entering year four.

This year, I'm under orders from my mother to lift the standard of Christmas decorations. 'No more of that minimalist rubbish,' she says. 'I'll make silver swans for the table, like the ones I made when I was nursing in Darwin during the war. You couldn't buy even a yard of tinsel so we nurses created Christmas out of nothing. And it was beautiful enough to make you cry.'

To please her (and to be honest, to make a childish point) I go overboard. Burrawang and cabbage palm fronds are cut and sprayed with gold paint. For two days, fumble-fingered and indelicate, I sit on the verandah threading gold sequins onto thin wire to wind around the fallen dead branch of a spotted gum I've spray-painted white. This is the designated Christmas tree. Yards of cut-price ribbon are tied into glittering bows and stuck everywhere from door handles to table legs. And still the house looks moderate. I cut and paint more burrawang fronds until every corner glows. It looks like Palm Sunday. Then the sitting room is *festooned* with gold beads. On bookshelves, around the edge of tables, draped around picture frames. By the time it's finished, it's blinding.

'Think this will make her happy?' I ask Bob at the end of a long day of draping and festooning.

'Christmas is about family. That's all she should care about.'

'You tell her that. I wouldn't dare.'

The day before Christmas, I walk in her front door to collect her for the boat ride across the water and then a few days with us.

'All ready?'

'Yes,' she says. Not moving.

'Got your pills? Got your toothbrush? Got a sweater in case it gets cold?'

'Yes.'

'Shall we go?'

'Yes.' But she doesn't attempt to get up.

'Is there something I've forgotten?' I ask.

'It would be nice if you gave me a hug,' she replies. Her expression is deliberately casual, as though her request is of no real consequence either way.

'You'll have to stand up. I can't lean over without bringing on a hot flush,' I say, making a joke to lessen the moment, as she so often does.

I wrap my arms around her. When did she get so small? When did the stocky little body with muscly legs and tennis player arms turn into empty flesh? My mother is old. I expect too much of her. Let this be a year of softening and compassion, I tell myself. I help her into the car with uncharacteristic tenderness, steady her in the boat and tuck her in the seat.

'There's a bit of a strong wind. Water might be a bit choppy,' I say. 'Think you'll be ok?'

'Of course I will.'

Her chair has swivelled a little, so she's sitting skew-whiff. When the boat rises before settling into a plane, she'll tip out sideways.

'Can you straighten up?'

She makes a feeble effort. I rotate the seat like she's a helpless child. I feel as though a piece of my heart is being chiselled away. Out on the open water, a swell rolls in from Broken Bay. We rock and roll and I hold her arm to steady her. It is all too much. Too hard.

'Sorry about this,' I say, turning to her and slowing the boat so we surf the waves instead of bouncing over them.

'Don't slow down,' she shouts, grabbing the front of the boat to hold on tight. 'It's better than a roller-coaster!' Her face is ecstatic. We both laugh. I gun the motor, until she nearly falls out of her chair. For a second, we both forget age.

At the pontoon, I tie up alongside the big *Tin Can*. 'Can you step over two boats?' I ask.

'I can do anything!' she replies. And she steps easily from one to the other and then onto the pontoon where Bob is waiting with one hand out and the other holding the *Tin Can* steady. Does a hug make you stronger? Or does it make you try harder?

She climbs into *The Pug*, a grunty, beetle-orange truck that looks like a golf buggy on steroids, which we bought to replace the old ute because I never mastered driving up the hill frontwards and never even tried to reverse blind.

'Let's go, kid,' she says, grabbing a handle on the dashboard.

I fling her half-zipped suitcase and six plastic bags filled with God-knows-what into the back. Bob drives her up the hill and I dash up the steps. I want to be there when she walks inside the house and sees the decorations.

At the back door, she stops. 'Where's the wreath? Every door has to have a wreath at Christmas.'

'Wreaths remind me of Anzac Day and funerals,' I mutter darkly. 'Loathe 'em.'

I dump her stuff in her bedroom, waiting for her to notice the golden hallway. But there's not a word.

'How about a cuppa? Why don't you sit on the sofa and I'll bring you one?' I suggest.

She shuffles, playing the weak old lady again, tapping the floor in front of her with her foot as if she's blind. If I hadn't just seen her leap across two boats I might have fallen for it. It makes my heart harden. A lifetime of my mother's Sarah Bernhardt moments comes racing back.

'Hurry up,' I snap, opening the door. The room glitters.

Esther looks around. 'I thought you said you'd put up decorations,' she says.

Bob sees I'm about to explode. He grabs my arm, steers me into the kitchen. Then he goes back to my mother, who is already lying on the couch. I am absolutely seething. She's done it to me again.

'Look around, Esther,' says Bob. 'Susan's spent days creating this.'

And she realises she's gone too far and back-pedals. She reaches in her handbag for her glasses, puts them on slowly and carefully. And her face fills with fake delight. 'Oh-h-h!' she says. 'Now I can see. I'm as blind as a bat. Oh yes, it's lovely.'

'Keep her away from me,' I whisper to Bob in the kitchen. 'I need a cool-off period.'

'You never learn, Susan,' he says. 'It's a game. If you play, your mother will always win. Don't play and you'll both be much happier.'

I think back. As a kid, I never tried hard enough unless I was pushed. My mother knew – and still knows – that about me. She learned how to force me to do my best and she's never lost the habit. Or perhaps I still need pushing.

18

THE DAYS SLITHER BY, fat and glossy. Boats. Weather. Seasons. Food and friends. A community that staggers here and there but never loses its heart. Family, too, of course. Although we lob up less and less at Bob's children's front doors, with grins and suitcases, the dog bed, and an empty picnic basket from the long drive. I am selfish with my time, I know I am. Or perhaps my energy doesn't stretch as lavishly as it once did.

Bob is my wider world, now. I am also aware that I sometimes spit out advice when it is least sought. If there is any real curse that comes with age, it is the sneaking certitude – misplaced, I hasten to add – of wisdom. Words tumble out of my mouth before I think to swallow them and I occasionally trample over good hearts unwittingly. Anyway, this world is so different from the one that first bent me into shape. What do I know? Not much. Well, I *do* know that.

Chip Chop is aging. She is nearly eight years old and the energetic independence of her youth has drifted into quiet steadfastness. Once she grabbed my trouser legs in her teeth and dragged me to the door each morning for her walk. Now she lies at my feet under the desk – or on a sheepskin on the daybed in the study – waiting patiently for when I turn to her and say: 'Shall we go? What do you think?' Then she instantly snaps out of somnolence. Oh, how I wish I could do that! Her tail thumps. She eyeballs me with what I firmly believe is complete knowledge and understanding. *Let's go!*

How I love this little dog who lay beside me in the thick days and nights of chemo, like a living hot water bottle. She stilled the shivers of illness, lightened the bleakness of moments that roared back unbidden from the past and threatened to flatten me. A touch, that's all it took. Silken white fur, the sigh of another living being close by. The deliciously earthy smell of a healthy body, a scent so wholesome it deadened the burning stench of treatment. Her sister, Vita, always at a distance. Even at night, she slept lightly curled at the foot of the bed, facing the doorway. Ready to bat back the demons, I liked to think in those demon-filled days.

When another winter is gone and I count, as I do every spring, these *bonus* years, I call in to see Jeanne for no other reason except that I have come to love her and she inspires me. When we're drinking tea on her porch, she reaches for a pamphlet at the far end of the table and shoves it across to me.

'You and Bob might want to come along to this. A fellow called John Pearman is talking about Hardy Wilson.'

I flick open the brochure for the Australian Garden History Society. Pearman's talk, titled 'The Road to Kurrajong', is on Sunday morning at the Hawkesbury Heritage Landscape Seminar at the Hawkesbury campus of the University of Western Sydney. There's a short biography on the back page where all the speakers are listed in alphabetical order. It tells me: 'John Pearman is a retired academic with an interest in the life and work of architect Hardy Wilson, a designer best known for "Eryldene" in Gordon. John will talk on Hardy Wilson's little known but eccentric plans for a new town at Kurrajong.'

I hesitate. Sunday. Bob and I treasure Sundays. Probably out of habit because, really, every day is a Sunday when you've leapt off the mouse wheel. But it's the day we fizzle around doing fiddly chores we've been putting off all week. If the weather is warm enough, we have a slow lunch on the verandah. Nothing fancy – a sandwich or maybe an omelet if the egg supply is overpowering – but I set the table properly, perhaps because Sunday lunch – always a roast – was a ritual of my childhood.

'It would be great if you came,' Jeanne adds. 'John is one of those eco-warriors who doesn't own a car and we need someone to pick him up and drive him to the campus. I'd hitch a lift with you, too.'

Could say *no*, but there's no real reason. And anyway, I can see by the barely suppressed grin on her face that she knows she's got me.

'Ok, I'll be there. Bob might not come, though.'

'Of course I'll come,' he says, later that night. 'Like to hear what he's got to say.'

'How you doing? Ready to rock and roll?' I ask when Jeanne opens her door (only a crack so the cats don't escape) a few days later. She looks frazzled and fraught.

'I feel like I'm running a soup kitchen,' she mutters. 'There's the cats, the brush turkeys, the kookaburras, the pigeons, the finches and Horace, the peacock, who's more demanding than them all. And now a bloody great goanna turns up every day, bold as anything, like he's waiting for me to cook him a chicken. And Lilly's missing,' she replies, her voice full of anxiety. She clutches her bag, her keys, a jacket. Closes and locks the door behind her.

'She'll be fine, Jeanne. Cats are tough.'

'Not Lilly.'

Bob jumps out of the front seat to make room for Jeanne but she stops him. 'I love being driven. It's luxury. And it's always more comfortable in the back.' She pushes him out of the way and plants her backside down firmly, holding a printout of a map.

'Thought there'd be more peace and quiet in the back,' Bob mutters.

'We're going towards St Ives,' she instructs. Bob reaches for the street directory.

'No, no, I've got a map,' Jeanne says, waving an internet printout behind his head. But Bob asks for the address anyway, and looks it up. 'He who trusts busts,' he often says.

John Pearman's house, *Moonview*, is a concrete bunker at the end of a cul-de-sac that backs onto a nature reserve. Gum trees soar above a roof that – impossibly – appears to be growing grass. It is an alien amongst the decorative redbrick classics. Every angle is sharp and straight and the house is so colourless, it fades into the monochrome landscape of the Australian bush. At first glance, it could be a small factory in the middle of nowhere.

Jeanne gets out and tramps down a pathway overhung by blady grass, and disappears around a corner. In a few moments, a tall, thin man with a tweed cap and a long sallow face follows her back to the car. Jeanne introduces us. He nods and touches the peak of his cap.

'Hello. It's very kind of you to take the trouble to come and get me,' he says in a rich, formal voice. Or perhaps he is so accustomed to lecturing, the casual lightness of everyday conversation is foreign to him.

It turns out that Pearman had a twenty-year friendship with Professor Waterhouse, Hardy Wilson's closest friend.

'How did you meet the professor?' Bob asks.

'When I was twenty-one years old I was asked to give a lecture on the diseases of camellias to the Camellia Society,' he explains as we drive along. 'After my talk, Gowrie's wife, Janet, asked me to morning tea at *Eryldene*. Gowrie was an expert on camellias. A fascinating man, charming, amusing, erudite. He spoke half a dozen languages and interviewed Mussolini in Italian in the thirties. Later he interviewed Hitler in German.'

'He must have been much older than you,' Jeanne says.

'Yes, well there may have been a fifty-year age gap but we were kindred spirits from the moment we met. Often, he asked me to drive with him around the countryside to look at houses designed by Wilson. That's how I became interested in Wilson's work.'

Twice a week, if he could manage it, Pearman helped the aging professor water more than one thousand camellias growing in tubs in the garden.

'It gave us a lot of time to talk,' he says, smiling.

Pearman is a great raconteur who weaves colour and atmosphere into his words. Gossip, too. The kind that goes on desultorily between people and only later comes back as glorious little insights.

Hardy Wilson, he tells us, was a frequent visitor to *Eryldene*: '"Billy" and Gowrie were great friends. Partly, perhaps, because Gowrie was probably the only client who never questioned Billy's ideas. Gowrie said he'd never known an architect with more mastery of the finer details.'

'Did you ever meet Hardy Wilson?' I ask.

'No. I wish I had. But Gowrie said he was always immaculately dressed and walked everywhere, in great, striding steps, often sketching as he went along. He was a wonderful artist who had a great understanding of light and shadow, although he brooded about lifting the level of taste in Australian homeowners. He was a reserved man, too, which some people mistook for arrogance.'

'Maybe Wilson was just tall. Tall people can look arrogant, when mostly they're not.'

'Perhaps. Now tell me, where do you live?' asks Pearman as we get close to Richmond.

'Lovett Bay,' Bob replies.

'Ah! Lovett Bay. I seem to recall Gowrie saying that Billy did a house there for a poet. Dorothea Mackellar.'

Bob and I look at each other. I glance at Jeanne's face in the rear-vision mirror. She's got that smug 'I told you so' expression, again. To our credit, none of us leap in with exclamations although I feel like thumping the steering wheel and yippy-yay-yaying like crazy.

'Really?' I say, faking nonchalance. 'Why would Professor Waterhouse know about her?'

'Well, Mackellar was a regular visitor to *Eryldene*, of course.'

'Did you ever visit her house on your jaunts with the professor?'

'Oh no. It was far too difficult to access. As I recall, you needed a boat.'

It's a few lines in a casual conversation based on hearsay. Is it enough to make a judgement? While the conversation drifts around me, I go over Pearman's words in my head. As a journalist, I know it's often a throwaway line that gives you the link in a story or reveals a truth you thought you'd never find. But is it enough in this case? Probably not. Academics want facts. I need tangible evidence that Hardy Wilson was personally involved in the design of *Tarrangaua*. Or not.

Later in the day, Pearman gives his talk about Hardy Wilson's plans for an imagined city called 'Kurrajong', self-published by Wilson in a modest little paperbound booklet when he was seventy-four years old. It was his last work before his death. Wilson came up with a detailed layout of a completely self-contained city exquisitely drawn as though it was a mythical kingdom in a magical land. It was art you could hang on a child's bedroom wall to keep them fascinated for hours.

Wilson's city, named after an Aboriginal word meaning 'look-sit-see', included council chambers, a sun temple, civic centre and a library. There was a parliament house, a temple of heaven which catered for all religions, a university, an open-air theatre and even an airport and helipad. It was a grandiose and utopian view of how he thought people could live in harmony surrounded by the beauty of nature.

'Mankind aims to subdue nature in its working on him. He must not forget that he is, and always will be, one of Nature's expressions of life. He is not the superman he has come to believe himself to be, but is as dependent on the sun as are the birds and insects . . .' Wilson wrote. And the words still resonate – perhaps even more loudly than in his own lifetime.

On the trip home, we tell Pearman about the quest to pin down the architect of *Tarrangaua*.

'Is there some doubt?' he asks.

'More like lack of evidence,' Bob replies.

'I seem to recall – in fact I am sure of it – that Gowrie mentioned the project and it's not likely he would make something like that up.' Then he sighs. 'I think I am right, but as I grow older . . . my memory . . . I wouldn't swear on a stack of bibles. Have you tried the Mitchell Library? There must be records of building the house.'

I explain the search and where it has led.

'The answer is almost always in the details,' Pearman suggests. 'Check the mantelpiece over the fireplace, see if the design is similar to any others. Is it a Marseille tiled roof? Wilson hated them but they were all he could get in the early twentieth century. Bagged walls, yes? Is the design symmetrical? Well, if I were you, I would stop looking for the reasons why the house is a Wilson design, and instead ask what is the case against it.'

'Perhaps I'll track down those heritage architects who started this whole ball rolling. I wanted to contact them when I found proof – if I found it. Thought that was the best way to go. But you've spun my thinking around. Heard the other day that one of them has a sister who has a weekender in Towlers Bay. Might give her a call and ask her to open the door for me.'

'It never ceases to amaze me,' Pearman says, 'that we are all separated by so little. That the world, if you like, is so small.'

A few months after his talk, Bob and I visited Pearman, curious to see how his eco-friendly house functions. He showed us water tanks, a waterless, composting toilet, shelves made out of recycled timbers and double-glazed windows. The key to it all, though, was an 800 millimetre thick layer of soil on the roof which he says is the ultimate form of insulation. And the grass I saw on the roof suddenly made sense.

'When you all sweltered the day Sydney hit forty-six degrees, inside *Moonview* the temperature was a comfortable twenty-two degrees,' he said with only a hint of self-congratulation.

I recalled our trip to the rug weaver in her remote village in Turkey. How she proudly pointed out her new tiled roof – a sign of wealth – that had replaced rammed earth. Much easier, our weaver told us, because at the end of every winter earth roofs must be rebuilt and tiles last for a lifetime or two. Is it possible for ease and sustainability to coexist? Or is it the point where balance breaks down?

I wonder whether, like Wilson when he designed *Purulia*, Pearman shocked the neighbours into mild revolt when he built *Moonview*.

'Oh yes,' he replies. 'Everyone was against it. They didn't understand what I was trying to do. But you see, I wanted to build an environmental teaching house, to show how we can live sustainably even in big cities. I was told I would cause house prices to collapse in the street, but as far as I can tell, prices simply keep rising.'

January swings in fast and furious and there's no time to follow up Pearman's suggestions but I have rung my neighbour and I have a phone number and email address for Howard Tanner, one of the heritage architects who is an expert on Hardy Wilson. I'll call him after the Tassie boat trip. Big Dave organises the Hobart pre-departure dinner. Crew and assorted partners – who have insisted with quiet inflexibility that they will not be joining us *under any circumstances* – sit around the heavy timber table on Big Dave's front terrace. Only a few metres away, *Intrepid* hangs sedately off her mooring, as though she is patiently waiting for Big Dave's bugle call. Does he laze on his deck on warm evenings with a beer in his hand, gazing at her with a mushy look on his face? Boats have a way of filling you with romance. Anyone who's ever spent time at sea, though, knows what the ocean can hurl at you and snatch from you.

Jackie hands around her famous homemade deep-fried wontons. Crisp on the outside and moist inside, they're so good we eat too many.

'I'm bringing a few packs of cards. I'm also going to teach everyone to play ten-card rummy. We'll have lots of time and not much to do,' she says. 'There'll be music on board but feel free to bring your own. As long as it's not doof or country.'

I glance around the group. Annette and her husband (who isn't coming). Middle-aged. Kerry and her husband (also a non-starter). Middle-aged. Bob and me. Middle-aged. No. No chance of doof.

'We've got two bathrooms, two double beds, a couple of single bunks, a fridge and freezer big enough to store food for three months and space for six people around the table,' Big Dave says. 'There's a washing machine, a press button toilet' – which sends up a sigh of delight from the women – 'and plenty of deck space out the back for pre-dinner drinks and snacks. The wardrobes are spacious, so pack as many clothes as you like, – another sigh – 'and the hot water never runs out' – almost applause.

'Bring your own pillows, if you want to,' Big Dave adds. 'There's bed linen but if you prefer, you can bring that, too.' Bed linen on a boat instead of sleeping bags? It's maritime luxury and we all know it.

Big Dave fires up the barbecue and the men drift towards the flames. Marinated chicken breasts hit the hotplate with a hiss. Jackie puts a rice noodle salad laced with hot red chili and coriander on the table. Big Dave goes to the kitchen and returns with a platter of barbecued pork belly he's bought in Chinatown. He slices it with the delicacy of a surgeon. Annette reads out meals she thinks would be suitable for the trip from a very long, very organised list. Spaghetti bolognese, lamb korma, curried chicken . . .

'What do you reckon?' she asks. 'A few of these in the freezer?'

'Yep,' we all nod. 'Sounds better than a restaurant.'

'I'll make a fruit cake, too,' I say, wanting to contribute.

'Don't eat cake,' says Big Dave.

'I don't eat cake, either,' Jackie adds.

'Never been fond of fruit cake,' Annette says.

'Thought I'd try to lose some weight,' Kerry says.

For a minute I'm miffed. But who cares? 'Just bring enough for Bob and me, then. We're partial to a sliver of something sweet with a cuppa.'

'Is it one of those cakes you put a lot of rum in?' Big Dave asks, only slightly curious.

'Yeah. Plenty.'

'Had a cake like that once. On a Sydney to Hobart race. Some bloke's mum made it. When we unwrapped it, the cabin smelt like a distillery. Magnificent, it was. Every bloke who'd hated fruit cake all his life got into it. Fought over the last couple of slices.'

'Well, I'll make a big one and we'll see what happens.'

'*No need for a big one!*' everyone shouts at once.

Fleury makes one last attempt to get me off the boat. 'I'll wait for you at Middle Harbour,' she says. 'You're gonna hate this trip if you go all the way.'

'Yeah, you're probably right. But I've signed on for the long haul. Don't waste your petrol.'

I sailed from Melbourne with Bob on my only other small-boat ocean experience. We were helping to deliver a yacht to Sydney. Time was short because we had to be home for a wedding. Ours. We hit a squall eight hours out of Hastings that ripped the mainsail. I was so sick I couldn't move from my bunk. I lay there for three days in full wet-weather gear with a bucket tucked into the crook of my arm, stinking like a dead fish. But Bob promised me Refuge Cove would answer all my prayers. I dreamed of hot showers, café latte, clean clothes, a rental car. We arrived in the dead of a black winter night, so I didn't realise we were in the middle of a perfectly pristine national park until the sun came up.

'Where's the marina?' I wailed.

'There's a freshwater creek,' Bob offered enthusiastically. 'You can have a good wash.'

The smell of toasted egg and bacon sandwiches filled the boat. My stomach lurched, settled, then erupted.

'Great honeymoon, huh?' he joked, emptying my bucket while I considered calling off the wedding.

When we made it to Eden, I stood under a hot shower in a motel room for thirty minutes then booked a flight to Sydney. Then bad weather delayed the boat for so long, Bob nearly missed our wedding. Stacky offered to act as proxy 'as long as there's full conjugal rights, mate', he teased. Miracle, really, that Bob and I ended up married. Thing is, he always made me laugh, no matter how crook I felt.

Fleury is aware that the trip to Tasmania will be a repeat performance. People who get chronic seasickness rarely get over it. But I don't want to be held back by a body that won't always do as it is told. 'I'll call you from Hobart,' I tell her. And all she can do is shake her head.

Two weeks later, departure time is set for 10 am and Bob and I wait for Big Dave to come by in his commuter boat to pick us up from the Lovett Bay ferry wharf. There was some drizzly rain overnight and it is still overcast, which takes the worry out of leaving Pittwater at this time of the year. The damp should stall any bushfires for at least a couple of weeks. But it's not enough to end the drought. A cool breeze flutters over smooth waters, changing the colour of the sea to deep grey. We clutch our favourite pillows. At our feet, there're insulated bags filled with food: chicken with olives, tomatoes and preserved lemon, boeuf bourguignon, lamb stew with dried figs, cold roasted pork for sandwiches. The fruit cake. Some stewed apple and rhubarb with a few frozen raspberries added, to have with our breakfast cereal. A dozen fresh eggs from the E-chicks, along with the teapot, loose tea, some cheese, dry biscuits, milk and yoghurt. Just in case . . .

'Looks like we're setting off on an international expedition,' Bob says, taking stock of the supplies.

'Well, we're going to Tasmania. That's sort of overseas.'

He sighs. It is excessive, I know it is, but I cannot help myself.

Big Dave's boat comes into view, a bright yellow plastic tub taking a short cut through the moorings instead of hugging the honeycomb shoreline. No-one follows that route at night. It's too easy to run up the nose of a yacht and take your head off.

'Morning,' he says, smiling and skilfully bringing the boat alongside the wharf with a quarter of an inch to spare. He reaches out and grabs a step to hold the vessel steady. Bob passes him our pillows, wet-weather gear, kit bags, boxes, food bags and tightly packed reuseable supermarket bags. The laptop, the GPS and navigational software. When we're securely loaded, he points south east to *Intrepid*'s mooring. He doesn't say a word about all our gear.

'This is so exciting,' I gush idiotically. I'm not sure why because what I really feel is anxious.

Big Dave grins. Up ahead, *Intrepid* sparkles: glossy white

paintwork, varnished woodwork, buffed stainless steel. She's ready for the Hobart Wooden Boat Show.

'Morning,' Jackie calls, leaning over the stern and waving. She looks excited. In a worried way. If we are lucky, we will live the dream of days and nights rocked gently by kindly seas. The engine will never falter and the head will never get bunged up. But we all know oceans are capricious.

Bainy emerges from the main cabin. 'G'day,' he says, touching the peak of his black cap politely.

'Bainy! Come to say goodbye?' we ask hoping he's not here to repair the engine . . . or anything.

'Having a few problems with the oil gauge light,' Big Dave explains.

'Oh.'

The back deck is chockers when we clamber up from the commuter boat, knee-deep with food. Bob was right. There's enough for a voyage from one side of the world to the other. It's reassuring – and mortifying. Truth is, missing a few meals here and there wouldn't hurt any of us.

I grab our clothing bags to put in our cabin. Whack! Bang my head on the edge of the stairwell. I tell myself to get used to it. Jackie's made the beds with matching sheets and doonas. It looks so cosy I feel like lying down already. Oh no. Queasy. Not even off the mooring yet. Am I mad? Should I climb into a tinny and motor home, turning back only to wave goodbye? No. One day, if I am lucky, I will be truly too old for this, but not yet. Bugger, where are the pills? I dash from below to the fresh air of the back deck, almost tripping over Bainy's backside which is half in, half out of a cupboard full of wires. Jackie's got the kettle on, bless her. Tea always sorts chaos. And what we've got is chaos on a major scale.

'What time do you think we'll be away?' Bob asks casually.

'Depends on Bainy,' Big Dave replies, looking enquiringly at his rear end.

'No pressure or I'll walk off the boat,' Bainy shouts from his wire cupboard.

Big Dave rolls his eyes. Bob laughs. Bainy's running true to form.

Jackie passes around the tea and opens a plastic container. She's baked a spice cake and a banana cake. It is only the second time she's baked cakes in her life, and her thoughtfulness makes me teary. Then I greedily grab a slice of each and hit the back deck where my stomach settles instantly. I whack a couple of seasick pills down my throat to be sure. What's the rule for a dodgy belly? Stare at the land. I gaze at Bells Wharf, the pale blue shed and canary-yellow steps like a waterfront doll's house. Further along, there's the brown timber house I rented when I first moved to Pittwater, raised a metre higher and with new deck rails. Nothing stays the same.

As Bainy labours, the southerly swings around to a nor'easter, a perfect rear-end shove for the journey ahead. Everyone cheers. Around us, yellow moorings pop out of the water. Fenders hang over the sides of boats like giant teeth. In Jackie and Dave's front yard, a mahogany Buddha looks down on us benignly. Once I would have seen it as an omen, but I've long stopped searching for omens to have the courage of conviction.

Bainy is struggling. Sweat pours down his face, the wire cupboard's cramped and stuffy. Bob stands alongside to give him a hand. Bainy's too buggered to tell him to piss off.

Tony delivers Annette and her pile of bags to *Intrepid* in one of the new plastic boats that seem to be gradually replacing the banged-up tinnies on Pittwater. Perhaps they're a sign of the increasing affluence of the area. Today's technology gives many more people the choice of working from home. The new 'bath-tubs', as I like to call the plastic boats, come in rainbow colours – canary yellow, sky blue, hot pink, purple, red, grey, green and white. They are easy to maintain and manoeuvre, and stable enough for a person to balance on a corner of the stern with the risk of going overboard. They're the best thing that's ever happened at Commuter Dock: no more worries about jumping into a boat and sinking it.

Tony, Annette's husband, ties the boat to the stern and comes on board to wish us luck. Most of Annette's bags are full of food, too. What are we all frightened of? But I know. We could get blown off course, hit a horror of a storm and end up lost at sea for weeks. Ancient fears that don't really fit in the age of satellite navigation. But they lurk in the bottom of every bag of food.

Kerry's still missing.

Dave's dry goods get stored in rough order under the green banquettes. There are nibbles to have with drinks, and rice, pasta, pasta sauces, tinned fruit and vegetables. No. No chance we'll starve.

Kerry and her husband Pete finally nuzzle up to the splashboard at the stern. Kerry's dithery. The leap from tinny to boat has her flummoxed. When to jump? Now? Or now? Big Dave reaches across, grabs her and pulls. She wails, looks tippy for a second then straightens in triumph. Pete ties up and comes on board. Tinnies hang off the stern like baby ducklings. The last link with land.

'Look!' says Kerry jubilantly, holding up a package. 'I've brought custom-made seasick bags. They fit over your nose so there's no mess.'

'More luxury!' we all chorus gleefully.

By late afternoon when commuters start returning from work, we're still anchored on the mooring. They slow as they pass, their tinny's nose rising like it's sniffing the wind before dropping back onto the water, a bit baffled. We should be long gone. They're wise enough not to ask any questions, though. It's a good way to get your head bitten off.

'Have a great trip,' yells Steve.

'Good luck,' calls Lewis.

'Enjoy,' says Lisa.

The summer sun's about to sink when Bainy calls it quits. 'You can take off now,' he tells us. 'Just give her a short trial run and you're on your way. Might as well take her to The Point. Wouldn't mind a rum and coke.'

We all look at each other.

'Sleep on the boat tonight but leave departure until tomorrow, d'you think?' asks Bob.

'Nah,' we all agree. 'Let's get going!'

Pete goes home. Kerry looks abandoned, then reaches for a ciggie. This trip is her symbolic leap from headmistress into the next stage of her life. Whatever it may be. She can't weaken now. 'I've got a heap of new, matching, uncrushable outfits for cocktail hour every night,' she announces brightly. But really, it's to hide her fears.

As we untie from the mooring, Annette dives into the freezer for her spag-bol sauce, Jackie drags out a packet of dry pasta from under a seat. No-one even thinks about parmesan, probably because we can't remember where we've put it.

'Never thought thirty-five years ago that one day I'd own an ocean cruiser,' Jackie says, shaking her head at the wonder of the way life turns out. 'My mother was a servant in an English home in Malaysia.' And we both get emotional as we wait for the water to boil.

Bainy docks us at the Church Point ferry wharf with a feather-light touch. We're all grinning madly. He jumps off and waves. Big Dave rolls the palms of his hands over the control levers and we pull away. Everyone at The Point waves. Then hands stop, mid-air. Faces lose their smiles.

'Shit,' yells Bob.

'Dave!' yells Jackie.

'The fucking bow line's still tied on,' Bob yells, racing forward. *Intrepid* is about to smash the pontoon. Everyone sees it coming and, unperturbed, steps well back. I suddenly remember why boats are an acquired taste. There's always a crisis. Dave slips the gears into neutral, Jackie races to the stern to fend off the pontoon. *Intrepid*'s just had a new paint job for the Wooden Boat Festival. Bit early to scratch it.

We're finally away, unscathed. We all look at each other.

'This calls for a glass of bubbles,' Jackie says.

'To celebrate,' Kerry replies. But it's probably to settle our nerves.

'How do you feel?' Bob asks me.

'Fit as a flea!'

We clink plastic glasses, backslap a little. Bob opens the laptop and keys in our position. Pittwater! Glorious and smooth as a baby's bottom. Annette sets the table.

Kerry pulls a journal out of her handbag. She says she won't bother to change for dinner on the first night. 'I'll change tomorrow. And . . . I'm going to write a diary,' she tells us, opening the journal at page one. She's also ship's purser. 'Ok, expenses. What's been spent so far?' she asks, looking at our faces.

'Ah, let's leave all that till tomorrow,' we insist. 'This is too good.'

Lights come on along the shore, like stars anchored to the earth. Occasionally a tinny scoots past close enough to wave but we are a self-contained, self-sufficient little metropolis. And from now on, there's no escape.

19

DINNER'S OVER BY THE time we reach Barrenjoey Point where the sinister profile of a hook-nosed witch bulges out of the ochre cliffs like an evil nemesis. It's barely visible in the dark. From here, we plunge straight into the uncertain waters of the mighty Pacific Ocean.

It takes about half a minute for me to realise I am about to bring up my dinner. I dash outside. Puke. Facing the right way so it doesn't blow back in my face. It's one of the first rules you learn when you're a puker.

Half an hour later, I'm fully dressed in my bunk with a sick bag over my face, paralysed by nausea. Under the hull, I can feel the currents of the ocean, Broken Bay and the Brisbane Waters, clashing and corkscrewing the boat. My stomach heaves. I try to think of Canadian geese flying across a field of pumpkins in upstate New York, a sight I saw once and will never forget. The image has soothed me through many a rough time. But I'm sick again. 'There are fairies in the bottom of the garden', I recite, like I used to when I was a kid to help me fling a nightmare into space. But nothing works. Then Jackie hits me with a pill.

Sometime during the night, I vaguely hear Big Dave giving Kerry and Annette a crash course in navigation before they begin their first watch. Two hours on, four hours off. Twenty-four hours a day.

'No drinking at all,' he says firmly. 'No-one is allowed alcohol on a watch. It's an unbreakable rule.'

By the time I wake up early the next morning, we're well on our way to Eden with a perfect tail wind and Jackie's on her bunk with a stack of sick bags. Big Dave's talking to *the girls*.

'Putting whisky in your coffee is the same as drinking straight alcohol,' he says.

'It was *hot* coffee, Dave. That's different,' explains Annette.

'Yeah,' Kerry adds, 'the heat burns off the alcohol.'

Dave sighs loudly. 'No. It doesn't.'

'But we needed to stay awake,' Annette says. 'And it was the tiniest, little-est amount.'

'No more whisky on a watch. That's final.'

Bob comes in to our cabin with a bottle of water.

'Sounds like Dave's got a mutiny on his hands,' I joke.

'Annette and Kerry are doing brilliantly,' Bob says. 'They're amazing, actually.' He unscrews the lid and passes me the water. 'You've got to get some fluids into you.'

'Thanks.'

When he leaves the cabin, I hide the water. If I drink it I'll have to pee. To pee I have to get up. If I stand, I'll puke. Slight dehydration seems like the lesser of two evils. I struggle into my pyjama bottoms lying down. It's a start. When my stomach settles, I'll have a go at changing into the top. I take another pill. Sleep, surely, is the greatest of all cures. I roll back and forward in the bunk in time with an ocean rising on a two-metre swell. Above, Kerry and Annette are flattening their bums against the galley cupboards to keep them steady while they fix breakfast, lunch and dinner. All day, laughter floats down the stairwell. Bob's right. These two middle-aged women who have leapt into the unknown are handling the rough conditions like they're on a picnic.

'I kept waiting to hear a whinge,' Big Dave said later. 'The sea got rougher and rougher and I thought they'd crack it because it was hard going. But they never did. Even when they got blisters on their backsides from trying to stay steady.'

At some time, I don't remember when, I bang my top lip and it is bleeding. Occasionally I wake to hear Big Dave, Bob, Kerry and Annette laughing.

A girlish voice giggles. 'I'm pole-dancing. Look at me. I've always wanted to pole-dance.' There's more laughter. I feel as envious as hell.

We average seven and a half knots and slide into Eden late on the second night. The anchor hits the water with a splash, the engine gives a final throb, the deck levels out. The crashing and banging ends as though a switch has been flipped. Peace. Everyone bunks down and no-one moves until the sun comes up, bringing with it a cool, light breeze. It's a perfect day. My stomach flips back to normal. It's as though seasickness was nothing but a bad dream.

In the morning, Dave manoeuvres *Intrepid* into a slot alongside the jetty between two yachts. After tying, testing, tying again, throwing out fenders the size of large gas bottles, we jump ashore. Everyone except Kerry.

'What's the problem?' we ask. We're lined up on the wharf like sailors ready to salute.

She's wearing one of her new off-boat outfits, her hair is washed and she's got makeup on (didn't matter how rough it got, Annette, I was told later, *never* appeared on a single morning or watch without eyeliner and mascara!).

'There's a gap,' she mewls, pointing at a six-inch space between the boat and the jetty.

We all look at each other in amazement. This is a woman who's just completed a rough passage on what boaties refer to as a *confused* sea (rocking, rolling, corkscrewing). She's cooked, cleaned, stuck her head in the freezer and fridge and even managed to light a ciggie on the back deck in a howling gale. She's learned navigation, how to steer a boat and done her share of the night-time watches. She's been tough, stalwart and utterly courageous. Six inches?

'Oh, get over it,' we say. And some terror deep inside her lets go. Her shoulders fall, her face relaxes. She steps onto the gunnel, grabs Bob's hand, and jumps.

'Nothing to it,' we say, turning towards shore.

'Yeah. Nothing to it.'

'Breakfast first! What do you reckon?'

My appetite is ferocious. Bacon, eggs, a vanilla milkshake, toast. We skip the tea when we see another customer being handed a cup of hot water and a teabag.

Bob shakes his head. 'I can't believe how quickly you bounce back,' he says.

'Easy,' I reply.

We hit the local library to get a weather report. 'Not looking good,' he says. 'If we don't leave this afternoon, we'll be locked in for a couple of days. There's a strong sou'easterly coming in.'

'Bugger.' There goes a night in a quiet, level motel room and time with Bob alone.

We find the others in the supermarket. Bob gives Big Dave the news.

'Why don't we talk about it over lunch at the club,' Big Dave says. 'See what everyone wants to do.'

We order deep-fried fish, scallops, prawns and calamari. The dining room is nearly empty except for the tinny ring of pokies which drifts in from somewhere out of sight.

'The weather's building,' Big Dave says, pushing his plate away. There's plenty left on it. He looks a bit pale. 'We could hang around for a couple of days until it goes past, or we can race it. What do you want to do?'

The vote is unanimous. Race it!

Outside the shelter of Eden, the boat slaps back and forth like a pendulum on even more *confused* seas. I grab a handful of sick bags and stagger below. I hate the weakness of it, am ashamed I am no use to anyone. Loathe, even more, that there's not a damn thing I can do about it. Drifts of conversation from the main cabin float through the pill haze. Jackie's almost well although she's taking it gently. Bob is invincible. Big Dave thinks he might have food poisoning. He's gonna rest up till his watch. Annette and Kerry are planning a proper cocktail hour. They, too, are invincible.

Bob, Big Dave who's still feeling crook, and *the girls* share the four-hour watches. Then the sea isn't confused anymore, it's rough as guts.

On day four from Sydney, we make it to notorious Bass Strait. Unbelievably, the water mutes to a smooth little tango, dipping and teasing. It's dark and oily instead of ferociously unkempt. I climb out of my smelly lair, struggle into the shower and wash off two days' stink. My stomach is almost under control and I'm fit enough to do a watch. Ten pm to midnight, longer if I'm able to.

'I'll sleep on the sofa. Wake me if you're worried about anything. And I do mean anything!' says Bob.

I grab the helm although we're on automatic pilot, run my hands over the wood. The boat smoothly surfs the swell. Everyone creeps off to bed. Big Dave says he's feeling better and we're all relieved. Bob pulls up a blanket and closes his eyes. Outside, moonlight frosts the water. Within a few minutes, the boat is silent. There's just the sound of water licking the hull and the steady, reassuring beat of the engine. I have memorised my instructions: *Watch for lights. If they're green, don't worry. It's a boat that will pass safely. If they're red, be careful. If they're red and green, change course immediately. We're on a collision course.*

A thin film of cloud softens the moonlight and we float like a matchstick on a sea that rises and falls as steadily as a heartbeat. It's a pure world.

Nearly two hours into the watch, eyes strained from searching the horizon for lights, I jump. From the outside deck, a black hand reaches for the door into the cabin. My heart thumps, panic pushing aside reason. It's an illusion. There is nothing but emptiness.

I check the time to see how much longer it is before the next watch begins. Then I notice the date. February the fifth. My brother's birthday. It's thirteen years since he died and out here on the water with no-one to hear, I have a long conversation with him. To bring him up to date. On the sea, with only unknown depths and a vast universe for company, it seems a completely normal thing to do. 'Life's good,' I tell my brother when I have nothing more to add. 'Life's good.'

We race the weather and make Wineglass Bay on the east coast of Tasmania before the wind builds to thirty knots and the seas turn black and ugly. A pod of dolphins escorts us through the entrance passage. It is a moment so exquisite none of us can speak. Inside the protective headlands, the turquoise bay is flat and almost tropical. The dolphins frolic around the boat, sticking their heads out of the water and grinning at us before plunging deep and swimming back out to sea. I lie on the bow in the sun and count clouds. Then Jackie gets out the vaccum cleaner. Kerry mops the floor. I cook lunch. Annette washes the dishes.

'Feeling a bit crook,' Big Dave says, scrunching the skin on his chest into a ball. 'But I'll be right.' He helps Bob lower the tinny from the deck to the water so we can go ashore for a walk. Kerry climbs aboard, no problems. On shore, we follow the curve of the white sand until *Intrepid* looks no bigger than a dinghy in the distance.

The next morning, boats not as lucky as we were limp in.

Someone's broken a wrist, another an ankle. It is hellish rough beyond the bay.

Big Dave says he's having back spasms. We discuss calling for a chopper to airlift him to hospital. His face looks green, yellow sometimes, too.

'It's not a heart attack, though,' says his wife, who's the midwife. 'He'd be dead by now.'

'No chopper,' Big Dave says. 'No way.' But he doesn't eat much lunch. Or dinner. He sleeps through breakfast. It's such uncharacteristic *Big Dave* behaviour that we think of overriding his orders and organising to evacuate him. He threatens to whack the first hand that reaches for a mobile phone.

A day later, the weather report sounds ok. Big Dave looks a little fitter.

'Must've pulled a muscle,' someone suggests.

'I reckon it's his gall bladder,' says Kerry.

'Nah. He doesn't fit the profile,' I tell her. 'You've got to be fair, fat, female, fertile and forty.' I know, because I've had mine out.

'Well, at least it's not his heart. The rest can be fixed in Hobart,' says Annette.

Bob doesn't even try to guess. 'He looks crook, though, that's for sure,' he says.

We up anchor and make our way south. The weather is kind, the water smooth. Sleek dolphins appear out of nowhere and dive through our wake, wild and free. Along the coast, breaking waves surge towards the rugged shore. Shoals of fish scoot in glittering turmoil. Terns skate, smooth and precise, barely breaking the surface. Then the dunny blocks up. Bob finds a thick ball of hair – Annette's colour. She's cleaned her hairbrush.

'Don't do that again!' Bob pleads.

'Sorry,' she says, mortified.

Late in the afternoon, we cut through the waterway between Cape Pillar and Tasman Island. Lobster pots marked by colourful buoys linger outside mysterious dark caves that must fill and empty with the tide. Seaweed sways like ballroom skirts from the hemline of the rocky shore. Surrounded by a bleak, forbidding landscape of iron-grey escarpments and arid peaks razored flat by wind and weather, the cliffs are like prison bars, an echo of the island's violent past. It's impossible not to shiver.

We anchor in smooth, protected waters near the convict ruins of Port Arthur. Red bricks, wreathed in brutal history, ring the roofline like broken teeth. The sky turns black as thick low cloud creeps towards us from the south west. Inside the cabin, even the cheery yellow sunflowers printed on the tablecloth fail to shift the gloom. Big Dave's face is a pale shade of green. He rallies to find some local lobsters to buy for dinner. Our moods lift. But when they're cooked and waiting lusciously on our plates, split down the middle and fat with pearly flesh, he takes a few bites then goes below to lie down. His expression is hammered, his eyes cloudy with pain.

Jackie throws together a handful of pills and gives them to him with a glass of water.

'What do you think is wrong?' we ask her anxiously.

'How would I know? I'm a midwife!'

In the morning, Big Dave says he's definitely feeling better, but he doesn't touch breakfast and his skin has turned yellow.

'Next stop Hobart,' someone mutters. 'Let's get going.'

Rounding Cape Raoul into Storm Bay on the final leg of the voyage, the weather blows up hard and fast. It's so rough the boat is tossed from side to side and water pours over the gunnels to drain away at the stern.

'Feels more *confused* than usual,' I say, grabbing a sick bag and lurching towards the cabin. Halfway down the steps, I puke.

'Oh no,' Bob groans. 'Thought you'd broken through the

barrier on Bass Strait.' He grabs my soiled bag, hands me another. 'I think this might be your last ocean voyage, my dear,' he adds.

'Like hell!' Wretched times, after all, are so quickly forgotten. Or at least the pain of them. What I *will* remember is sliding into the captain's chair, reaching for the helm, being part of the glistening night. Navigating dark waters. In such synchrony with the physical world, for a moment or two I felt immortal.

'I don't want to go to my bunk. I'll miss our arrival. Does anyone mind if I hang on the sofa? If I promise not to puke again?'

Bob looks at the girls, his eyebrows raised. 'Go for it!' they insist. I stretch out with my head on one of Jackie's red and gold brocade cushions where I have a perfect view of the outside world.

'Ah shit,' we hear Big Dave yell from below. 'We forgot to put out the stabilisers.'

Two massive and awkward weights known as 'fish' hang from outriggers on each side of the boat to moderate motion. They surfed alongside us from Sydney, just under the water, like faithful guards, until they were stowed in Wineglass Bay. Until now, the seas have been so placid, we all forgot about them.

'There's Iron Pot,' Bob says, pointing at a boxy red and white lighthouse on a barren, rocky island at the mouth of the Derwent River. 'We're nearly there.' Inside the sheltered waters, the sea reduces to a simmer but the wind is even more ferocious.

'Why is it called Iron Pot?' I ask.

'See the flat rock at the base of the island?'

I nod.

'According to legend, whalers dragged carcasses onto the rocks for butchering, then they boiled the meat in iron pots. It's theory, though. No-one's sure.'

At Constitution Dock, Big Dave, sick and weak, manoeuvres *Intrepid* in a 25-knot wind with a gearshift that takes twenty seconds to lock in.

'He's captain,' Bob says. 'He won't let anyone else take the helm and he's right.'

The old Hobart dock is racked with neatly nestled, pretty wooden yachts, steamers, barges and working boats, many of them historic and antique. Done out in cushions and covers, with flags flying in celebration, they have been lovingly tarted up for the festival. One wrong move and Big Dave could reduce them all to scrap wood. He reverses, moves forward, over and over, gaining an inch, a foot, a yard. Sweat pours down a face the colour of an oyster. Time after time, yachts bear down on us from the Derwent River. Are they blind to our strife? No. It's just that the wind's so strong everyone's stampeding to shelter.

When it seems we'll never make it without destroying the fleet, a rogue gust lifts the boat and carries us in the right direction. Big Dave gets a clear swing into the berth. We nick the paint of a tender boat hanging off the back of a multimillion dollar catamaran, but it's not even worth a touch-up. We cheer.

Big Dave slumps over the wheel. Then he looks up and smiles.

'Feeling a bit better,' he tells Jackie. 'I'll wait until tomorrow to see the doctor. I think I'm coming good.'

We yell at him, then Jackie grabs his arm and forces him off the boat.

A day later, a surgeon removes his gall bladder in the Hobart hospital.

'A few hours away from septicaemia,' the doctor tells Big Dave. 'You're a lucky man.'

'How soon can I get out of here, Doc?' Big Dave wheedles as charmingly as he can in a too-small hospital gown, tubes hanging out of his arm.

'You were a terrible mess, mate. You don't recover overnight. You'll be here a week. At least.'

'But I'm gonna circumnavigate Tassie,' he moans. 'I've got crew.'

'You a yachtie?' asks the doctor. 'S'pose you could be out of here in three days. Your wife's a nurse, isn't she? I do a bit of sailing myself . . .' And he settles on the end of Big Dave's too-short bed for a chat.

The big circumnavigation never happens. The weather gets grouchy and the Tassie coastline, especially the west coast, kills you if you treat it with anything less than total respect. I have an assignment in Western Australia, so I can't continue with the group. Bob and I book a swank hotel room for my last night in town. I fill the bath as soon as we check in and we sit in it for hours, drinking champagne.

'Wish I could do the trip home with you,' I say.

Bob shakes his head. 'We'll find more suitable adventures,' he says. 'The world's full of them.'

At breakfast the next day, before I leave for the airport, we're all gathered over French toast, bacon and eggs. Porridge.

'We need another fella for the trip home,' Big Dave and Bob agree. And out of the blue, an old buddy of Big Dave's wanders past and yes, he's got a bit of time on his hands. He signs on. I later heard he looked up an ex-girlfriend when the boat docked at Eden. She turned out to be Kerry's niece. Weird coincidence? Maybe. But I've lived long enough to believe there are forces at work that none of us understands. A year after that fateful saunter past a Hobart café, Big Dave's friend is a new dad happily living on the south coast of New South Wales. He could so easily have said no to Big Dave but he took a chance and his world opened up.

Intrepid 11 arrives home two weeks later to a flotilla of welcoming tinnies. We all race up to the stern of that brave, strong, tough, reliable and thoroughly cosy old girl whose engine never skipped a beat, then tie on while she chugs sedately to her mooring. We jump aboard to slap backs, cheer, share a beer and welcome the great navigators home. Bob stands on the back deck, where only three weeks earlier we planned cocktails at sunset and afternoon card games. Delusional, we were, absolutely delusional. He slips his arm around my waist. He is unshaven and stinks, ever so slightly, of diesel. He is irresistible.

Three days after *Intrepid*'s return, Fleury calls with distressing news. 'Katie's not well,' she says. 'We're all worried.'

'What's happened?'

'She's having tumours taken off her lungs. It means the experimental chemo didn't knock out the growths,' she replies. 'Her emails are full of energy, though, and she's prepared a new exhibition. She's focusing on that. And with Katie, you never know. She's beaten the odds so far.'

About two days later, Sharon calls to say she's in hospital.

'Oh, Sharon, what's the problem?'

'Well, this is punishment, I am sure, for a lifetime of *toast with my butter*. My heart has staged a rebellion.'

'How are you feeling?'

'A little tired, dear. Yes. A little tired.'

'You'll be right, Sharon, you'll be right.'

The day after Sharon phones, it's suffocatingly hot. I'm lost amongst the spaghetti lanes of a motorway I didn't even know existed. My mother sits beside me, her hands folded in her lap. I'm trying not to let my frustration rub off on her. Two bunches of oriental lilies have collapsed on the back seat.

'If I could read maps, I'd try to help. Never been able to understand them,' she says.

'Now I know where I get it from.'

'You can blame me for a few things, but not everything,' she whacks back.

We're on our way to visit Sharon. I introduced my mother to

her when I took them both to lunch one day. It became a routine, afterwards, to take them together to restaurants where they could look at the ocean and feel the sun on their faces. They forged a most unlikely friendship. My mother is Miss Corn, Sharon is almost unbearably proper, but they bring out the best in each other. My mother stops trying to be funny and opts for a little dignity while Sharon drops her reserve and lets her sense of humour loose.

With Sharon's prodding, my mother decides that, after all, my cooking isn't too terrible and she wouldn't mind a few 'offcuts from the main house', as she calls it.

'You've always hated my cooking,' I respond, amazed.

'I love your cooking!'

'Well, why did you say *no* to everything I offered you?'

'I didn't want to bother you. You do enough. But if you're cooking for Sharon, I might as well get in on it.'

And my cheeks flush with shame. Is that what's gone wrong for most of our lives – I've misinterpreted consideration as rejection?

When we finally find the hospital, Sharon is sitting in a chair beside her hospital bed. Her arms are black with bruising, her ankles swollen to bursting. But her face is pink, her skin flawless. She is still incredibly pretty, with an Alice band holding her wavy white hair off her face.

'You look fantastic!'

My mother, who's never in her life kissed a single human being on the cheek socially, bends unsteadily and grazes Sharon's cheek.

'Love your nightie,' she whispers.

'I'm told it's a style that's sweeping the world,' Sharon responds, looking at her crumpled hospital-issue robe with three ties down the back.

'You don't look a bit sick,' I tell her, sitting on one of those dreaded hissing hospital chairs. The sound makes me want to flee, takes me back to that room of last resorts with a thin tube trickling a bright red chemical into my veins. The remembered smell of chemo is so strong, even the pungent sweetness of the lilies fails to dislodge it. I swallow old fears.

'Here, Sharon, some flowers.' I hold out the bunches. 'They should come good in a bit of water. It was shockingly hot in the car.'

'Ah, lilies. Lilies to lie on a coffin,' she says, softly. And I could kick myself. Hasn't my mother told me a hundred times that for her generation, lilies in a house mean death?

'No, Sharon. These are oriental lilies, not arum lilies.'

'Ah.'

But we both know lilies are lilies.

'What's the doctor telling you?'

'He says he does six pacemaker operations a day and they are all easy, but I am not easy. He needs time to think about my case.'

'Are you in pain?'

'No, not really. But I think I know what dying is like, now. And it's not frightening at all.

'You see, the night I was admitted, I remember lying in bed and seeing an old friend hovering in the corner of the ceiling. He held the most exquisite bunch of pink roses I've ever seen. I looked at him and felt a bit confused. I thought I'd been to his funeral about twenty years ago, but I asked him how he was and what he was doing. And he said he was well and he'd come back to see me tomorrow.

'When I woke, he'd gone. And he hadn't even bothered to leave me the roses. I was quite put out.'

'Do you think that was death, Sharon?'

'It was certainly strange. But I felt the most wonderful peace. It was quite seductive.'

'Was it your old flame, Sharon, the man you should have married, hanging from the ceiling?'

'No. Just an old friend.'

20

A FEW MONTHS LATER, wind blasts from the south, cold, bleak and so strong that eight trees fall on the back track. Palm fronds fly through the sky, boats break their moorings and run aground. The bays are empty. Not a tinny in sight. The sound is cacophonous, the power frightening. The wind rages for nearly two days, building in ferocity until it seems every house and tree must surely be ripped to pieces and blown out to sea.

On the other side of the bay, a tree comes down and smashes between two houses, ripping out a wall and destroying a kitchen. Michael jumps in his tinny and races across the water. The house, thankfully, is empty. On the way home, waves spill over his bow as he weaves to dodge debris – bits of boats, houses, branches and fenders. He scoops up the fenders. Plastic doesn't rot.

Near Clareville, a 54-foot yacht breaks its mooring. It rams two other boats, crashes through a public pool and ends up jammed under a wharf. Bob decides to check the date that *Larrikin's* mooring needs a service.

Tarrangaua stands firm. Only Barbara's camellias lie flat in the back courtyard, their pots tipped over. They are miraculously undamaged. A large branch has fallen from a spotted gum, too, but only onto the lawn. It will make good firewood. The *Tin Shed* is also safe in its small hollow, protected from all winds except a westerly.

'Shocker of a couple of days,' says Michael when we are counting our blessings. 'Didn't know it could blow so hard.'

The wind brings rain, cold, hard drops that sting like insect bites. They slap the big leaves of the magnolia in the courtyard, sounding like tennis balls on a racquet. Then the deluge begins. The waterfall gushes white foam, the bush slowly raises its head and sloughs off the dust of the past five years. But we are all cautious. We have celebrated the end of the dry before only to see rain clouds move out to sea and forget to come back.

'Maybe it takes extremes to turn around weather patterns,' I say to Bob, which makes him smile because he says I always have to find a reason to explain even the smallest changes. Until I had cancer I didn't care much about whys or wherefores. Now, perhaps because I'll never really know why my cells went nuts and turned on me, I insist on trying to find explanations. Even if they're far-fetched. 'This *could* be the end of the drought.'

'Let's wait and see,' he replies.

The rain goes on for seven days. No-one whinges. Then the sun returns and washing machines crank up all over Pittwater, clotheslines aflutter. Windows and doors are flung open and mould rubbed away with vinegar.

'Is that all we're going to get?' we ask each other.

Then the rains come again and again, steady and heavy. This drought, at last, is over. Colour erupts. Angophoras: white. Grevilleas: pink. Banksias: orange and yellow. Wax flowers: girly pink. Flannel flowers: off-white. Boronia: pale pink, dark pink and almost purple. Hardenbergia: purple. Blueberry ash: white with purple berries. Pittosporums: white. Lilly pillys: cream with deep red fruit. Goodenia: bright yellow. Brachycome: deep mauve.

Pseuderanthemum: so shy and delicate, pale lilac. Commelina: vivid blue.

For the first time in my life, I see dwarf xanthorrhoeas in bloom. Lemony bottlebrush flowerheads on five-foot long slim stalks that shoot from the ground like fairground lollipops.

'Walk with me tomorrow,' I implore Bob. 'I want you to see them.'

Two days, that's all we had to look at them before they vanished. Wallabies must find their sappy heads delectable. They will not bloom again until fire and rain come together closely.

In the gullies along the back track vines explode from the ground fingering from tree to bush until they form a thick canopy, a swaying roof that changes the pecking order of the plants. How quickly the landscape grows lush in the right conditions. Like people.

On walks spiders are rampant. St Andrews cross: elegant, with long, yellow stripes and pincer legs they bring together until they look like four instead of eight. Black house spiders: squat and black with furry legs, desperately ugly with a nasty bite. Jumping spiders with yellow-green horizontal stripes, beguilingly beautiful. Daddy-long-legs, fine as X-rays. Huntsmen: fawn and sleek with fine hair like a dog's, some of them so big they give you a fright. Where are the golden orbs this summer, with their glittering webs and banded yellow legs?

Thin, sticky wires span the back track. They wreathe the court-yard in hundreds of perfectly spun threads like stars or cut diamonds and on them, the spiders wait, ever so patiently, for the kill. In the tinny, a huntsman takes up residence. He drops from a crevice in the windows one morning and my first instinct is to jump overboard. Then I remember: *I am strong.*

Apple-green inch worms dangle at the end of gossamer threads along the back track. They fall down our shirts, crawling, until we strip and shake them out. The air turns thick and steamy, sticking to our lungs when for so long it slipped in and out of us dryly, leaving only the dusty scent of parched eucalyptus leaves. On the track, water runs in busy little streams, gouging out new pathways to the bay below. Water, water everywhere. We put on gumboots to slosh through the mud. The noise of the waterfall wafts around the bay sounding like birds in flight.

The golden orbs appear in late February, thousands of them. They hang from their webs immobile, like pretty brooches. I am so relieved to see them. They appeared so late, I worried for a while that some dreaded, unseen calamity was at work, like the worldwide death of busy lizzies. There are leeches, too, that cling between our toes until they are big and fat and we scream and pour salt on them to make them drop off, and blood fills our shoes for a while, warm and wet. And ticks. Sly and vicious. A quick sting turns into a throbbing, itchy welt and we try not to scratch but at night, in our sleep, we tear at our skin until it bleeds.

Katie lived long enough to know her exhibition at the Redfern Gallery in London was a success. A sell-out. She died in her new home on the banks of the Thames, with her husband Alex and her sister, Carol, by her side. Working her massive antique printing press in the light-filled eyrie at the top of the house until she could no longer find the strength to sign a print. She was not a woman who understood the concept of *giving up*.

Alex plans to come back to Pittwater soon. We will gather at Stewart and Fleury's and toast Katie in a way we know she would love. On a summer evening as dusk coats Towlers Bay in a silver slick, with a good bottle of red – or two – and some fabulous cheeses. If we can, we will sing. But that might be too hard.

Sharon moves into a nursing home not far from the retirement village where my mother lives. It's pleasant enough but it wrecks me to go there to sit with her. Is it the indignity all around? Waxen faces, ropes of white hair, bodies lying on beds with eyes closed and mouths open, hanging on grimly to every last breath?

'Don't you ever put me in there,' my mother orders.

'Don't worry. I'll club you if you even get to the semi-coma stage.'

'You won't have to. I'll take care of things myself.'

But how do we ever know what we will do until we are faced with the decision? And I, of all people, know that life in just about any form is precious.

'Long way to go yet,' I tell my mother. 'For both of us.' And I hope with all my heart that it's true.

After a while, Sharon is able to walk again with her frame. She dresses with care each day and sits in an armchair beside her bed. She is witty, charming and self-deprecating about the cursed restrictions of old age. There is never a single moment when she lapses into self-pity. The closest she ever came to a complaint was to confess she sometimes craved a simple tomato sandwich.

'I can make you one of those,' my mother says, 'whenever you like.'

She abandons the sofa and summer sport on television to take charge of Sharon's welfare and we deliver the food together, or she calls a taxi if I'm not available.

'I think she saved my life,' Sharon says when I visit her. 'For the first four days I was here, the kitchen brought me food I knew could kill me. Swimming in fat. Your mother came with a banana. It could not have been more perfect. I ate it in a single mouthful. Well, almost. And she went home and brought another and another.'

Each day my mother devises new treats. Ham off the bone in

a white bread sandwich, no butter, plenty of slices of tomato. Smoked salmon salad with red onion and capers and drizzled in lemon juice. Chicken, skin removed, alongside an old-fashioned iceberg lettuce salad.

'Your mother arranges each plate like an artist, as though she's going to paint it,' Sharon tells me.

And I begin to see this mother with whom I've battled for so long through the eyes of someone else. I have been judge and bully. Off-hand and unthinking. I have held back praise and affection when it would have cost nothing. I have looked for gratitude for every small gift and given none in return for a lifetime of giving. *She nursed me like a heart patient after I had scarlet fever, for God's sake!* And through how many other childhood dramas? Adult, too, here and there. Although I never had the guts to tell her about my seediest moments.

'You have done everything with your life that I dreamed of doing with mine,' she told me one day. And I realised I am who I am because of – not despite – her.

Did I get my love of cooking from her? Did she insist I listen to music until I heard the passion in it? Did she tell me books were the key to the universe? Did she withhold praise only to make me try harder? Did she know – and of course she did – that there would be times ahead when the framework we all build to make us feel secure would come tumbling down and unless you have learned toughness, you crash with it? Of course she did. Did I dismiss her as frivolous because I failed to see it was her way of handling tragedy? Did I close my eyes to her long empty nights after my father died as I pursued my own dreams?

If she were someone else's mother, would I see her as my friends tell me they see her? 'She is strong,' they say. 'She is a character. She's tough. And she's very, very funny.'

≈

The doctor tells Sharon there is nothing he can do for her. She needs surgery to implant the pacemaker but she is not strong enough to handle it. And even if she were, there is the matter of cancer. All he can do, he says, is make her as comfortable as possible.

Sharon is devastated. She thought she was getting better and would soon be well enough to return to her villa. For a day or two she reels. Then she puts the *small matter* of death aside and calls my mother. 'Do you have a needle and thread?' she asks.

'Yes,' my mother replies.

'Could you bring them with you the next time you come? I have a button to sew on.'

'I'll bring it with your fruit.'

My mother phones to tell me what the doctor has told Sharon.

'What did you say to her?' I ask.

'I said, "Sharon, I've never lost a patient yet and you're not going to be the first."'

'That was good.' But I want to cry, because her words are perfect. And my mother didn't even have to think about it.

'I'd like to bring someone to lunch,' my mother says in the middle of the supermarket. She leans forward on the trolley, and it supports her through the aisles. Slower than slow. I am tempted to grab it and whip around quickly while she sits and waits, but I hold back. She is heading for ninety and she still takes care of herself. And Sharon. She is, in fact, amazing.

Her trolley is full of custardy desserts. 'Would you like some eggs? Bacon?' I suggest, trying to move her beyond sugar.

'Don't be silly. They're fattening. Oh, shut up,' she adds, although I haven't said a word.

'So who do you want to bring to lunch?'

'Just someone I've met at the village. We get along very well. He's extremely interesting.'

He?

She reaches for soy milk. 'I'm allergic to dairy,' she explains.

I look at the desserts, zip my lips. With luck I, too, will be her age one day and able to do as *I* damn well please.

'Sounds ok. When do you want to bring him over?'

'Whenever.'

'Is this some kind of . . . fling?'

'Don't be ridiculous. I am an aging woman. We just get along. We think alike.' Then she smiles. Looks coquettish. 'Your mother,' she says, 'has still got it, kid.'

At home, I tell Bob the news. 'A bloke,' I say, 'she's got a bloke. And he's young enough to have his driver's licence. Maybe she'll be off our hands for a while.'

Bob looks at me. 'Doubt it. Just means we could have two of them to look after.'

I finally contact heritage architect Howard Tanner, and he kindly agrees to take a look at *Tarrangaua*. This will be my last step in the search to discover who designed the house. I have no regrets about taking on this funny little personal quest to ensure that the correct man doesn't have the credit snatched from him as time blurs the line between fact and fiction.

Researching the past has opened new doors, led to knowledge, given me a tiny insight into what it must have been like to take on the challenge of settling here in the early days of last century. Mostly, it has stopped my world from shrinking. What was it the Bangalow rug seller said? Knowledge keeps you young?

Tanner arrives with his wife Mary on 28 January, the final day of a sunny, breezy, Australia Day long weekend. I do not realise, until a few weeks later, that he chose a singularly appropriate date: Barbara first saw the house on 28 January 1993, when she and Bob walked through the bush. The same day a year later, they took possession of it.

Tanner, a neat man, stands at the front of the house, near where the Australian flag flies strongly from the top of the flagpole with the small plaque: *Barbara Story 1943 – 2000*. He looks at the roof lines, asks how many foundation piers there are. Bob gives him the information. Then Tanner wanders along the verandah. 'In Mackellar's day,' he tells us, 'summers were often lived on the verandah. People covered them with daybeds, tables and chairs, sofas. It was cooler than the house. And thought to be healthy.'

'I can never understand why there are so many doors into the main room,' I say, leading the way inside.

'So the servants could access both ends without walking through it,' he replies.

'And the locks on every single cupboard?'

'Servants,' he repeats.

After he's had a thorough look, we have tea and cake on the verandah, in the same spot the Buddhist nun tells us Mackellar ate her lunch: 'She always kept an eye out for kookaburras. They often waited patiently on the dead bough of a spotted gum for the moment they could safely snatch the steak from her plate,' Adrienne said.

Two hours after he arrived, Tanner stands to leave.

'I had a feeling I should have checked the dates about Dods before wondering if he might have been involved in the design,' Tanner says. 'But the columns are such a feature of Dods' style, it seemed to make sense.'

'What's always had me stumped,' I say, 'is why Wilson, Neave and Berry would have designed a septic tank for the house if they had nothing to do with the rest of it.'

Tanner smiles. 'A defining point,' he concedes.

≈

'Now the rains are here, what do you think about a paella down by the little beach?' I suggest.

'Do you mean light a fire?' Bob asks.

'If it's safe enough.'

'So wet we might not get it to start,' he replies.

'You're the combustion engineer. And you like a challenge.'

We load the blackened steel washing machine drum in the back of The Pug along with enamel plates, mismatched cutlery, a camp table, folding camp chairs and an old kilim – with holes chewed in it by one dog or another over the years – that I bought for my brother as a wedding present when I travelled through Afghanistan in my twenties. Before I discovered his new bride preferred silk carpets. We take a plastic groundsheet to go under it.

There are gas lanterns, fishing rods, bait, two big cast iron pans. I cheat, though, and fry the onion and garlic in the house. The rice, tomatoes, spices, prawns and chorizo go in a plastic container, homemade stock in a plastic screw-top jar. There are crusty baguettes to sop up the juices. Wine and beer, water with home-grown limes and mint from Bob's herb garden in the courtyard. Dessert is butter, almond and coconut cake with blue-berries and cream. I've poached some nectarines, too. And made a custard with vanilla beans, cinnamon and star anise. What's a picnic without dessert?

I call Stewart and Fleury, Nick and Ann, David and Caro and John and Therese, who have moved from the *Tin Shed* into a home of their own. They are just a little further along the shoreline in Lovett Bay, so we have not lost them from our 'chosen family'.

'Miss the shiny-headed old bugger poking around the boatshed every morning,' Michael said not long after they set up in their new house on a point with views to Palm Beach. 'He was part of the routine.'

We call Michael and Mary Beth, Ric and Bella, Jack and Brigitte and the new tenants living in the *Tin Shed*, Martin and Ulrike, who are from Germany.

'Maybe the rain has brought back the fish so bring your rods,' we tell everyone on the day of the paella. 'We've got plenty of bait.'

Under a sky splattered with stars, we friends and neighbours eat and talk and reminisce. I feel like my life really began when I moved to this wondrous little bay. And again, I am struck by the irony that I needed to face death to understand life.

'This is the stuff of magic,' I say to Bob. He threads bait onto his hook and casts his line from the pontoon where our two tinnies are tied side by side.

'Life doesn't get much better than this,' he replies.

I nod, cup my hand around his face and lean against him lightly. The moon is a yellow crescent in a purple sky.

EPILOGUE

TO CELEBRATE MY MOTHER'S eighty-seventh birthday, Bob and I take her to a swish restaurant with kind young waiters and views of Whale Beach and the Pacific Ocean. When we ask Esther if she'd like to invite her new beau, she shakes her head. 'He's a friend, I've told you that. Just a friend.'

'You can still ask him along.'

'No. I don't mind talking about other people, but I'm not going to have anyone gossiping about me,' my mother states firmly. 'At my age, anyway, you get too selfish. And people think you're nothing but a silly old woman.'

My mother wears a tan and white suit that hugs her figure. She looks wonderful, and she knows it. She flirts outrageously with the waiter and then kisses him on the cheek as we leave. 'If only I were sixty years younger,' she tells him.

'If only . . .' he replies, smiling beautifully and playing the game. He makes her feel desirable, which is the best birthday present of all.

Big Dave is looking for crew to make the passage across the Pacific Ocean to the island of Vanuatu on *Intrepid 11*. He spins tales of syrupy tropical nights, white-gold beaches and azure waters when we meet as we pass through The Point. The light of passion flashes in his eyes. Then he looks at me and shakes his head. 'Might be better if you fly and meet us there,' he suggests. 'But Bob . . . what do you think? Want to have a go?'

So far, Bob has resisted, but as we turn away I see a glimmer of desire on his face. 'Why don't we go?' I ask once or twice.

'We'll see what happens,' he replies.

The rain comes down for thirteen days straight and mould rampages through the cupboards. Leeches become so bold they hover, heads swaying like dancing cobras, at the back door, hoping to latch on to us with their sharp little teeth.

Then a southerly wind turns the temperature from cool to cold and the idea of a smooth little dish of Spiced Cottage Cheese Custard is irresistible. I follow the directions from Mackellar's handwritten notes perfectly, a first for me. The result is a lovely old-fashioned and very easy dessert, although it's worth mentioning that there's a missing quarter of a cup of sugar in the list of ingredients.

I make it a second time with a few changes: I infuse the milk with a cinnamon quill and vanilla bean because the cinnamon powder makes the custard look a bit *curried* in colour which I find a little off-putting. I replace the cottage cheese with ricotta, and instead of stirring the mixture, I whiz all the ingredients in the food processor except the hot milk, which I stir in before pouring the mixture into cups. This method makes a smoother dessert. I use canned baby apricots and canned whole baby pears. The apricots are richer.

Just when I think I've put the *Tarrangaua* architect question to bed forever, John Pearman, whom we invited to see the house a few weeks earlier, calls to say he's been doing some research. Would we care to hear it?

'Yes!' I reply, emphatically. And Bob and I make a date to meet him at *Moonview.*

It is a wet, clammy and cold day but none of us dares to complain. It would be blasphemy to wish the rain away when so much of the country is still powdery and parched. My Uncle Frank says it will take ten years of steady rain in the right season to restore lushness to his land. 'And when have we ever had that in this country?' he asks. For the first time ever, there is a hint of resignation in his voice. The final six rows of peach trees, he then tells me, have just been ploughed in. The old orchard, due to be sown with pasture, will be put up for sale in spring. But I can't help thinking that farmers are optimists and that if it rains this winter and the dams fill to overflowing, the family will plant new trees and stay on. Life is always a gamble of one kind or another, no matter where you are. But Uncle Frank is past eighty now, and bouncing back is no longer so easy.

At *Moonview*, John leads the way inside and points at a small square table with two chairs in the library. Bob and I sit down. John steps back a little and in his deep, mellifluous voice says: 'I have had a quick look at Hardy Wilson's houses and I believe there is evidence to support the view that *Tarrangaua* was built by Wilson, Neave and Berry.'

Bob and I are silent. John, still wearing his tweed cap, his wind-cheater zipped over plain, green cotton overalls (he has an identical pair for each day of the week), looks us in the eye. The room is filled with a sense of drama.

'*Tarrangaua* is a no-frills house,' he continues. 'There is none of the scholarly detail you would expect from Hardy Wilson. But they were probably left out because of access problems. *Or* . . . pared back to adapt to the site. The house is brilliantly situated and has a fine sense of proportion, which is what Wilson did best. His imitators are never quite as clever,' he says, making his first point.

'One of the most obvious missing details is shutters. Wilson used them prolifically and they were his trademark. He believed they were an excellent way to keep houses ventilated. But that doesn't mean he never designed a house without them. In 1926, the year after it is believed *Tarrangaua* was built, he designed a home for Mrs Ryan in Kiama, also without shutters.' Pearman opens a folder filled with copies of plans of Wilson's buildings. He points to a drawing of Mrs Ryan's house with its unadorned windows.

'Now, look at this. The back to back – or twin – front steps were used for the first time at *Tarrangaua* but they appeared again here, at *Barford*, which was built in 1931 for Hardy Wilson's niece, Betty (Wilson) Fairfax. Admittedly, Wilson was no longer part of the practice, but the precedent is there.'

Next, Pearman reaches for a copy of *A 20th Century Colonial*, published by the National Trust to celebrate the centenary of Wilson's birth. He points to a drawing of a cottage in Burwood, built for Mrs Murray in 1914, listed in the '*Inventory of Architectural Works*', which I notice was compiled by Howard Tanner. Would Tanner, I can't help wondering, add *Tarrangaua* to this list in the future?

'Let us look at columns, such a feature of Wilson's work. He favoured elegant, detailed and tapered columns, yet they are unadorned and muscular at *Tarrangaua*. Well, the pergola at *Macquarie Cottage* at Pymble' – Pearman opens Zeny Edwards' biography of Wilson to page 203 and points to a photograph – 'has identical columns. So, too, does *Andreas House*.'

He closes the book and returns to the folder of architectural drawings from which he selects a copy of the plans for *Andreas*

House. 'You see? They are substantial. It is also worth noting that the pavilion in the garden of Wilson's home, *Purulia*, had similar columns.'

He then makes a series of quick points: 'The sleep-out at the eastern end of the verandah was typical of Wilson. In those days, people were expected to get up with the sun.

'The bagged brick walls were a Wilson trademark.

'Wilson also approved of the Arts and Crafts Movement, and on page 160 of his biography, there is a drawing of cupboards designed for a dining room in 1916. The metal latches and slab doors are similar at *Tarrangaua*.

'Although the fireplace at *Tarrangaua* has been interfered with, the mantelpiece is very similar to the one in *Purulia* and the large main living room is typical. So, too, is the "circulation" corridor connecting all the rooms.

'The rear courtyard is also found in many Wilson homes. The Chinese, whom Wilson admired greatly, believed they brought light into dark areas. They were known as "wells of heaven". A wonderful description, don't you think?'

He closes his books and puts away his reference materials with great care.

'You have been very kind and diligent, John. Thank you,' I say.

His face breaks into a smile. 'Oh, not at all. It was great fun. Learning and discovering, well, what else is there?'

Later, after we have toured his amazing home again, he tells us he's worked hard to regenerate the nature reserve that is his back-yard. Once it was infested with lantana and privet and even the wreck of an old Austin car with an English numberplate and the keys still in the ignition. 'There was a skull on the front seat, too, but it was porcelain. Part of an elaborate practical joke.'

His environmental house, he adds, and the beautifully restored bush, will be bequeathed as an environmental educational centre to show people how they can live sustainably in the city – like

Jeanne, who plans to leave her house and garden in trust for the people of Australia to enjoy. 'It is my legacy,' Pearman says.

Legacy. Such an old-fashioned concept. More noble, somehow, than 'inheritance', which reeks of greed and never seems to do anyone much good anyway. Certainly not Dorothea Mackellar. What would she have been capable of, if she'd had to strive? 'There was too, too much money,' a Mackellar family friend told Jyoti Brunsdon. Mackellar may have left a fortune when she died but she believed her *legacy*, the single thing that defined her life, was her poem, 'My Country'.

'In truth, none of us owns anything, especially land. We are only custodians for a very short while,' Pearman says. He gazes through a window. 'Brush and comb gardens are dead compared to living in the bush. When the land is left wild, it is full of *wonder*.'

A while later, we lunch with an old friend of Pia's who transformed a tiny, dark old fibro shack in Frog Hollow into a sleek, modern house with solid sandstone walls and light-filled open spaces.

'Who did the design?' Bob and I ask.

He tells us a local architect did a sketch of the ground floor, then he passed the job on to someone else. 'But I ended up taking over the project myself,' he says.

'So who would you designate as the architect?' I ask, curious.

'Does it matter?' he replies. 'Either the house works or it doesn't.'

A couple of weeks later, I arrange to look at the plans for Dorothea Mackellar's septic tank at the Mitchell Library. The only evidence linking Wilson with the house. Bob and I set off together. At the library, we are taken into a room and seated at an old dining table. The plans are put in front of us — two small drawings, that's all. This is printed neatly in the lower right-hand corner of the plan along with a small outline of the house:

RESIDENCE AT PITTWATER
FOR MISS D. MACKELLAR
1/2" SCALE DETAIL OF
SEPTIC TANK
WILSON, NEAVE & BERRY – ARCHITECTS
UNION HOUSE, 247 GEORGE ST. SYDNEY.

It is listed as 'DRAWING No. 17'. There is no date on either of the papers.

'Guess that's that, then,' I say, unable to hide my frustration. I felt sure, absolutely sure, that there would be a date.

'Don't be too disappointed,' Bob says.

'I would have liked a firm date, that's all. One tiny little unassailable fact.'

'Would it make any difference to our enjoyment of living there?'

'No. Of course not.'

'Then let's go home,' he says, grabbing my hand.

APPENDIX

HOWARD TANNER, WROTE THIS report after his visit to *Tarrangaua* in 2008.

TARRANGAUA, LOVETT BAY, PITTWATER

Tarrangaua is arguably the most poetically sited and most architecturally distinguished house on Pittwater, an expansive salt-water estuary to the north of Sydney. Commissioned by the wealthy poetess Dorothea Mackellar (1885–1968) on land she acquired in 1925, the design of the house is attributed to the well-known architectural practice of Wilson, Neave and Berry. The firm's founder William Hardy Wilson (1881–1955) actively promoted the Colonial Revival style of architecture in Australia. His friend and contemporary, Arthur Stacey Neave, and John L. Berry, a partner from 1920, were both excellent architects in their own right, as their role in the practice in the 1920s (when Wilson was sometimes abroad) and their work together in the 1930s (after Wilson had gone to live in Tasmania) reveals. The attribution derives from three specific sources:

- Kath Strang, Dorothea Mackellar's cousin, stated to (DM's biographer) that the house was designed by WH Wilson.
- John Pearman, closely associated with WH Wilson's famous *Eryldene*, Gordon, and its owner, Professor Eben Gowrie Waterhouse, recalled EB Waterhouse telling him that WH Wilson had designed a house for Dorothea Mackellar on Pittwater.
- A drawing from the (Wilson), Neave and Berry archive held by the Mitchell Library, Sydney, for a freestanding EC (Earth Closet, as opposed to Water Closet) for Miss Dorothea Mackellar at Pittwater.

While I have observed the house from the water many times from 1956 onwards, and appreciated its formal architectural qualities, and its splendid setting on a promontory amongst tall-shafted spotted gums, my first detailed inspection of *Tarrangaua* occurred on 28/01/2008. Having studied Wilson's work closely over many years and visited many, and provided architectural advice on a number of the practice's buildings, it is interesting to note the elements which most closely relate to Wilson's other houses from the 1920s:

- The simple, formal massing, with a strongly pitched hipped tile roof, with a pair of secondary wings to the rear.
- The primary architectural elevation, symmetrical about centrally placed stairs and entry, and with columns edging a wide verandah, the latter enabling healthy outdoor living. The proportions of the verandah and its railing details are found in other Wilson houses.
- The primary elevation received most of the architect's attention, with side and rear elevations being simple, rational and unadorned.
- The formal planning, with a major room at the front, and a cross

hall separating the secondary rooms to the rear, all about a central rear courtyard (faintly reminiscent of *Eryldene*, Gordon).
- The refined beading to architraves and bookcases (though this was typical of all quality joinery of the period).
- The use of narrow hardwood flooring boards.
- The pre-cast concrete window sills (as at *Struan Lodge*, Woollahra).
- The chimney with its 'gothic' capping, derived from Colonial examples (as at *Macquarie Cottage*).

However, *Tarrangaua* has elements which I have not seen on other Wilson, Neave and Berry buildings. These include:

- The use of verandah columns which are neither slender, finely detailed timber Colonial columns (as at *Eryldene*) nor major tapered masonry columns, somewhat 'Old South' or Antebellum in character (as in projects at Burwood and Killara). Here at *Tarrangaua*, the columns are substantial cylindrical drums, with no entasis, capital or base; simply bagged like the rest of the house.
- The non-alignment of the door and window heads – Wilson usually resolved this by providing a finely patterned fanlight above the doors.
- The provision of one large room for sitting and dining across the full width of the main block of the house.
- The use of beamed ceilings with little or no detailing.
- The use of joinery with minor or no detailing. The main chimney mantelpiece offers a degree of Georgian-derived elaboration in painted timber, reasonably close to other Wilson models, but is not undercut on the projecting lip, as occurs in his better work.
- The heavy-duty ledged doors and the use of simple iron latches, all rather in the c.1900/1910 Arts and Crafts tradition – I have not seen these details in other Wilson buildings.

Reflecting on the house, and an architect's experience with a headstrong client, and realisation by a good, standard builder conveniently away from any easy viewing by the discerning members of the architectural team, I surmise:

- The plans were prepared by Wilson, Neave and Berry, probably with all their usual attention to detail, especially in the joinery of fanlights and chimney pieces.
- Perhaps Dorothea Mackellar emphasized to the architect that this was to be a secluded retreat, and more informal than his usual architecture.
- The site was then remote from Sydney, making easy inspection by the architect difficult.
- The house, designed of full brick and tile, perhaps with little regard for the problems and expense of water access by barge and motor boat, was realised by a competent local builder.
- The builder formed a close working association with the owner, and simplified the house's detailing to ensure easier realisation, probably with the owner's agreement, and possibly causing alienation of the architect.

In the past I wondered if *Tarrangaua* could be by Brisbane architect Robin Dods (1868–1920), who later practised in Sydney. This idea grew out of the robust columns (relatively uncharacteristic of Wilson) and the more gutsy qualities of Dods' work, as seen in formal residential designs such as *Clayfield*, Brisbane for Mrs J. Reid (Plate XLVI in *Domestic Architecture in Australia* produced by *Art in Australia* and published by Angus and Robertson in 1919). Espie Dods has confirmed that Robin Dods and Dorothea Mackellar were friends, but alas Dods died in 1920, and *Tarrangaua* was erected in 1925 or shortly thereafter, and is unlikely to be based on plans prepared in 1919.

Tarrangaua as part of the formal, Georgian-derived architecture advocated during the 1910s and 1920s, was bound to have been known to individuals such as Sydney Ure Smith, publisher of *Art in Australia* (1916–) and *The Home* (1920–c.1940), and his wealthy friend and backer Charles Lloyd Jones. *The Home* had its favoured circle of fashionable and tasteful architects, which included Wilson, Neave and Berry, Professor Leslie Wilkinson, John D Moore, and occasionally BJ Waterhouse. All were extremely competent architects who, from time-to-time, built houses with some characteristics similar to *Tarrangaua* – its concept and character derived from primary ideals evident in the better domestic designs of the period.

As the above text is largely based on memory, key dates and facts (such as the EC drawing in the State Library) deserve checking.

Howard Tanner
Architect
28/01/2008

THANKS

I would like to thank the people of Pittwater for letting me write about them once again. And for being part of what I like to think of as my 'chosen family'. I am extraordinarily privileged to live in this quite magical part of the world amongst a community that is kind, caring, creative and never, ever dull.

Thanks to Jeanne Villani and Ann Reeve, who never cease to inspire and who demonstrate each day, how to live a useful and fulfilling life at any age.

My thanks to my mother, too, for her incredible generosity of spirit in once again letting me write about the ups and downs of our lives. She didn't flinch. She never does. She has the most amazing heart and, I have finally learned, would make any sacrifice for her rather flawed daughter. Thank you, Esther.

Thanks too, to my agent, Caroline Adams, a good friend and fellow dog walker, who guided, shaped and influenced this book with all her usual subtlety, humour and wisdom. Caro, every suggestion was gold and this would have been a much lesser book without your input.

Thanks too, to publisher Nikki Christer, for her invaluable

advice, support and insight, and to lovely Katie Stackhouse, who eased all the hard moments with her gentleness and compassion. Jo Jarrah, who edited the manuscript, is that wondrous rarity – an editor who saves you from yourself and makes you a better writer than you are. Thank you, Jo. And of course, Margie Seale, whose confidence gave me confidence.

Then there is Bob, without whom I would never have found the courage to begin.

Also by Susan Duncan

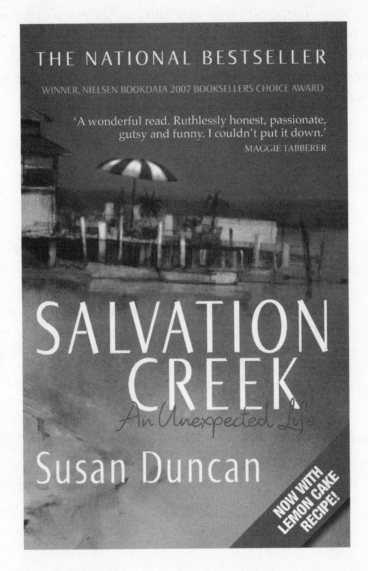

THE NATIONAL BESTSELLER

WINNER, NIELSEN BOOKDATA 2007 BOOKSELLERS CHOICE AWARD

'A wonderful read. Ruthlessly honest, passionate,
gutsy and funny. I couldn't put it down.'
MAGGIE TABBERER

SALVATION
CREEK
An Unexpected Life

Susan Duncan

NOW WITH
LEMON CAKE
RECIPE!

ABOUT THE AUTHOR

After a 25-year career spanning radio, newspaper and magazine journalism, including editing two of Australia's top selling women's magazines, *The Australian Women's Weekly* and *New Idea*, Susan Duncan woke up one morning and chucked in her job. The decision followed the deaths of her husband and brother. After struggling to begin again, she finally found her own patch of paradise on earth only to discover it might already be too late when she was diagnosed with cancer herself. Today Susan lives with her second husband, Bob, on the shores of Pittwater at *Tarrangaua*, the beautiful home built for poet Dorothea Mackellar in 1925. Susan's bestselling memoir, *Salvation Creek*, won the Nielsen BookData 2007 Booksellers Choice Award and was shortlisted for the prestigious Dobbie Award, part of the Nita B. Kibble awards for women writers.